SECOND EDITION

the
performer

IN MASS MEDIA

connecting with television and online audiences

William Hawes
UNIVERSITY OF HOUSTON

Beth M. Olson
UNIVERSITY OF HOUSTON

Holcomb Hathaway, Publishers
Scottsdale, Arizona

Library of Congress Cataloging-in-Publication Data

Hawes, William.
    The performer in mass media : connecting with television and online
audiences / William Hawes, Beth M. Olson. — 2nd ed.
        p. cm.
    Includes index.
    ISBN 978-1-890871-99-4
    1. Performing arts—Technique.   2. Mass media.   I. Olson., Beth M.   II.
Title.
    PN1590.T43H3 2010
    791.028—dc22

                                        2009034071

Photo Captions and Credits

All photos reprinted with permission. **Page 1,** New England Patriots quarterback Tom Brady talks with CBS sports anchor Jim Nantz at Super Bowl XXXVIII. Photo by John P. Filo/CBS. © 2004 CBS Broadcasting Inc. All Rights Reserved. ▪ **p. 17,** Astronaut Neil Armstrong films Buzz Aldrin on the moon, July 20, 1969. Courtesy of Carlos Fontanot, chair, ISS Imagery Working Group, ISS Mission Integration and Operations, NASA Johnson Space Center, Houston, Texas. ▪ **p. 23,** Hal Eisner reports live from outside Dodger Stadium covering the Los Angeles Police Department's Medal of Valor winners. © Bryan Frank. ▪ **p. 41,** Veronica Griffin is an anchor/journalist for WDJT-TV, Milwaukee, Wisconsin. © Jamie Zahn. ▪ **p. 65,** Robert Arnold reports on Hurricane Dolly from South Padre Island, KPRC-TV, Houston, Texas. © KPRC-TV. ▪ **p. 91,** Sheletta Brundidge appears as host of *Crossroads,* a public affairs series on KSTC-TV, Minneapolis. Photo by Roxane Battle. ▪ **p. 113,** Anchor Mike Rush reports on Fat Tuesday at the scene for WPMI-TV, Mobile, Alabama. © R. Steve Huffman. ▪ **p. 127,** Amy Davis reports on contaminated garden mulch for KPRC-TV, Houston. © KPRC-TV. ▪ **p. 151,** Fred Schultz directs from the control room at KIAH-TV, Houston. © Pathik Shah. ▪ **p. 159,** Fujio Watanabe photographs former President Jimmy Carter for KUHT, Houston. © Francisco Castro. ▪ **p. 181,** Julie Tam, reporter, and Mike Olmstead, photographer, set up a shot for WDRB-TV at Thunder Over Louisville. © Saqib F. Siddik. ▪ **p. 197,** Mike Barajas and Melinda Spaulding, co-anchors, hurry to the studio for Fox 26 News, Houston. © Alex Luster.

Holcomb Hathaway, Publishers, Inc.
6207 North Cattletrack Road
Scottsdale, Arizona 85250
480-991-7881
www.hh-pub.com

10 9 8 7 6 5 4 3 2 1

ISBN 978-1-890871-99-4

Printed in the United States of America.

Contents

Appearance   41

Voice   65

Movement   91

Succeeding as a Performer   113

The Television Studio   127

Specialized Performances   159

Technology and Performance   181

The Business   197

"I want to be in front of the camera."

"I want to be a television anchor."

"I want to be the next Oprah."

e have all heard such statements, from prospective students and students enrolled in our classes. It is not surprising to hear these types of career aspirations from a generation that grew up in front of cameras. From birth through each birthday party, sporting event, choir performance, band competition, and graduation they have seen themselves on screen. They have sent photos and video images to friends via cell phones and computers. They have created personal MySpace and Facebook pages, and may have posted video images of themselves on YouTube. They are familiar with being on camera but not necessarily with performing effectively on camera. Being a performer is hard work, and it may not be glamorous. But motivation, drive, and guidance can make performing rewarding. *The Performer in Mass Media: Connecting with Television and Online Audiences* can help provide that guidance.

This book is written to address primary and secondary audiences. The primary audience consists of students who have aspirations to work in a visual medium as talent, as career performers. The secondary audience is non-career performers—individuals who by virtue of their jobs, organizational memberships, citizen journalist functions or activist status, find themselves appearing on camera as spokespersons, witnesses, subject experts, or in a variety of other roles, and who want to present their messages effectively.

Those wanting to appear on camera no longer find themselves limited to landing a broadcast or cable position for which scores of people have applied. Finding employment in television may be challenging, but other digital options are now available, made possible by the Internet. Due to the prevalence of small, inexpensive cameras and additional broadcast technologies, opportunities to perform are everywhere. Performers must be prepared to present their best image at any time. This book is intended to help readers prepare for a variety of possible jobs. When someone says "I want to be a reporter" or "I want to create my own Internet show," or "I will appear on camera for my job as a company spokesperson," this guide will help them work toward achieving those goals.

The heart of this book grew from 40 years of producing a student-lab television magazine program, *Video Workshop,* at the University of Houston. This program sends many students into successful performing careers. In the workshop, students prepare field packages, conduct live interviews, produce demonstration segments, and serve as hosts for the program. Each of these tasks encompasses a variety of on-air skills that need to be learned and polished, and *The Performer in Mass Media* is organized around the needed skill sets. Readers are encouraged to build the various elements that translate into "the total package" and help make them marketable, including pleasant appearance, appropriate dress, expert makeup, and the ability to speak well and move and think on their feet. They will learn to be well-prepared, rehearsed, and calm, to perform with energy, and to communicate effectively to the audience.

Most chapters focus on individual on-camera skills, such as understanding the communication process, the importance of creating content, and various aspects of performance for a visual medium: the look, voice, and movement. General television and online performances are the focus, but information about specialty performances such as weathercasting, sportscasting, and hosting a talk show is also included. Additional chapters present an overview of the functions of a television studio, the basics of field reporting, and advice on succeeding in the business.

Since this textbook is grounded in pedagogical experiences, it offers a range of helpful features, including:

- Real-world advice and examples from working professionals
- "Try it out" exercises that allow readers to immediately practice and hone their performing skills
- End-of-chapter student activities for practical application of chapter concepts
- Clear key terms bolded in each chapter
- A book-end glossary of key terms to familiarize aspiring performers with industry terms

A guide to the running and organization of the *Video Workshop* experience in a classroom setting is also available for instructors who have adopted the book for their course and wish to use it as a model or resource.

While skills and talents may be shaped and perfected, readers who study this guide are often reminded that on-camera performance is an intimate endeavor, connecting the performer to the audience. ABC anchor and reporter Diane Sawyer described the successful formula for her work on the network morning show: ". . . it's a conversation that you're having with people who are distracted, and people who are paying attention, and people who are sleepy, and people who really are curious and want to know things. So in that sense it's personal." *The Performer in Mass Media* shows potential performers how to ensure that their on-camera "conversation" will captivate and motivate their audience.

Acknowledgments

Our thanks to Jerry Goodwin, assistant professor at the New England Institute of Art in Brookline, Massachusetts, for his suggestion that we re-introduce our book *Television Performing: News and Information* to the classroom. His kind words and a suggestion from Nancy Hawes Wagner of Maricopa Community College, Arizona, prompted this revision. Colette Kelly of Holcomb Hathaway, Publishers, expressed interest, and with feedback from several reviewers we improved the direction for the book. We wish to thank the following reviewers, whose constructive input helped us to improve the book: Robert Kelber, Breyer State University; Greeley Kyle, University of Missouri; Timothy Lewis, Lyndon State College; Beverly Love, Southern Illinois University; James Lumpp, University of Mississippi; and Elizabeth Spencer, Naperville Community Television, NCTV17.

Publishing a book requires lots of input, and we are grateful to others who spent time on this project. From the Valenti School of Communication at the University of Houston we particularly want to thank *Video Workshop* coproducer Craig Crowe, Manager of Media Productions Ward Booth, their staff, and those who mentor students at KUHT, Channel 8. We are also grateful for the technical assistance of Kent Hawes at The Production Company, Austin, Texas.

We are always pleased to recognize our many former students who are now career professionals in news and information, some of whom are pictured in this book. They include Robert Arnold, Mike Barajas, Sheletta Brundidge, Amy Davis, Hal Eisner, Carlos Fontanot, Veronica Griffin, Jim Nantz, Mike Rush, Fred Schultz, Julie Tam, and Fujio Watanabe, who are working from coast to coast or appearing on local stations serving the needs of the greater Houston/Galveston community.

We deeply appreciate the support of all these contributors.

William Hawes
Beth M. Olson

About the Authors

illiam Hawes, Ph.D. (The University of Michigan), is a professor in the Jack J. Valenti School of Communication at the University of Houston. He has produced more than one thousand television programs, and is creator of the school's workshop that has provided community programming on commercial and public stations for over forty years. He has produced a dozen short films and is the former manager of three FM radio stations. Dr. Hawes is the former head of radio-television-film at the University of Houston and Texas Christian University. Between academic appointments he was briefly at WTOP-TV, Washington, D.C. He has also taught at Eastern Michigan University and the University of North Carolina at Chapel Hill. A specialist in media history, criticism, and production, he taught in the UH London Program in 1984 and 1994. He was a J. William Fulbright lecturer to National Chengchi University, Taiwan, in 2001 and was a scholar at the Rockefeller Foundation's Study and Conference Center, Bellagio, Italy, in 2003. Among his six books two are on performing. Dr. Hawes has been a consultant to industry, publishers, government, and attorneys.

eth M. Olson, Ph.D. (Indiana University), is director of the Jack J. Valenti School of Communication at the University of Houston, where she is an associate professor. The school has about 1,600 students, nearly 100 of whom are pursuing a master's degree. The faculty numbers just under 25, with support staff of about 14. Since joining the faculty in 1990, her teaching areas include electronic news, media effects, and gender and media. She contributed to Mitchell Stephens' *Broadcast News* in 2005 and has published articles in *Journalism and Mass Communication Quarterly*, *Journal of Broadcasting and Electronic Media*, *Sex Roles*, *Mass Comm Review*, and *Southwestern Mass Communication Journal*. Dr. Olson worked in radio and television for six years as a reporter, producer, and on-air talent. She was the voice of the University of Houston's telephone student enrollment services for the nearly 15 years it was used. She has been director of the Valenti School since 2003.

Cue, You're On

INTRODUCTION

Chapter 1 creates a foundation for thinking about performance by providing communication models applicable to the performance process, describing types of performers (career vs. non-career performers) and levels of performances (live or prerecorded, the audience interpretation of the performance, and the remembered performance). The outcome of the performance process is performance itself, and it should be a memorable one. Finally, the importance of a performer's image cannot be underestimated and is, in fact, the theme of this book.

The Performer Takes Center Stage

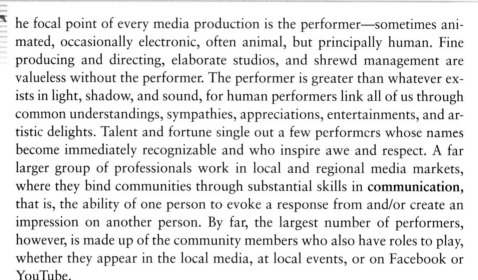

The focal point of every media production is the performer—sometimes animated, occasionally electronic, often animal, but principally human. Fine producing and directing, elaborate studios, and shrewd management are valueless without the performer. The performer is greater than whatever exists in light, shadow, and sound, for human performers link all of us through common understandings, sympathies, appreciations, entertainments, and artistic delights. Talent and fortune single out a few performers whose names become immediately recognizable and who inspire awe and respect. A far larger group of professionals work in local and regional media markets, where they bind communities through substantial skills in **communication,** that is, the ability of one person to evoke a response from and/or create an impression on another person. By far, the largest number of performers, however, is made up of the community members who also have roles to play, whether they appear in the local media, at local events, or on Facebook or YouTube.

This book is about human beings as performers—who they are, what they do, and how they do it. The instant someone appears before a camera or speaks into a microphone, that person creates an impression, favorable or unfavorable, in the minds of hundreds, thousands, or even millions of viewers and listeners. Knowing how to be a strong performer can make a difference both in a career and in life.

Who Is a Performer?

Performing has become more commonplace with the increased availability of media, ranging from a video created with a handheld camera posted on the Internet to worldwide production and satellite distribution. With the prevalence of media in our society, relatively unknown individuals get caught in news-making circumstances. For example, a community member who discovers an environmental issue and a doctor who wishes to obtain funds for critical medical research may find that in order to gain favorable attention, they must make media work for them. The rapid dissemination of information and entertainment by mass media makes everyone, whether performing in the media professionally or nonprofessionally, likely to engage in the role of a performer.

Who is a performer? In general, a **performer** is someone—newscaster, actor, minister, teacher, social activist, and so forth—who uses the media to impart information so that people respond through action, such as purchases, political support, or intellectual endeavors, and/or to provide entertainment. Of course, these days just about anyone who wants to be on television or online can be, at least for a short time. In a way, all of these people are performers. The use of *performer* in this book, however, refers to those who want to become or are employed as communicators of news, information, or entertainment. They perform as part of their job, though they may not necessarily base their entire career around performing.

This book specially focuses on two groups: the career performer and the non-career performer.

CAREER PERFORMERS

Traditionally, **career performers** are those whose income comes primarily from performing and whose occupation revolves primarily around performing, whether on television, on the stage, or in the movies. They are professional performers who use media consciously to influence an audience. Career performers include news anchors, sportscasters, weather reporters, and other journalists; disc jockeys, motivational speakers, masters of ceremony, hosts, and other **announcers;** singers, actors, dancers, musicians, variety artists, and other entertainers.

At the outset of your performing career, you decide whether you are a reporter of news and information or an entertainer. Fundamentally, a **newscaster** tells about other people and events, while an **entertainer** is the event. There is a sanctity and responsibility about journalism that prohibits reporters from considering themselves primarily as entertainers. Those in entertainment do not want to give an account of the lives of other people; they generally want to act as other people or characters—meaning they portray a personality separate from their own. The truth they seek is in the spirit of what they do: they are artists. By contrast, journalists seek to present the truth in the literal description of persons and events from a factual, accurate, and balanced perspective.

How do you decide whether you belong in news or entertainment? The answer is: intuitively. You already know your preference. Even though you like both information and entertainment to some extent, here is the test: If you could do anything you want in the world of performance, what would you do? Set aside the advice someone else (who may never have been a performer) has given you, and set aside the obstacles, real and imagined, to obtaining your goal. Now ask yourself what you really want to do as a performer during your lifetime. Your decision will be based on heartfelt desire, background, aptitude, perception of opportunity, advice from others, and whether you are willing to pay the price for being a performer.

The path of a career performer

Although a few people attempt performing professionally later in life, most become interested in performing while in their early years at school. Interactions with media can range from preschool children who present a "show and tell" to third graders who face cameras and microphones in their libraries, where they present daily schedules, lunch menus, and weather. High school students often produce sophisticated newscasts or videos related to class subjects.

Following high school, future professional performers often continue at colleges and universities to use media technology to develop personally and experiment with its impact on audiences. An outgrowth of media knowledge for the current generation is the fearless utilization of media for personal goals and for classroom and distance learning. At the center of such instruction are the teacher and students as performers. These performers are eager to give and take lessons in virtually every subject, devoting a great deal of time to performance because of personal motivation. Usually future professional performers do not have to be told to practice for long hours. They use every opportunity to appear before the public, whether in church or school or at some community event. These performances are frequently recorded and distributed. This experience is readily obtained in college in departments of communication, journalism, music, and other liberal arts. Future professional performers may pursue related activities like theater, dance, or athletics. Depending largely on the courses available, they may enroll in areas where specific performing interests can be developed. As performers gain experience and as their work becomes better known, more opportunities arise.

Breaking into the professional world

Arguably, it is more difficult to be a performer on television than in some other outlets, such as radio, or in the role of a company **spokesperson,** serving as a representative and the voice of an organization. However, none of these professionals knows when or where the first paying job will come and how long it will last. These are the uncertainties with which people live as long as they are performers. Frequently, novices begin by either working in another medium or accepting whatever position comes along in television with the hope that once they are in the station, their performing ability will be recognized. Young professional performers accept out-of-town assignments, one-night appearances, and benefits, and they are aggressive in asking for work and showing what they can do. The aspirant is willing to work for free if it will achieve a goal. For example, one man who wanted to get into a local television news department demonstrated his journalistic fortitude by waiting out a hurricane as it hit the Gulf Coast in a particularly vulnerable location. Another wrote to a network offering to pay his own way if the network would allow him to join the sports staff when on location for a tournament. Both were hired. A woman joined a civic organization so that she could make its public service announcements. She, too, was successful.

Blending a strong academic curriculum, preferably at a major college or university with an established internship program, and the job potential of a major broadcast market gives beginning performers the best chance of accumulating both a degree and commercial credits—that is, a record of commercial experience—at the time of graduation. By establishing this record, the performer has a strong foundation.

With such a foundation a professional performer may be fortunate enough to be hired full-time by the local public media station after working part-time while attending classes. Some students, awarded internships in various communities, may be hired after the internship is complete. To further their careers, however, performers must go wherever the work is, realizing that professional life is transient. The first job may last six months to two years; the second a bit longer. A performer needs to be looking for the next job constantly, and therefore may seek the assistance of an agent. Even professional performers who are lucky enough to be hired in hometowns or cities where they attended school rarely stay for an extended period. Personal ambition and the necessity for station revitalization force the turnover of even excellent employees. Broadcasters often are told to get experience in smaller communities before trying larger ones or the networks. The road to success can be discouraging, but it must be traveled if a performer is to be recognized. While most professional performers do not become well known until they have worked in media for many years, some do make it rather quickly. There is no one formula for success.

NON-CAREER PERFORMERS

Non-career performers are those who have another occupation but who may use the media to communicate with the public. Included in this group are politicians, attorneys, physicians, research scientists, diplomats, business executives, government officials, members of the clergy, athletes, educators, various advocates, and activists. These individuals may use performing as a way to draw attention to their organization, their cause, or themselves.

In recent years, the number of people who are non-career performers has increased substantially as more people attempt to use the media to obtain their objectives. Today's performers in the mass media come from all walks of life. These non-career performers are often highly skillful in their occupations but seldom skilled in media performance. Why do many Sunday sermons seem so long? Why do many politicians appear incompetent? Why do so many bank presidents look stodgy? Why do public relations officers for oil companies appear to be against the interests of the community? They use media *ineffectively.*

Those people who have learned how to use media effectively wield it as a powerful tool. The president and members of Congress, as well as local politicians, are aware that their reelection may depend upon how successfully they use the media. World tensions rise and subside with statements made by deplaning diplomats. Water bonds are voted, a city attorney's staff is increased, streets are improved, and the public attitude toward its police force changes when the power of mass media is mobilized properly.

The subject expert

One type of non-career performer who appears on television is the subject expert. This professional is on camera to offer knowledge of an area or to offer commentary. The subject expert may or may not be paid directly by a television company and instead will probably be compensated by the business, government, or institution that hires the expert principally for the person's knowledge of the subject. Television exposure is secondary to another kind of valuable service. For these specialists, television appearances recognize and enhance their roles in life.

Business and industry, recognizing that media must be used purposefully, hire experts to make statements to media in the event of off-shore well fires, plant explosions, train derailments, airplane crashes, and other instances of public news interest. Physicians are interviewed to comment on the policies of a local hospital. Managers of automobile companies present a direct personal sales appeal to gain public confidence in their business. Athletes depend on media to perpetuate their reputations through play-by-play action, locker room comments, and interviews. When the playing field is no longer a career option, many athletes become professional performers by joining the sports staff of a radio or television station.

An increasing number of school administrators realize that they may be using media as presenters. In elementary schools, morning announcements, once made on public address systems, now are televised. Children and teachers are also presenters; both are highly motivated by media. In high schools with limited resources, fewer teachers can be hired for the languages or arts, and so these kinds of teachers may become critical performers using distance education. In large school systems, administrators who once had orientation sessions in auditoriums now deliver them over closed circuit television.

Both community experts and concerned citizens are increasingly realizing how they can accomplish their objectives through proper use of the media. Social activists, including minority group leaders, clergy, civil rights lawyers, or indeed anyone with a cause, may plan to take advantage of the media. Many non-career performers simply do not know how to use radio and television, but they are learning through evening classes held in community colleges, churches, schools, and other common gathering places. Non-career performers compete with the most glamorous celebrities when they appear on the media. In addition, the family, friends, and colleagues of the non-career performer are concerned about his or her appearance. They want to be proud of that person, as many of the reality television programs continue to illustrate.

The community spokesperson

A performer may represent a racial, religious, or sexual minority, the medically disabled, veterans groups, the elderly, or crime victims, among others. As the media serves more diverse interests in the future, more spokespersons for these groups will be needed.

In the past, the media has depended on those already on staff to identify and to lead discussions concerning special views and experiences of such groups. However, their demands require more background than most media generalists, such as community affairs directors, can address. Thus, individuals with unusual backgrounds have emerged to present social issues to the public in a positive way. Some high-profile celebrities represent special interest groups. This performer is frequently part of the group—he or she has the disease, is blind, is a victim of assault—and steps forward to use his or her reputation to raise money, create awareness, and urge change. In recent years the value of previously marginalized people has been reassessed thanks to the increased visibility of these spokespeople. For example, elderly performers have advocated that retirees instruct children and adults who cannot read, while news media spokespeople seek to differentiate Hispanics as Mexicans, Salvadorans, Nicaraguans, and Cubans, and to serve other national interests.

As news and information programs refine their content, many more exceptional talents will emerge to add a diversified list of media celebrities drawn from around the world.

Commitment To Performing

egardless of the circumstances, no matter what anyone utters aloud, almost everyone who appears in the media for any reason wants to look good, sound intelligent, and be admired. To be effective in the media, whether you are a career journalist or an entertainer, an information expert or a private citizen, requires forethought and skill. You will need to know how to control your image to the extent that in every circumstance you seem to be at your best. This book should be a helpful guide in reaching your objectives as a professional performer in the increasingly complex world of news and information.

Keep in mind that being a performer can be a highly beneficial beginning to your life and career. The experiences you have in attempting to be a performer may lead to other kinds of professional opportunities later in life. A reasonable way of approaching performing is to set short-term goals that are realistic. Nevertheless, if you want to be a performer, especially a career performer, then you must commit to it. Few reporters are part-time and few actors are part-time in their commitment. Their employment may be only sporadic, but their commitment is full-time. If you cannot make such a commitment, or if you vacillate, or if you do not intuitively know you are a performer, chances are you will not succeed. You may appear as a performer occasionally, but your life's work will probably take some other direction.

Types of Performance

 performer's work can be observed at various levels and in different contexts. First, the performance may be **live,** allowing the viewers to experience the total context of the performance, or it may be **prerecorded,** allowing some control over the context. Second, there is variation between the *commu-*

nicated performance, what the viewer/listener actually experiences within the environment of the performance, and the *remembered* performance, the fragmented parts that remain in the listener/viewer's memory.

LIVE VERSUS PRERECORDED PERFORMANCE

In a live performance, whatever performers say or do on-camera and microphone (when they are **on the air**) can be transmitted, altered, or eliminated through noise substitution (**bleeps**), **blackouts** (audio/video deletion), or **cutaways** (alternate video) as their message is processed through the media. Despite this fact, performers can be relatively certain that most of what has been said and done will be viewed and heard. In the case of live performances, producers have little recourse for alteration except through obvious censorship. Call-in programs on radio or television are examples of a common "live" format where any changes made to a performance are obvious. In this format, responses from participants calling in are delayed a few seconds so that producers can exercise the option of deleting potentially injurious or litigious words or actions. Some unedited interview programs noted for their candor have guests who are aware of legal limitations and who use discretion.

Although most programs are audiotaped, videotaped, filmed, and/or digitized for permanent use and storage, it is only recently that day-to-day life is also recorded. Cameras are everywhere and an alert public seems to be ready to capture newsworthy events as well as in-home activities. Whether a person is at home, at work, or in a store, he or she is probably on camera at certain times in these environments. These spontaneous "performances," usually aired online initially, are examples of "live" news or entertainment recorded for broadcast, but the performers who take part may be unwitting.

Prerecorded edited events are referred to as packaged or **canned,** meaning completed and ready for airing. The opportunity for alteration of material in prerecorded programs is great. For example, an interview may consist of only carefully selected questions and answers from an extensive session recorded over many hours. In its final form, the discussion may be edited to a half hour; thus, a great deal of information is eliminated. Although the remainder may be offered for viewing online, this presentation will be outside the original program.

Thousands of hours taken of a performer may be condensed into a one-hour documentary. Errors the public might see in live performance may be eliminated. In short, performers appear at their best because the work has been carefully edited; consequently, edited programs may create the illusion that participants are always articulate, witty, brilliant people. Electronic alterations enable singers and dramatic artists to reach nearer perfection than they could when appearing live. As a result, the viewer/listener sees and hears a careful selection and condensation of what really took place.

THE COMMUNICATED VERSUS
REMEMBERED PERFORMANCE

A communicated performance is one the viewer/listener actually experiences and absorbs despite multitasking, daydreaming, or other interference. Viewers/listeners experience a live or prerecorded performance in a unique environment: a mental and physical mixture of their own thoughts and miscellaneous, uncontrollable distractions. A bombardment of stimuli, frequently a result of multitasking, disrupts the **continuity** of a performance. What is retained are those bits of information or emotional experiences that activate and reinforce preconceived notions, thoughts, and feelings. If the performer's message is compatible with the person receiving it, the viewer/listener will be motivated to action: to buy a product, to react spontaneously (laughing or crying), or in a multitude of other ways. Only then has the performer communicated with someone at this level. However, that communication can be affected by what the audience chooses to take away from the performance. A performer has to consider whether and how the performance will be remembered. The recollection of a performance is based on the viewer's/listener's mental and emotional state when the performance is experienced and will probably deteriorate with time, causing a confused recollection of it. If viewers/listeners like the work of the performer a great deal, they may remember the performance in some idealized or romanticized way, resulting in a large audience and favorable **publicity** (free, often favorable attention) that may make the performer famous. A viewer may be primed to accept or reject a performer's work. To place it in perspective, consider the role of media critics, who often articulate the assets and liabilities of a performer's work for posterity so that the performer's work can be evaluated. A performer's work can be greatly enhanced by constructive critical judgment, but the critics' comments can have an effect on how the performance is remembered by others as well.

Image Control:
The Performer's Public Perception

Of prime concern to performers is what an audience thinks of them, professionally and personally. Close associates such as an agent or a producer know what performers think or do or how temperamental they are behind the scenes, off-camera and off-mike, but the audience knows only what they see and hear while the performers are on media. Appearances, interviews, and news items in all media tend to be selected by a performer's associates, so the performer will always seem to be at his or her best. The relatively few characteristics the performer and associates wish to convey about the performer constitute the **public image.** Mastery over what the public sees and hears is called **image control.** The performer and associates select what they want the audience to see and hear so that the audience has a high regard for the performer professionally and personally. The task is complex and difficult because an audience forms its opinion the moment it sees and/or hears the performer, continually changing its opinion as the performer provides new stimuli.

Performers, especially the most visible performers such as newscasters, are subject to comments from the public regarding every detail of their appearance, voice, and conduct. In one instance, a quarterback whose image was touted to promote the team and the city lost several games, and media critics blamed him for being aloof, for not admitting mistakes, and for limiting media access. Politicians, reporters, or entertainers can quickly lose their public appeal by using offensive words in an unguarded moment, and their work may be remembered always for this incident.

The term *image* refers to the public's acquaintance of a person through the media, not to the person as a human being. If, for instance, media reveal a performer in a socially acceptable context pursuing virtuous activities exclusively, the public will likely think of that performer as virtuous. High-status performers have to protect themselves from missteps that might not benefit their public image. They often do this by using surrogates to speak for them: agents, attorneys, publicists, and other press information specialists.

Although image control is expected for **anchors,** who provide continuity for news and information programs; movie stars, who often depend on the public's perception to maintain popularity; and other media professionals, what about a non-career performer such as a community expert who becomes a media performer? How important is image control for that person? If his or her appearance is fleeting and the occasion pleasant, then image control is of little importance. If, however, the person sincerely wants to influence an audience to enact legislation, to propagate an idea, to raise money, to sell a product, or to disseminate information, the community expert must make a convincing presentation. In effect this person must compete with career performers. Anyone who plans to use media should know how to use it to advantage. Nowhere is this clearer than on television/radio station editorials or news shows where qualified representatives of opposing views are invited to state differing perspectives. Often the response from the community expert can be inept, because the person is debating not only an issue but also a media professional who depends on media to make a public presentation. Thus it has become increasingly evident that it behooves a community expert who appears as a performer to use the media as skillfully as possible.

Let there be no doubt that image control is the same kind of media control that politicians use to create the impression of a just government working to benefit the people. Image control, whether by government officials, professional athletes, or industry executives, is a form of thought control. But there is another facet to the matter of image control: the public view. The public, weary from decades of media persuasion, does a great deal of selecting on its own. An audience tends to select what it wants to believe. It is acquainted with the illusions of the screen world. Publications concerning media manipulation have alerted the public to those techniques designed by media experts to create favorable public opinion. For example, the promotions department at CBS had to admit that the photograph of Katie Couric used in promotional materials in 2006 had been digitally altered so that she appeared to be thinner.

Needless to say, an ongoing selective search for truth requires the public to be more discriminating in believing performers on media. The ramifications of this fascinating study can only be hinted at here; it is enough to remind performers that today's audience, raised on mass media, is paradoxically astute and naive. The performer must respond to this paradox in the public.

The Communication Process

In order to become a successful performer, you will need to understand the communication process and the transactional relationship between the performer and the audience. The time-honored adage "What goes around comes around" applies to the communication process performers use. By means of the communication process, a performer connects with viewers. In response to them, the performer is prompted to modify his or her performance. Today's media enable instant reaction from media audiences. Networks, newspapers, and the Internet separately or together encourage responses. Performers want to know if anyone is paying attention to them, and audiences want performers to respond to their reactions.

The communication process in mass media can be summarized in six steps identified by Wilbur Schramm:[1]

1. The performer (communicator) conveys stimuli (messages) via appearance and voice.
2. The stimuli are designed or formalized (encoded) in language, sounds, and pictures by the performer.
3. The formalized message is transmitted through radio, television, film, the Internet, or another medium (e.g., DVD) to the listener/viewer (communicant).
4. The listener/viewer selects stimulating impressions from the message and decodes or makes sense of the message.
5. The listener/viewer (now in the role of communicator) responds emotionally, such as with applause or laughter, or with questions or comments to provide stimuli (feedback) to the performer. (Feedback is so necessary for performers that live studio audiences are required stimuli for some top performers. For example, performers on *The Tonight Show* depend heavily on the reactions of a live audience, and viewer feedback from e-mail, Internet message boards, and telephone, and on television **ratings,** the number of people tuned into a broadcast program. As another example, the *CBS Evening News* asks viewers

at the beginning of the week to choose from previews of small-town features which ones they want to see at the end of the week. The viewers' choice is then played.

6. Performers respond to the contact they have made with the audience in proportion with the message either being heightened or eventually terminated. A performer must evoke response from the audience.

The communication process is an empathic or **circular response.** Schramm illustrated this feedback loop in his model, the Interactive Model. He included the concepts of a sender encoding the information (deciding what to say and how to say it) and a receiver decoding the information (interpreting the meaning the sender intended), as shown in Figure 1.1. This principle of a communication model when applied to performance means that upon appearance or utterance a performer instantly conveys information through media to the audience, the audience reacts, and sooner or later the performer reacts to the audience reaction. In a live performance, all this occurs more or less instantly and continuously, such as at a political convention. When a performer works through the media, however, **feedback** from the unseen audience may be delayed, for instance, after making a documentary, although it can also be immediate via email, Twitter, and so forth.

Schramm also added the concept of context when he included the term "field of experience" as an element of both sender and receiver. In that model, performers bring the sum of their own experiences and biases to the communication situation. For example, the sender may have a biased or prejudicial

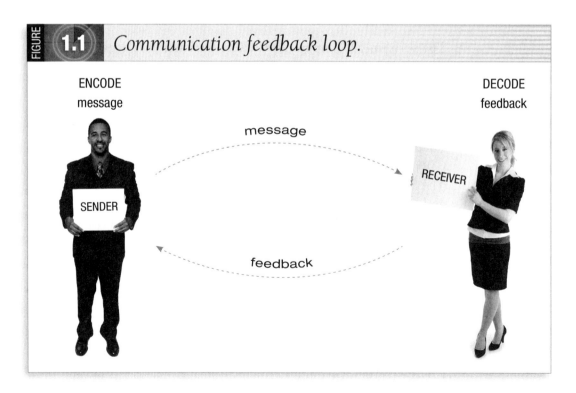

FIGURE 1.1 *Communication feedback loop.*

ENCODE
message

DECODE
feedback

message

SENDER

RECEIVER

feedback

frame of reference when she writes a script using words and images that are offensive to a minority group. This person's frame of reference has yet to include aspects of sensitivity as to races or ethnicities. Members of the minority group could become offended and insulted by the message; however, some audience members with experiences or biases similar to the writer may interpret the message in the same manner as the writer and not be offended.

Both parties (sender and receiver) in a communication scenario must have at least something in common at the most basic level—perhaps language—in order for the sender to encode a message so that the receiver may decode the message. Each receiver may "read" the message differently, meaning they arrive at their own individualized interpretations, even though all receivers were presumably exposed to the same message. Early communication theorists soon discovered that receivers were not all alike in their interpretations of messages.

In David Berlo's book *The Process of Communication*,[2] Berlo's sender-receiver-channel-cognitive model advanced the idea that *meaning* is transmitted. Information may be transmitted from person to person via various channels, but the sender does not always communicate the information effectively and the receiver does not always understand the information. The cognitive aspects of encoding and decoding represent how misunderstandings may result from communication.

PROCESSING AND RECALLING INFORMATION

In years subsequent to Berlo's work, the cognitive aspects of the communication process have continued to be explored by cognitive psychologists. The information processing theory may be of particular interest to performers, because the theory attempts to analyze and explain the way people process or make sense of information—how they attend to it, process it, reflect on it, and recall it. The box below presents a brief summary.

People are bombarded with information every day. Obviously, not all the information can be processed or decoded. People may devote some level

 The Information Processing Theory

Information processing theory describes the way people handle input from their environment. Steps in this mental process begin with awareness of the stimulus or information, followed by attention and a decision to code that information or store it into memory. Next, the person needs to be able to retrieve the information at a later time.

Sometimes the steps occur in serial order and other times steps may occur simultaneously, such as attention and coding. The information processing theory is often compared to the way a computer processes information: data reading, data processing, and storage.[3]

of attention to some of it, but they may process even less of it, and retention and recall of the information may be poor. People do not so much process the information as they avoid the information.[4] How might a performer adjust? The information you convey as a performer has a greater chance of being seen, processed, and recalled if you are able to structure your material in such a way that a viewer's cognitive processing is enhanced. For example, most of what we convey in communication is not verbal—it is nonverbal, as you will read later in this book. As a performer, you may use slight vocal intonations or subtle facial gestures to make a point. And rather than attempt to bundle as much material as possible into the time allotted for your performance, information processing theory dictates that less is more. You want your information to stand out, to be attended to, and to be recalled.

One example of the difficulties that arise when audiences are given too much information to process may be found in television news. Research indicates that when people attend to a complex or vivid visual image, the ability to process the verbal or audio content suffers. And the reverse has also been found—when people focus on intricate verbal statements, they are less able to attend to the visual images.[5] This phenomenon has been called dual-coding theory, a reference to the tendency of humans to allocate attention to one or the other, but seldom both, especially if the two are unrelated. So, what's a performer to do? Reinforce each component with the other. In other words, make the audio or spoken element of information match the visual element. This adds emphasis to both the audio and video messages. If you have critical information to convey, do not pair it with a striking or intricate visual image. Or if you have compelling video, perhaps of a tornado, simply let the image "speak for itself."

According to one study on audience recall of television news, the viewer retains almost nothing from the viewing experience. Dennis Davis and John Robinson's research included interviews with more than 400 viewers of the three major network news programs.[6] They determined that several characteristics of news stories made the stories easier to recall. Stories that were complex, not surprisingly, were difficult to remember, whereas human interest or feature stories told with simple yet powerful story lines were easy to comprehend. However, most participants tended to confuse details from one story with details from another, and hardly any of the participants were able to recall as few as one or two elements of the news stories they viewed. Although this may seem discouraging, rather than accept this finding as an indication that nothing you tell an audience will be recalled, you might, instead, permit this to challenge you to pay close attention to the advice found in the remainder of this book about ways to match content and performance to maximize your impact.

COMMUNICATION THEORIES FOR TODAY

The media landscape continues to change, requiring continual evaluation of older theories and the creation of new ones. More recent writing about the future of mass communication predicts a profound change in the way we think about communication, most notably how communication is driven and changed by the Internet. In the past 60 years, the concept of a more active audience has taken precedence in mass communication theory. The growth of the Internet and our reliance on it, and its wide-ranging capability both in content and in audience, have changed the way we think about transmitting and receiving communication messages.[7] It is difficult to predict, though, just how Internet information will be processed cognitively. The Internet as an amalgamation of text, audio, and video presents a complex challenge to cognitive psychologists. Research indicates that text, audio, and video are each processed differently, and considerable work remains to be done concerning how Internet messages are understood.

Results of one study showed that recall of news stories read on the Internet was similar to the recall of news stories read in print. Yet the Internet recall was higher than typical findings of recall from stories listened to on the radio or watched on television.[8] The mixed results indicate that information on the Internet is indeed processed differently than material presented via traditional methods of mass communication.

On the other hand, in some ways "new" technology is not that new after all, since it includes the familiar formats of text, audio, and visual information. This approach about how to think of new technology has been called the "mix of attributes."[9] For example, television has traditionally been thought of as a visual medium, whereas newspapers have been considered a print or text medium. The Internet mixes these attributes by combining the traditional components of television (visual) and newspaper (text). It is more difficult to know how people process information from the Internet. Is it more like television or is it more like print? The Internet also possesses varying degrees of interactivity, organization (its structure), amount of control the user has, and channels (audio, visual, or both).[10]

Regardless of which of these opposing views you like, knowledge about how best to transmit information via the Internet effectively ought to be a concern for the conscientious performer.

The Emergence of the Broadcast and Radio Performer

As early as the 1920s, radio announcers for news and music began broadcasting regularly from individual stations. In 1929, radio programming became formalized under the National Broadcasting Company (NBC) and the Columbia Broadcasting System (CBS). Of course, radio could only provide a sound version of an event, and until 1927 motion pictures could only show a silent picture rendition. During the 1930s television technology began to improve picture and sound quality substantially. Radio, however, which came into homes with advertising-supported programs, was just right for the mass public suffering through the Great Depression.

During the 1930s, a tumultuous time leading up to World War II, the public received its news largely from newspaper conglomerates that owned radio stations, movie newsreels that accompanied feature pictures, and radio. The power of radio and mass media was first indicated as early as the 1930s when President Franklin D. Roosevelt delivered his first inaugural address to an audience of millions. "Roosevelt's fireside chats to audiences of 62 million people suggested the amazing potential of the radio medium—one individual, in a moment of time, bringing to bear upon a nation at large the full force of his vocal effectiveness."[11] His speaking style was direct, friendly, and comforting at a time when the nation needed strong leadership. Several radio broadcasters with journalism backgrounds began to gain prominence as World War II materialized. The radio broadcast pioneers had distinctive voices, well suited to the messages they were broadcasting to the public. Their voices were dignified, and some of them could even sing. Milton Cross became well known for his broadcasts of the Metropolitan Opera, and Graham McNamee was a major sports broadcaster.

Information programming in education, politics, health, finance, and weather developed along with news and sports. The public service program format was established. It consisted of a warning of a tornado, for example, followed by appeals for aid to the victims. Bulletins were often issued, but it was Lowell Thomas who began a hard news regular broadcast five times a week on NBC-Blue in the fall of 1930. Major wire services, such as the Associated Press, United Press, and International News Service, extended their news coverage for newspapers to radio, after press attempts to limit broadcast news failed. In 1936 UP became the first news service to offer a special radio wire transmitting news summaries written for delivery. Soon radio reporters were covering domestic and international news. H. V. Kaltenborn, a master of several languages, could translate the events of the Munich crisis in 1938.

As World War II came to Europe and spread, CBS had 14 full-time employees in European capitals, and listeners began to hear the soon-to-be-famous voices of Edward R. Murrow from London, Eric Sevareid in Paris, and William L. Shirer in Berlin. Each of them would describe the events of World War II—the bombing of London; the Japanese bombing of Pearl Harbor; the fall of Paris; the invasions of North Africa, the South Pacific, and Europe; D-day; and the death of Franklin D. Roosevelt—in a gripping, dramatic narrative style. Eyewitness coverage brought the war to the public with devastating immediacy. Evening commercial network time devoted to commentators, news, and talks went from 6.7 percent in the winter of 1938–1939 to 12.3 percent in the winter of 1940–1941. CBS led the way, NBC's Red and Blue were second, and Mutual was third.[12] By 1944 news and specials made up 16 to 20 percent of network program schedules. Many recordings exist of the announcers and the events of the war, and they are available in libraries and on the Internet. Radio and television news as it is known today inherited the news traditions of this period when broadcast news came of age.

Principal newscasters during the war years carried over to the postwar period of 1946 to 1952. *Meet the Press* began as a way to present interviews with members of congress. CBS and NBC had 15-minute newscasts in the networks' first seasons. The NBC *Camel News Caravan* had John Cameron Swayze narrating clips of newsreel film, and *Douglas Edwards with the News* was the CBS counterpart. Several special events drew public attention, such as President Truman relieving General Douglas MacArthur of his Korean command and the Estes Kefauver crime investigation that showed the public the depths of organized crime in America. Radio's *Hear It Now* became *See It Now,* the first continuing documentary series on television. These programs were the work of Edward R. Murrow and producer Fred Friendly, who had teamed up in the late 1940s. The best known program was aired on March 9, 1954, when Murrow used filmed speeches of Senator Joseph McCarthy, a Republican from Wisconsin, to expose the senator's bullying tactics during an investigation of communism in the U. S. Army. The controversial program drew a great deal of attention from the public because the senator had manipulated facts and damaged people's reputations. In 1956 Chet Huntley and David Brinkley began a shaky odyssey for their long-running newscast *The Huntley-Brinkley Report.* With the reserved Huntley in New York and the amusing Brinkley in Washington broadcasting from a tiny studio with a lecture stand at WRC-TV, the duo became a prominent national habit for news watchers. Walter Cronkite came to prominence during the 1960s, reporting on the assassination of President John F. Kennedy and narrating the live, riveting moon landing in 1969. By the end of the decade, Cronkite was the most trusted news man in America.

The news journalists had become anchors and celebrities, and had gained growing respect and trust for being fair and balanced in their presentations. With increasing profitability at the networks and local stations, celebrity status and dependability bolstered the reputations of television newscasters, especially during times of crisis and when the public looks to informed television leaders to bring perspective to complex issues. During the latter decades of the twentieth century Tom Brokaw at NBC, Dan Rather at CBS, and Peter Jennings at ABC assumed these responsibilities by hosting political debates, conventions, and elections. During the first decade of the twenty-first century, changing of the guard occurred at all three broadcast networks, with Brian Williams at NBC, Katie Couric at CBS, and Charles Gibson at ABC.

A multitude of documentaries has provided in-depth looks at the most complicated events, inventions, and changes that have impacted society. Feature programs such as *60 Minutes* have consistently included current issues, investigative reports, and personal insights from our country's storytellers. The number of women with prominent roles in news and information programming continues to grow but is still small. Women such as Jessica Savitch, Connie Chung, Barbara Walters, Diane Sawyer, Meredith Vieira, and the highly visible anchors and reporters of *The News Hour with Jim Lehrer* on PBS, such as Gwen Ifill and Judy Woodruff, have made significant contributions. These journalists and many others who have been major reporters during the wars in the Middle East continue the highest standards of television performing.

The Emergence of the New Media Performer

The revolution in transition from analog to digital media content, discussed in more detail in Chapter 9, is simultaneously a boost and a burden for performers. It has made it much easier for an aspiring performer to gain access to media, to create messages, to record them, and to distribute them. In the past, barriers to participation could be found at nearly every turn—available slots for talent were limited, and just as limited were the power brokers who selected performers and made it possible for their performances to be seen. Unprecedented avenues exist for beginning performers to be seen, thanks to the Internet and the less expensive production tools they now have at their fingertips. This experience is intensified as children in elementary schools learn the techniques of television broadcasting and develop as performers and producers. As students continue to learn and enter college, these future performers will have perfected their pragmatic skills and will look for strong, intellectual programs and courses in the future.

Performers as Leaders in Society

ews and information specialists inherit the responsibility of upholding important traditional values in society as surely as fictional characters in dramas, and perhaps more so because they are real. For example, an anchor learns that she is going to have a baby. As she continues to work on-air every day while she is expecting the baby and as a new mother, she becomes a symbol of dual achievement to her viewers.

Heroes and heroines, both real and fictional, exist at different levels. The performers who portray these figures are in fact leaders in sports, medicine, religion, education, and government and serve as inspiring role models for television viewers. A leader's highest attributes include the following:

- consistent pursuit of what is right and good
- self-sacrifice for a worthy cause or another person
- love and understanding of human beings, collectively and individually

Over the past few decades, television has depicted heroes and heroines as contending with an increasingly complex universe. On television (usually as actors in fictional dramas), these heroes and heroines may be super heroes and super heroines with nuclear, genetic, or bionic characteristics; less powerful, extraordinary mortals such as police, firefighters, professional people, and sport stars, among others; and ordinary human beings who act bravely under unusual circumstances. All of these performers serve in media, and in their personal lives, as an inspiration, especially to youth.

Despite their own human deficiencies, newscasters, subject experts, and the multitudes from other professions who take on performing roles must give perspective to a world in crisis. Although there is controversy over violence in media, it is the news anchors, contributing reporters, specialists, and producers behind the scenes who attempt to make sense of world events for a public that would be largely lost without them.

In summary, the talented are often thought of as leaders, as heroes, and as those who embody the best qualities of humankind. Performers, whether comfortable in the roles they play or not, are likewise thought of by the general public as bigger than life. If you are fortunate enough to be talented, use your talent to benefit your television viewers and you will reap untold rewards.

Using This Book

his book presupposes that those who wish to be performers will locate video equipment and facilities so that their work can be recorded and analyzed. Each chapter discusses the essentials. The first half of the book concentrates on developing the individual performer with chapters addressing material, appearance, voice, movement, discipline, and talent. The second half discusses the studio and on-location experiences, technology that makes field production possible, Internet news, and the business considerations in making the transition from a training program and internship to being a professional performer.

Summary

onsummate television performers make their job look easy, and some people may aspire to be part of the fast-paced, seemingly glamorous world of television, thinking it will be easy for them, too. However, you may already be aware that talent and skill combine so that the performer's communication appears effortless. Performers may be pursuing a career on camera as their primary occupation, or they may be non-career performers who are employed in a position that requires them to appear on camera. This chapter introduced you to the communication process and the complicated media world in which we live—creating challenges for any performer to present a clear, understandable message. Becoming a performer and gaining access to the opportunity to influence, educate, or persuade audience members comes with responsibility. The privilege of a platform should not be abused, and if your image becomes tarnished there often is little you can do to restore it. The media landscape is routinely littered with performers whose actions have left their careers in decline, while leaders in the field of journalism, throughout its history, have provided examples of how to get it right. Naturally, nothing of value happens on media without a carefully crafted plan or material, formalized as the script. This is where we will begin.

Notes

1. Wilbur Schramm, *The Process and Effects of Communication* (Urbana, IL: University of Illinois Press, 1954).
2. David K. Berlo, *The Process of Communication* (New York: Holt, Rinehart, and Winston, 1960).
3. Donald Eric Broadbent, *Perception and Communication* (London: Pergamon Press, 1958).
4. Stanley J. Baran and Dennis K. Davis, *Communication Theory: Foundations, Ferment, and Future.* (Belmont, CA: Wadsworth Publishing, 2006).
5. John E. Newhagen and Byron Reeves, "The Evening's Bad News: Effects of Compelling Negative Television News Images on Memory," *Journal of Communication* 42 (1992): 25–41.
6. Dennis K. Davis and John P. Robinson, "Newsflow and Democratic Society in an Age of Electronic Media," in *Public Communication and Behavior,* vol. 2, ed. George Comstock (New York: Academic, 1989).
7. Baran and Davis, *Communication Theory.*
8. Melvin L. DeFleur, Lucinda Davenport, Mary Cronin, and Margaret DeFleur, "Audience Recall of News Stories Presented by Newspaper, Computer, Television and Radio," *Journalism Quarterly* 69 (4) (1992): 1010–1022.

9. William P. Eveland, "A 'Mix of Attributes' Approach to the Study of Media Effects and New Communication," *Journal of Communication* 53 (3) (2003): 395–410.

10. Ibid.

11. Girard Chester, Garnet Garrison, and Edgar E. Willis, *Television and Radio* (New York: Appleton-Century-Crofts, 1963).

12. Christopher H. Sterling and John M. Kittross, *Stay Tuned. A Concise History of American Broadcasting* (Belmont, CA: Wadsworth Publishing, 1979).

Other Sources

Brinkley, David. *David Brinkley. A Memoir.* New York: Alfred A. Knopf, 1995.

Cooper, Anderson. *Dispatches from the Edge: A Memoir of War, Disasters, and Survival.* New York: HarperCollins, 2006.

Cronkite, Walter. *A Reporter's Life.* New York: Alfred A. Knopf, 1996.

Gale Encyclopedia of Childhood & Adolescence. Gale Research, 1998.

Humphrey, Hubert H. "Before Edward R. Murrow," (Speech). Center for Public Diplomacy, Medford, Massachusetts, December 6, 1965.

"Katie's Extreme Makeover?" Mediabistro.com, August 4, 2008. www.mediabistro.com/tvnewser/couric.

Mitchell, Andrea. *Talking Back . . .: To Presidents, Dictators, and Assorted Scoundrels.* New York: Viking Adult, 2005.

Nantz, Jim, with Eli Spielman. *Always By My Side: A Father's Grace and a Sports Journey Unlike Any Other.* New York: Gotham Books/Penguin, 2008.

Rather, Dan. *The Camera Never Blinks: Adventures of a TV Journalist.* New York: William Morrow & Company, 1977.

Shannon, C., and W. Weaver. *The Mathematical Theory of Communications.* Urbana: University of Illinois Press, 1949.

10:56:20PM.EDT.7/20/69. *The historic conquest of the moon as reported to the American people by CBS News over the CBS Television Network.* New York: Columbia Broadcasting System, 1970. Richard S. Salant, president, CBS News.

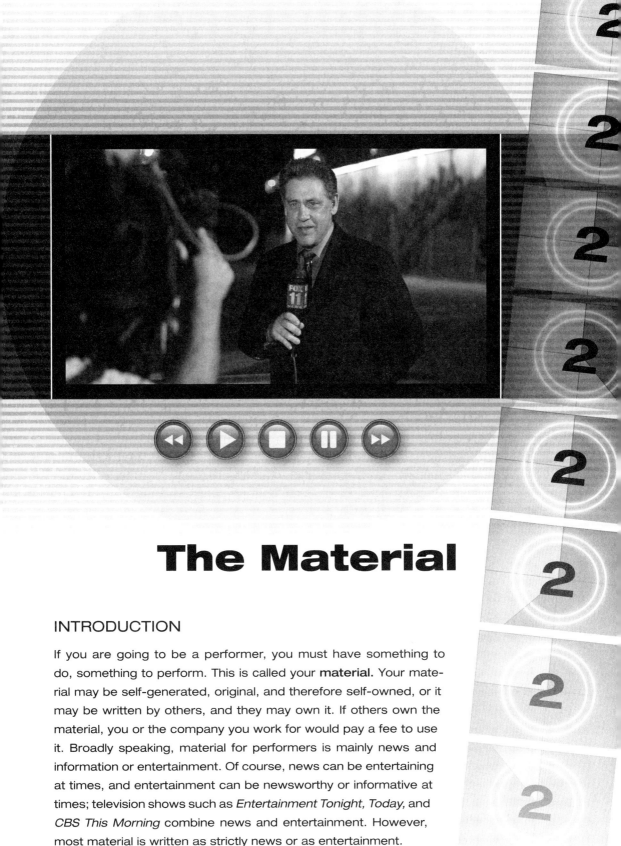

The Material

INTRODUCTION

If you are going to be a performer, you must have something to do, something to perform. This is called your **material.** Your material may be self-generated, original, and therefore self-owned, or it may be written by others, and they may own it. If others own the material, you or the company you work for would pay a fee to use it. Broadly speaking, material for performers is mainly news and information or entertainment. Of course, news can be entertaining at times, and entertainment can be newsworthy or informative at times; television shows such as *Entertainment Tonight, Today,* and *CBS This Morning* combine news and entertainment. However, most material is written as strictly news or as entertainment.

Your material is fundamental to who you are and what you do. Your material, for example, may center on reporting current events, and so you may be perceived as a world traveler: sophisticated and experienced; an acquaintance of world leaders and an eyewitness to political change, human sorrow, and triumph. This image may be different from that of a local news reporter, who dependably covers stories that impact a small community. But the changes and human problems that make local news are just as important to local people as world news is to those on the world scene. Your success as a news reporter will be measured by doing a good job wherever you are. Your value as a performer grows from the quality of your material.

Sources of Material

our material is constructed from basic units: the report, the interview, the demonstration, and the speech. These units, when arranged in a certain order, called a **format,** form newscasts, talk shows, magazine programs, and instructional presentations. After deciding what you want to do as a performer and what you want to share in news and information with your viewers, you are ready to consider ways to reinforce your material through the consistency of your image.

For the performer, the **sources** of material are the entire range of human experience. Traditionally, newscasts, documentaries, and informational programs are the types most commonly broadcast. Talk, advice, instruction, religion, product orientation, and sales programs are other categories that utilize performers. The information age offers abundant opportunity to gather material for every performer who has expertise to share. For most performers, the following are common sources of material and data:

1. Being an eyewitness, as, for example, if you saw a tornado touch down, or you were on the front lines of a war.
2. Gathering information at the scene from participants, such as those involved in an accident.
3. Getting data from government and officials, such as investigators in a fraud case.
4. Using domestic and foreign wire services.
5. Quoting from other news companies, such as newspapers and other broadcast and cable facilities.
6. Searching records, public libraries, and databases, such as those maintained by newspaper and broadcast companies.
7. Surfing the Internet, although you must be certain your source is reliable.
8. Interviewing those with specific experiences (such as veterans or world travelers), occupations (such as chefs or union leaders), and lifestyles (such as athletes or stay-at-home parents). The list is as varied as the performer's imagination.

The key to success in developing any material is selection. For example, a journalist may select a specialty or two within the broad range of news events. Even though journalists should be prepared to cover any story, they may want to be identified with an area or two in which they have special expertise. Fine arts, medicine, the environment, education, economics, and politics are just a few of the specialty fields available. Weather or sports may hold special interest. These two areas have high audience appeal and are usually part of news programs. Journalists may also find that further refinement of their specialty is necessary. In sports, for example, they may decide that although they can do play-by-play for major sports, they are better at one particular sport. Or some journalists may realize that they are better at feature sports or color background rather than calling the game. Selecting material is a part of determining where your abilities and interests lie. The material selected tends to define the individual performer.

The task, therefore, is to identify material that is appropriate for you to present as a performer and to develop skills in gathering the facts so you can structure a report for a newscast (inside or outside the studio), an interview, a demonstration, or a speech. Regardless of content, use a similar procedure:

1. Gather the data.
2. Organize it properly.
3. Write it up.
4. Deliver it to the public.

Performance Formats

ommon information formats are the newscast, the interview, the demonstration, and the speech.

NEWSCASTS

In most newscasts, the news content is determined by the news producers' behind-the-scenes staff, who actually run the program. Early in the day the stories that will be developed for airing start to emerge. This is an ongoing process. Most reports will have audio or visual support, but some stories will be mentioned only in anchor narratives. Short pieces, news stories that have just occurred (called *breaking news*) and have no visuals, or reports that are too expensive to cover will be read on camera by the news anchor.

Traditional newscasts are similar in structure. First there is a billboard (headlines) and then the top story of the hour (often this is a local story or a national story with strong local impact). The value of the news story depends upon its impact on large numbers of people. Natural disasters, wars, economic changes, and life-threatening events are potentially stories of heavy impact. They are **hard news** and exist in real time only. The objective of television news is to tell what is going on *now*. Stories taking place earlier in the day, last night, or yesterday require updating to current status. News, therefore, is highly perishable.

Because television hard news is so brief—about 9 to 12 minutes in every half-hour newscast—the top stories are clustered in two six-minute segments at the beginning of the program. They are followed by features, sports, weather, and a final human interest story, the kicker. Reporters, therefore, tell their stories in 20 to 90 seconds, though 90 seconds is a long story. It's rare to appear on-camera continuously for longer than about 20 seconds. Visuals and newsmakers keep the **pace,** the overall flow, of the news fast and maintain an aura of importance.

Usually, a reporter prepares a **package,** a tightly written set of easy-to-comprehend audiovisual reports, with a minimum of on-air exposure for herself. The exception to this is the live report from the scene, where the reporter stands in front of or near the event, usually at an accident, fire, or public building. The report may be partially prerecorded, but anchors at the station may ask questions also. The questions and answers are prepared largely in advance and coordinated with the journalist at the scene. The news department cannot afford to have its reporter quizzed without having correct answers. The live report creates the impression that the news team is giving the most recent update, and once the station has gone to this expense, it wants to make the venture worthwhile. Little pondering can be done on camera. Smooth **ad-libbing,** the ability to say words on the spot that are not in the script, and finesse in talking with celebrities, politicians, and sports figures are essential to a reporter's prestige, credibility, and personality.

The basic news story

The report or story is the basic unit of a newscast. The nature of the report is mainly current information with high impact, called **hard news,** or supplementary information that does not require immediate delivery, called feature or **soft news.**

Keeping journalism's "five W's and an H" (Who, What, When, Where, Why, How) in mind, the reporter focuses on what the public wants or needs to know while using all the elements of compelling storytelling. As these facts are gathered by the on-camera reporter, a photographer records shots that will correlate with the action of the event (increasingly, the reporter and photographer roles are being filled by the same person). Later, in the **editing** process at the station, the words and the pictures will blend into an **audiovisual** presentation that will explain the event to the public in a concise, understandable narrative.

That narrative is usually chronological, but occasionally it is topical. If the narrative is chronological, it has a beginning, a middle, and an end, often presented in sequential time. To capture immediate attention and to create an aura of excitement, a reporter will probably introduce or **lead in** the story with the current status of the event. Thus, the chronological order may be reversed or altered; that is, the end of the event (or current status) is presented first, and then the reporter fills in the background.

Whether the reporter already has the data or gathers the data at the scene, there are obvious questions the public wants answered. The reporter determines the order in which the main events will be told. The rest of the story consists mainly of verification, such as testimonials from officials and participants, and insightful photography. Because a guiding principle in television is "show, don't tell," reporters are often on-camera for a brief lead-in and wrap-up, providing voice-over narration in between. A **wrap-up** usually projects the future, that is, what in the best judgment of the reporter is likely to happen next.

Hard news events are reported as they happen and have a major influence on large numbers of people. Soft news and features add substance and depth to hard news topics and may be part of an ongoing public discussion. Some feature stories are humorous or anecdotal and have little or no impact on public activity. Even so, a news story follows a typical pattern, whether the event is scheduled and anticipated or unscheduled and unanticipated. What follows are some examples of typical types of news stories.

A scheduled story: Hard news

A mayor is giving the State-of-the-City speech. You must glean from the speech the essence of what the public needs to know to quickly understand the actions of city government. In a hard news story told as it unfolds at a scheduled news event, you lead with what the mayor says that is most important, such as plans for new city programs, new taxes, or new trends. The format would be similar to the basic story in Figure 2.1.

FIGURE **2.1** *Scheduled news story structure.*

Who	The mayor wants to
What	build a new dam near the
Where	north end of Blue Lake
	if the taxpayers will vote for
How	ten million dollars in
	bonds. The mayor says
Why	the dam is essential to
	water reserves in the
When	decade ahead. Public
	debate begins next week.
Speculation	The mayor expects to get
	her way on this issue.
Signature	John Doe reporting live
	from city hall.

An unscheduled story: Hard news

For a hard news story reported in real time at an unscheduled event, the lead is similar. What happened is briefly summarized, as in Figure 2.2.

A news feature: Soft news

A feature may be a multipart series on hunger, drugs, or other urban problems. Or it may be a humorous, inconsequential footnote on the day's events called a kicker, which is usually placed at the end of a newscast. Figure 2.3 has a sample feature format.

Sports news

Sports news must begin with hard news; that is, sports scores of local and national games. This may be all the time allotted to sports. Usually, however, the sportscaster also manages to include one or more feature items. Celebrity acquaintance is a big asset to sports reporters, so if you specialize in sports, you will want to develop associations with key figures. Typically, a brief soft news interview highlights a game as in Figure 2.4

FIGURE 2.2 *Unscheduled news story structure.*

Who	Sixteen-year-old Mary Brown
What	is dead. She was shot at about
When	3 p.m. at her home in the
Where	1600 block of E Street.
Attribution	Police say she was shot by
	her boyfriend, 18-year-old
	Bob Jones. They reportedly
Why	were playing Russian roulette
	when the gun discharged.
	Jones is in custody. Charges
Speculation	are expected to be filed
Signature	tomorrow. Maxine Dayton
	reporting.

2.3 *Soft news story structure.*

Who	The alarm rang. Bill Bryan walked into the
Where	shower half awake. He turned on the water.
	As he stepped onto the floor, he felt it
Attribution	move. Bryan says he made a yell Tarzan
What	would have been proud of. A 12-foot boa
	constrictor was lounging on the shower
	tiles. But Bryan's yell was one of joy. You
Why	see, Hefty, his pet snake, disappeared over a
When	year ago. But today, Hefty is home. That's
Signature	the news. I'm Dave Stone. Thanks for watching.

2.4 *Sports news story structure.*

	Davis:
Who	The Ace team's top pitcher Abe Aronson was
What	a major reason for the team's victory tonight
When/Where	at Home Stadium. What is your reaction to pitching a no-hitter?
	Aronson:
Testimonial	It feels great, Duke. But no one wins a game alone.
	Davis:
Game highlight	The highlight for me was when Joe Player stole third in the eighth inning.
	Aronson:
	That was a great moment all right. Every player was great tonight. The other team was tough to beat.
	Davis:
Reporter comment	It's a happy locker room for the home team
	tonight. Thanks, Abe Aronson, for dropping by.
Speculation	Ace team goes against the Big Leaguers on Friday.
Signature	Duke Davis reporting from Home Stadium.

INTERVIEWS

Numerous in-depth programs are primarily interviews or a collection of interviews. Celebrities or public figures discussing their lives and careers make up much of the content. Some programs concern historical events, politics, philosophical and religious issues, business matters, and public concerns. Although the nature of the content may change, the interviewer's role remains fairly constant.

The key to a good interview is the same key that generates a good news report—a concept or **story angle;** it is a fresh approach that may suggest solutions as well as identify problems. Interview programs provide a good deal of insight but can endure criticism for a tendency of some program hosts to appeal to the seamier side of human life. Make sure you have a good reason for conducting the interview. Why do you want to talk to your guest? What do you have to talk about that the public wants to hear?

Prospective interviewees should not consent to television interviews unless they are willing to express personal views and feelings openly. Asking people to reveal personal information can be intense, so professionals don't get involved with interviews unless they are sure they can handle them. Many people are willing to be interviewed after they have written a book on a personal problem, not only to promote the book, but also because they are fully prepared to discuss the subject matter. If the topic is personal, the interviewee may try to exclude sensitive questions in advance. Naturally, good interviewers will ask them anyway, because they are the ones the public wants answered. The interviewee must be ready for candid questions. The interviewer must be prepared if the interviewee refuses to answer, gets angry, or even stalks off the set. However awkward, the interviewer must conclude graciously. It's important for both interviewers and interviewees to be prepared for the program, and this is discussed more in Chapter 8.

In an interview, be it one person to another, or one person to individuals in a group, all participants are referred to as **talking heads.** Nowhere is the importance of strong material better illustrated than in long formats involving talking heads. Oprah Winfrey and Larry King are both famous for creating engaging shows centered around interviews. Hot topics (often involving sex and violence) and major celebrities (preferably emerging from major projects) keep these programs going.

The typical structure for a television interview normally runs from three to 15 minutes. Half-hour magazine programs may use the shorter interview; one-hour shows may use the longer one. The interviewer begins with a 15-to-20-second lead-in to introduce the guest.

The basic format for a group interview may go as follows: The host provides a background of the topic, the guest or guests are introduced, the guests are interviewed, the audience asks questions, an expert may be introduced to lend some perspective to the topic, the host briefly summarizes, and then the host thanks the guests and audience.

In a one-on-one interview, the typical information pattern emerges: the current status and what the public wants most to know, the background details, and the future of the guest or of the issue. Twenty questions covering this structure will help focus the host, although only five questions may actually be covered. The questions should be open-ended so that the interview doesn't consist of "yes" or "no" answers. Through careful listening on the part of the host, the interview may be more insightful than anything the producers could have prepared in advance. This assumes that the interviewer is well read and can match his or her background with the guest's experience. The interview has a 20-second lead-in consisting of why the topic or person is worthy of public attention, the person's name and title as it relates to the topic, and a challenging initial question, followed by others the viewers want answered. Most beginners are afraid to ask tough questions but should ask them anyway. Those on the talk circuit expect them and so does the public. If interviewers don't ask them—politely of course, but clearly and directly—they are not working hard enough on behalf of the public. After all, the interviewers represent the public.

The closing of the one-on-one interview is the opening in reverse order: restating the question, thanking the guest, repeating the guest's full name and title or relevance to the topic, providing a **summary** or **tag line** for the interview, and then ending with the host's signature. Promotion for a future program may be included.

The following interviews illustrate the structure and typical questions. Some of them may seem commonplace by using a formula, but they are usually very effective.

Personality interview

For many years, Barbara Walters has been known for her skillful handling of sensitive personal subjects. Coming from a famous theatrical family, Walters has been acquainted with celebrities all her life. The key to Walters's approach is enabling the celebrity to present his or her point of view, or position, without restriction. Most of Walters's interviews are with people she has known for years, has helped to promote, and with whom she has maintained a friendship. This is their mutual comfort zone. Walters must ask the difficult questions the public wants answered, but she does so with grace, never seeming to attack the interviewee even though she is tenacious in getting the answers she wants. For example, after being diagnosed with pancreatic cancer, actor Patrick Swayze appeared on *The Barbara Walters Special—Patrick Swayze: The Truth.*[1] He knew that Walters's interview style would be respectful and would allow him time to talk about difficult issues in his own words. Video inserts provided background for his career, which emphasized hard work and a fighting attitude to survive. Even though Walters had ample time and network resources, her difficult one-on-one interview is similar to the more minimalist interview illustrated in Figure 2.5.

FIGURE **2.5**   *Personality interview structure.*

Interviewer's Perspective	Interviewer
Guest's name/title	Mary Megastar has been a film actress for more than 10 years.
Background	She has a handsome, successful husband and two bright children.
	She seems to have everything a woman could want.
Central focus	Yet, last June she attempted suicide.
Lead question	What would you like to say about it now?
List questions	1. What caused you to consider suicide?
Cause/effect	2. How have you solved your problems?
Current status	3. How are you feeling now?
Solutions	4. What suggestions do you have for others with similar problems?
Closing: Name/title of guest	Thank you Mary Megastar for being brave enough to tell us
	about your problem.
Repeat focus	
Information/source	If you want more information,
Promotion	Mary Megastar has a new book, *Survivor.*
Signature	Until next time, I'm Helen Hostess.

Issue interview

Important, complex issues are not usually solved on issue-oriented television shows, but they do allow a forum for discussion and explanation. For example, several years ago a Palestinian and an Israeli agreed to discuss the issue of living in separate states. Hostility was so intense neither person would look at the other or carry on a direct conversation. The student moderator had to arbitrate their views extemporaneously on the set. However, both sides wanted to be heard and would accept whatever airtime was offered.

Presenting opposing views is essential to public understanding; hence, the issue interview is important. Local issues are especially interesting to viewers, so often these kinds of interviews will include community figures and local representatives. In Figure 2.6, the example issue interview is with a policeman who is discussing an initiative that has officers visiting classrooms.

FIGURE 2.6 *Issue interview structure.*

Interviewer's Perspective	Interviewer
Lead	There's more to living on the streets
Central focus	with drugs than just saying no.
Guest's name/title	My guest is local police officer Dan Gilbert.
Lead question	Officer Gilbert, how many elementary schools do you visit each week?
List questions	1. What message do you give the students?
	2. Do they listen?
	3. Are you optimistic about the war on drugs?
Closing: Name/title of guest	My guest has been local police officer Dan Gilbert.
Repeat focus	He believes we are winning the war on drugs,
Comment	and so do I.
Information/source	If you want an officer to appear in your school, dial the information line 1-866-G-O-O-D-G-U-Y, or log on to our station's Web site at www.goodguy.com.
Promotion	Tomorrow's community focus is on the homeless.
Signature	I'm Lyle Boggs.

Lifestyle interview

The lifestyle interview acquaints the public with individuals with qualities or life circumstances that set them apart. For example, a guest may be afflicted with a rare disease, or may be an accident survivor or a savant. They are able to testify about the fragility and strengths of what it is to be human.

One student-hosted public affairs program consisted of guiding "unsighted" (a term the parents preferred) children around a television studio, allowing them to touch and listen to explanations about microphones, lights, and cameras. Three-dimensional objects such as a relief globe showed how the children were able to understand the object without sight. The parents and children were excited to participate, and to add this experience to their lives.

A typical approach to a lifestyle interview is laid out in Figure 2.7, where the guest is promoting a book about his extraordinary experiences. This interview format is frequently used for book promotion because the interviewer knows the guest is most likely well informed and is able to handle the questions the public wants answered.

FIGURE 2.7 Lifestyle interview structure.

Interviewer's Perspective	Interviewer
Background	*My Two Lives* is a new book by Jon Jones. Jon was injured in a
Central focus	car accident five years ago, leaving him paralyzed from the
	waist down. He knows what it is to be able-bodied and to be
	handicapped. John, what are the biggest problems you face?
Topic outline	1. Transportation
	2. Depression
	3. Financial problems
	4. Human relationships
Interviewee's Perspective	(Jones is attractive and neatly groomed. Jones exudes charm, but
	he seems genuine. The questions are short and his answers are
	short, too.)
	Jones:
Jones only answers what he knows and believes.	Transportation is my biggest problem. I can't drive, and so I have to depend upon others.
	That's tough. You aren't free.
	Interviewer:
	Do you get depressed?
	Jones:
He is optimistic.	Yes, I was very depressed right after the accident. But much of that is behind me.
	Interviewer:
	Have you adjusted in normal ways?
	Jones:
Jones wants to avoid embarrassing questions.	I have a girlfriend. That's fortunate. We just met. We are just getting acquainted.
	Interviewer:
Interviewer persists.	Can you have intimate relations?
	Jones:
Jones anticipates the question.	Having sex is complicated for many people, not just the disabled. In my case it's too early to say.

(continued)

2.7 *Continued.*

Jones tries to redirect the agenda.	My main concern is being self-reliant. Most disabled have difficulty finding work that is satisfying and arranging transportation.
	Interviewer: If you could say one thing to the viewer, what would that be?
	Jones:
Central focus	Employ the disabled.
Jones has a clear message for the public.	They want to work, too. (Jones gives a generous smile.)
	Interviewer: My inspiration today is Jon Jones. His wonderful book is *My Two Lives.* We'll be back, right after this message.

DEMONSTRATIONS

The demonstration is the third type of informational programming (along with the report and the interview). Demonstrations are particularly valuable as teaching tools. Other than through a lecture, how does one usually learn? Imitating someone else's demonstration is a key learning technique. Whether you want to teach a person how to drive a car, putt in golf, or prepare a meal, a demonstration will probably be the main means of instruction. An increasing number of programs demonstrating everything from how to operate a forklift truck to how to set a table require performers skilled in the task. The media markets that use demonstrations, such as talk shows, do-it-yourself cable channels, and on-demand exercise programs, are huge and growing.

Each demonstration will contain information that you will need to include so that the audience is able to learn. In the demonstration program, talk to the guest prior to the program so that you will know what the guest needs and plans to do. Clearly, most television performers cannot complete the entire task assigned to them within the time frame of the program. Therefore, advance planning is critical. First, the demonstration must be thought out step by step. Each step must be illustrated well enough for a viewer to understand it and to be able to duplicate it. Demonstration materials must be prepared beforehand in progressive steps and in a logical order. In other words, each step is partially finished before the actual demonstration is presented on television. Popular forms of demonstration shows include home improvement programs (such as those found on HGTV) and cooking shows (like those on the Food Network).

Demonstrations are carefully structured. Frequently, they are brief how-to-do-it programs. Viewers are told what is going to be accomplished, shown the easy steps it will take to do it, and then the attractive results are displayed, which should exceed a viewer's expectation. At the outset you must outline what is going to take place within the time period you are allowed. Whether you are painting a picture, grooming a dog, or orienting new employees to the operation of a company, outline what you are going to do and how you are going to do it. Then follow your outline, step by step, and finally tell the viewers you have done what you said you would do. Try not to accomplish too much in any given program. Twenty minutes is the maximum attention span for most viewers in an instructional setting. Ordinarily, television watchers are not dedicated viewers, because messages so often interrupt program continuity. Demonstrations are seldom finished in real time. They are prepared in progressive steps, including the end result. Figure 2.8 walks through a basic demonstration.

FIGURE 2.8 *Doll-making demonstration.*

Demonstration	Making a doll
Memorized open (for a fluent open/close)	*Demonstrator:*
	Hi, I'm Doris Teacher, and I am going to show you how to make dolls out of scraps around the house. If your children want to watch, that's okay, too. I'm going to make this doll in five easy steps:
Script outline	*(Each step is started, but not completed)*
All items needed are placed on a table and identified.	1. Here are all the materials we'll need.
One pattern is cut on-camera; others are precut.	2. Now, let's cut the patterns.
One doll is assembled from materials on the table; other examples are completed.	3. This is how you can assemble the doll's body.
Doll is dressed; another doll nearby shows the completed look.	4. Dress the doll.
	5. Add finishing touches such as jewelry.
Several elegant dolls are displayed to show potential of the project.	Isn't she pretty?
Memorized closing	Making dolls is easy, fun, and inexpensive. You and your children will enjoy it. If I can do it, so can you. Thanks for following along.

SPEECHES

So far we have discussed the news story, the interview, and the demonstration. The fourth basic unit is the speech. Those performers who give speeches fall into three categories:

1. First are those career performers who give news reports. They are hired by a company to talk directly to viewers, such as anchors who are capable of maintaining an audience through both scheduled and unanticipated events. They often work endless hours for the privilege of being an eyewitness to great moments in history. Such a person is ABC's Charles Gibson, who narrated the inauguration of Barack Obama. Besides anchors, other single performers can include opinion writers (PBS's Anne Taylor Fleming), essayists (CBS's Andy Rooney), or editorialists, such as a local station's president.

2. A second group of career performers who use speech formats are those who give speeches in order to lead a discussion or performance. This may include hosting a discussion group or serving as a moderator of a round table. A distinguished moderator was NBC's Tim Russert, who hosted *Meet the Press*. These people are sufficiently charismatic to hold an audience with little visual support.[2] These performers may host an information program, be an unseen commentator, or be a voice-over reader of continuity for a documentary, such as John Chancellor was for Ken Burns's documentary *Baseball*. These performers may be permanent or contracted freelance employees of media companies.

3. The third and largest group that uses speech formats is the non-career performers who use speeches to get their organization or issue out to the public. For example, a professor may give a speech in the form of a lecture. These speakers have new information on topics they have studied for years, and the lecture may be compelling to a group dedicated to the subject and/or to the speaker.

Speeches are often presented with or without an audience. These people address their viewers through the camera lens, also. The organization of the speech or lecture is outlined right at the beginning. Sometimes the topics to be discussed are numbered. This makes the speech easy for the listener to follow. Many speeches are completely written out, referred to as a **prepared statement,** and may they be printed so that members of the press and viewers may obtain copies. Politicians, military personnel, salespersons, instructors, clergy men or women, and corporate executives are among those seen reading speeches from prompters or scripts in studio settings, at conventions, and in classrooms. A well-known example is the president of the United States delivering a speech, as shown in Figure 2.9.

2.9 *Basic setup for a speech to a large audience.*

1. Speaker   2. Microphones   3. Prompter   4. Lecture stand

Note: Media tower with cameras is several feet directly in front of speaker.

In most speeches, especially those that are televised, a teleprompter is an integral part. Audiences have high expectations of perfection, but speakers still want to appear as though their words come from themselves and not from a prepared document. Some prompters are part of the speaker's podium, while others may be directly below the camera(s).

Speeches are essays consisting of identifying the topic, providing background, outlining what you are going to talk about, commenting on each topic in logical order, summarizing, and concluding with a call to action or hopeful statement. Speeches usually begin with a summary of the background for the status quo. Then the speaker submits his or her outlook for each topic. These topics for change are listed and should be discussed in order. A general summary and conclusion will follow. Although each topic may be worthy of several speeches, time constraints keep all but the most important speeches to 30 minutes or less. See Figure 2.10 for an example of a short speech format for a corporate setting.

Some speeches lend themselves to audio or visual aids, such as PowerPoint, but the more important the speech the less distraction it needs. The president's State of the Union speech has been a direct presentation to each citizen since the days of President Franklin Roosevelt, and it shows how even on the largest scale, communication fundamentally remains a one-on-one experience.

FIGURE 2.10 *Speech structure.*

	Speaker:
Structure: Verbally outline what you are going to discuss. Include a friendly opening to attract audience attention.	Friends, tonight I want to talk about the future of our company. While the company is fundamentally strong, we need to improve three areas to help ensure continued success. The first is the quality of the product. The second is economic conservation through technology, and the third is the need for continued employee dedication.
Some background may be necessary for each topic.	*Body of the speech:* 1. Product quality 2. Conservation 3. Employee dedication
Finish on a positive note of hope and encouragement.	*Summary:* Remember that by increasing the quality of our products, by using the latest software to increase our conservation, and by reaffirming our dedication to the company, we can have another decade of success.
Thank the audience for their attention.	Thank you so much for your time.

Summary

U nless you are simply a model in front of the camera, you will need material that sources provide. As an old saying goes: You are only as good as your material! Typically material or information is generated in one of these four formats: the report or newscast, the interview, the demonstration, and the speech. Newscasts are made up of combinations of stories called hard news, soft news, and sports news, each having its own common formulaic framework. A story angle is necessary to provide structure to an interview. The interview may be about a celebrity or an issue of concern, or it may introduce viewers to the lifestyle of exceptional individuals. Demonstrations take a step-by-step approach in order to teach viewers how to do something, and they lead to the creation of an end product. The final category, speeches, may be delivered by career performers such as news anchors or moderators. These people have enough charisma to be the sole person on-camera and rivet viewers' attention to the screen. The non-career performers who give speeches are larger in number because it is a common venue or opportunity. Some people who give speeches write them out prior to delivery; others ad lib; either way, the content is carefully designed to maximize the success of the presentation.

CHAPTER 2 *exercises*

1. Write several 30-second news stories based on interviews or newspaper or Internet data. Use real events, data, and attribution.

2. Record yourself reading these stories aloud. If no camera is available, practice them in front of a mirror.

3. Prepare a script for interviewing a friend. Be sure to include an opening, probable questions, and a close. Focus your interview on one aspect of his or her life.

4. Outline a demonstration and set up the items you will need for it. Record people to emulate.

5. Obtain scripts from the Internet, such as from www.simplyscripts.com or from local stations. For example, WDNJ in Virginia has a script library at scholar.lib.vt.edu/VA-news/WDBJ-7.

Notes

1. ABC-TV, *The Barbara Walters Special—Patrick Swayze: The Truth* (January 7, 2009).
2. "A Good Life," *People* (June 30, 2008), pp. 46–51; Jon Meacham, "God, Politics and the Making of a Joyful Warrior," *Newsweek* (June 23, 2008), pp. 31–33. These articles discuss the life of *Meet the Press* moderator Tim Russert, 1950–2008.

Other Sources

Attkisson, Sharyl, and Don R. Vaughan. *Writing Right for Broadcast and Internet News.* Boston: Allyn & Bacon/Pearson Education, 2003.

Brooks, Brian S., George Kennedy, Daryl R. Moen, and Don Ranly. *Telling the Story. Writing for Print, Broadcast and Online Media.* The Missouri Group. Boston: Bedford/St. Martin's, 2001.

Callahan, Christopher. *A Journalist's Guide to the Internet. The Net as a Reporting Tool.* Boston: Allyn & Bacon/Pearson Education, 2003.

Kant, Garth. *How to Write Television News.* New York: McGraw-Hill, 2006.

Lieb, Thom. *Editing for Clear Communication.* New York: McGraw-Hill, 2002.

Richardson, Brian. *The Process of Writing News. From Information to Story.* Boston: Allyn & Bacon/Pearson Education, 2007.

Ryan, Michael, and James W. Tankard Jr. *Writing for Print and Digital Media.* New York: McGraw-Hill, 2005.

Yopp, Jan Johnson, and Katherine C. McAdams. *Reaching Audiences. A Guide to Media Writing.* Boston: Allyn & Bacon/Pearson Education, 2007.

Appearance

INTRODUCTION

This chapter presents key components of your "look," beginning with an assessment of the shape and features of your face. As a performer, you must learn how to control the muscles in your face; in effect, to smile when you don't feel like smiling. Your complexion and hair are perhaps the two key components of your appearance that you may be able to improve and transform. Other suggestions for how to improve your look include the topics of height and weight control, clothing, and a discussion of cosmetic and medical options. You are encouraged to conduct a self-analysis, scrutinizing each of these key elements. Though everyone has areas in which they might improve, your own attitude, displayed as confidence, may be the best feature you can develop.

Finding Your Unique Image

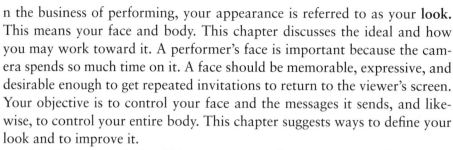

I n the business of performing, your appearance is referred to as your **look.** This means your face and body. This chapter discusses the ideal and how you may work toward it. A performer's face is important because the camera spends so much time on it. A face should be memorable, expressive, and desirable enough to get repeated invitations to return to the viewer's screen. Your objective is to control your face and the messages it sends, and likewise, to control your entire body. This chapter suggests ways to define your look and to improve it.

Ideally, your look should be consistent with your material. If you aspire to be a news reporter, then your look should suggest maturity and credibility. At the same time, you want to demonstrate energy and understanding, empathy for human problems, constructive curiosity, and fairness. Professional television performers who hold major positions are usually easy to recognize because their look is unique; it is different from that of anyone else. Therefore, your objective is to find an individual look that suits you. Even if your field calls for a more conservative look, such as for anchors, hosts, or field reporters, a personalized image can still stand out in the right way. A few feature reporters have made themselves distinctive through the originality of their material and their look. For example, consumer affairs reporter Marvin Zindler became an iconic figure on KTRK-TV, Houston, because of his outrageous speaking style (almost shouting at times), silver-hair toupee, stylish clothes (the family business), and an exhibitionist personality. He concentrated on using his media position to help the less fortunate, especially veterans, children who are disabled, and the poor. In each feature Marvin Zindler tried to reach a positive outcome and conclude with a big smile.

The viewers will decide whether they like you and are willing to see more of your work. Even if they do not respond to you immediately, continue to do the work you believe in. Many fine performers have, over time, gained the public's appreciation. If you are a dedicated performer, remember that recognition may take years or may happen overnight. Regardless, over time you will steadily improve your material and your look.

DECIDE WHAT WORKS FOR YOU

Controlling your dominant image begins by allowing others to help you find that unique quality that is fundamental to you, and performing on television gives you the chance to express it. Most likely your image will come from within yourself, and so you must diligently hunt for it. Sometimes you can find your image by defining what you like about other people. What draws you to someone else? Being friendly, open, smiling, and good natured are qualities that form a favorable image for some people. These characteristics attract admirers. But your dominant image comes from within you; it must be your own. You must find it, develop it, and project it.

BE CONSISTENT

When you feel comfortable with your image, write material that is consistent with it. Set aside material that doesn't foster that image. Focus your attention on what you can do best. Prepare and rehearse to perfection. Naturally, you hope to work with highly capable directors and crews and to benefit from the expertise of an excellent editor. You must appreciate that a certain amount of trial and error is part of what you do, and that opportunity and a great deal of luck must come your way. Even so, determining your dominant image and selecting the best material will add focus, direction, and momentum to a specific career objective such as news anchor, community expert, feature information specialist, or host of a talk show.

Defining Your Image

eep in mind that television does not reveal the whole truth about a performer, just part of it. Therefore, your objective is to show what you want to show and nothing more. This procedure is image control. To control your image, you must be aware of both the image you have and the image you want to project for the work you want to do in news and information.

In order to perform well, you must settle on an individual appearance that you can live with. This may not be as easy as it sounds. Some individuals are quite happy with who they are and how they look. If your appearance is consistent with your conception of your personal and professional life, you are fortunate. For many others this consistency is not so obvious and needs some adjustments. You are basically seeking a dominant image that the public will admire and remember. While your image may not express the true depth of your soul, it is who you are when you appear on television or in public.

ANALYZING YOUR OVERALL LOOK

As mentioned above, the key to visibility in broadcasting is having or cultivating a unique and memorable look. Visual recognition is the dominant identifiable aspect of television and other forms of broadcast. It is more important than voice, even though voice is very important. Although your appearance may not be unique, it should be pleasant and easily remembered by viewers. Being exceptionally beautiful, handsome, ugly, strange, exotic, large, thin, nervous, or energetic, however, can provide a strong basis for a memorable appearance. Your look consists of your face and entire body. Television, being a **close-up** medium, concentrates mainly on your face.

Perhaps you do not know how you appear to other people. Maybe you do not know what values others see in you. A simple technique for helping to identify what other people admire, or possibly dislike, is to stand up in front of a classroom of 20 strangers, such as new classmates. Ask them to write down a few descriptive words of what they see, and what reaction they have, as you stand before the group. Strangers do form an immediate impression.

For more than a decade, ABC's *20/20* television series has done studies on the value of being attractive. These experiments have shown that good-looking people have a better chance at employment, tend to be offered more money for the job, are considered more believable and friendly, and have other positive qualities automatically assigned to them.

Use this first impression test mentioned above to identify characteristics that you may want to improve or eliminate. Look for these key words if you aspire to be a journalist: *intelligent, serious, mature, credible, articulate,* and *attractive.* Descriptions for feature reporters may vary greatly: *funny, sporty, clever, unusual, perceptive,* and *pleasant.* These initial impressions suggest whether you are on the right track in projecting the dominant image that is consistent with the performing you aspire to do. Now let's consider in detail your dominant image.

ANALYZING YOUR FEATURES

If a performer wants to gain a reputation in news and information, facial characteristics should not detract from the messages the performer is attempting to convey. The easiest way to assess your face is to have someone take three close-up, high-resolution photographs of it: a front or head shot, and right and left profile shots. The photographs should not be retouched. Study these photos. Notice the shape of your head and face and appraise your features, muscle control, complexion, and hair. Be objective, but avoid being overly critical without reason.

Viewers are more inclined to watch people they consider to be attractive. Until recently, media standards and American standards of beauty have, for the most part, been dominated by the Anglo-American or classic Caucasian look, as preserved in European art for centuries. Internationally, however, we find that beauty takes many forms depending on the audience—opinions about performers and their appearance are as varied as the viewers who watch them. African, Asian, and Middle Eastern standards differ, but these alternate standards of beauty have now begun to be defined, discussed, and popularized in the United States. Progress continues to be made, as international media allow for other standards of beauty to be understood and more widely accepted. In fact, variations on the "typical" dimensions of attractiveness may in the long run be more memorable and therefore more suitable to television and other forms of broadcast.

Evaluate the three photographs mentioned earlier to get a sense of your facial structure. Determine your assets and liabilities by considering the questions listed in Figure 3.1, which are discussed in the following sections.

Analyzing your features.

What is most dominant about your appearance?

What is the shape of your face?

What are the color and shape of your eyes?

What is the shape of your mouth?

What is the condition of your teeth?

What is the shape of your nose?

What is the shape of your chin, jaw, and cheekbones?

Do you have good muscle control in your face?

What are the quality, color, and complexion of your skin?

What are the characteristics of your hair?

What is most dominant about your appearance?

Almost everyone wants to look pleasant. However, physical characteristics you prefer may not be so appealing to someone else. What you consider unattractive and highly noticeable, another person may ignore. How many physical characteristics do you remember about your close friends? What you do remember is important to you. Try to be objective in considering your own facial and body assets and liabilities.

What is the shape of your face?

Traditionally, faces have been described as primarily oval, round, square, or heart shaped. Figure out your face shape by tracing a close-up photograph of your face and comparing it to those in Figure 3.2. An oval face is generally considered the most pleasant for women, and an oval face with a rather square jawbone is favored for men. The classic face familiar from Greek statues divides the face into almost equal thirds: one-third from the top of the forehead to the eyebrows, one-third from the brow to the tip of the nose, and one-third from the tip of the nose to the tip of the chin. High cheekbones, deep-set eyes, somewhat angular jawlines, small, well-proportioned noses, and healthy skin and hair coloring are admired qualities.

What are the color and shape of your eyes?

For most performers, the eyes are the dominant feature. This is because the audience sees the expression in the performer's eyes—often in close-up—and interprets the credibility of a message mainly from them. The English language depends on nuances in delivery to convey ideas and feelings, and

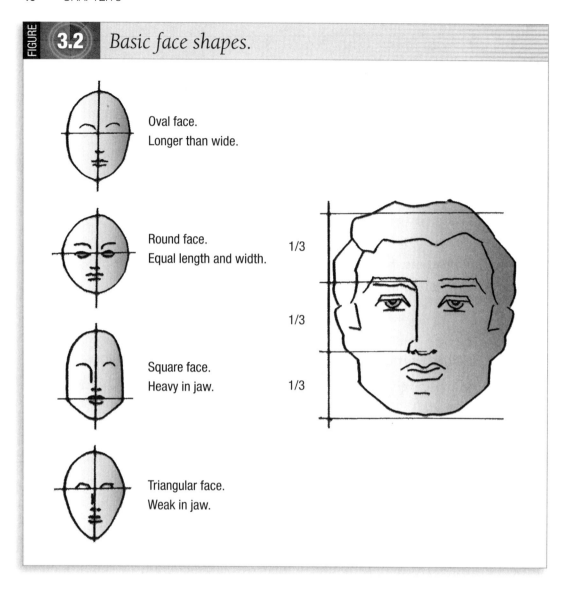

FIGURE 3.2 *Basic face shapes.*

Oval face.
Longer than wide.

Round face.
Equal length and width.

Square face.
Heavy in jaw.

Triangular face.
Weak in jaw.

1/3

1/3

1/3

these vocal nuances are reinforced by the expression in the face, especially in the eyes. Although most people have brown or blue eyes, other colors may be more useful in remembering an individual. Eye shapes include prominent, close set, wide set, round, or oval. The main thing is to use your eyes energetically, so they sparkle with life and expression. The best way to accomplish this is to think positively and enjoy what you are doing. Read your lines or news story in an upbeat way. Eye drops in each eye can help, too.

What is the shape of your mouth?

The second most dominant facial feature—although some believe it is the first—is the mouth. Surely, the most important movement a performer should learn to control is the smile. No action signals welcome, human approval, warmth, or friendship as universally as a well-motivated smile. Like the eyes, the mouth can convey a wide range of meaning. Performers learn to use the mouth for full expression.

What is the condition of your teeth?

Teeth should be straight, white, and even. At-home tooth-whitening kits have become readily available in recent years. The current generation has greatly improved teeth due to better lifelong dentistry and fluoride in the water. Visit a dentist regularly and consult with him or her about possible improvements, either by changing your habits or through procedures such as braces, caps, and veneers.

What is the shape of your nose?

The nose is often the most troublesome facial feature. It can be too big, too small, or un-evenly shaped. Too much bone or cartilage at the bridge or too much thickness in the skin may be reasons for the nose to appear out of proportion with other features. Yet in some cases the nose may be the most memorable facial characteristic. A distinctive feature may not be beautiful, but it may be memorable, and to the public it may be more important than beauty or conformity. A wise performer does not forget this fact.

What is the shape of your chin, jaw, and cheekbones?

In general, ideal characteristics for both men and women include deep-set eyes, a strong chin, and a jaw that is defined back to the ear. Makeup can help improve aspects of these features and will be discussed later in this chapter.

Do you have good muscle control in your face?

Muscles enable the performer to consciously and even unconsciously control the face. Speaking on cue requires muscle control to shape words and emotional energy to give them meaning. Holding a pencil between the teeth horizontally helps to limber up the cheek muscles and emphasizes the importance of smiling. Muscles surrounding the eyes are also very important. Eyebrow movement, opening and closing the eyes, and winking or blinking on cue can enhance or detract from the expression in the eyes. Quivering or muscle spasms, especially if involuntary, can cause problems for performers.

What are the quality, color, and complexion of your skin?

A healthy-looking complexion is especially important now that programming is in high definition. One of the main revelations of high definition television is skin quality. Blem-ishes once easily covered by makeup may be revealed. The objective of adding color to your skin is to improve its clarity and energy and to make sure the tones are balanced and seem natural to viewers. Fair-skinned persons can effectively change their skin color. A favorite color for many men and women is a medium tan, because it looks healthy, especially when heightened by a slight natural color of blush. Equally attractive is a white complexion highlighted by a touch of ivory or pink. Deeper skin colors such as blue-black, dark brown, brown, and some tawny hues require little or no makeup for television; some makeup may be needed for a matte finish, however. Performers with dark complexions depend on lighting to accent features and create a more three-dimensional appearance.

Another aspect to consider about one's skin is damage. Scars, blemishes of all kinds, poor color, heavy beards or unsightly stubble, large pores, and various allergies are among the problems some performers have with their skin. Moles are especially noticeable on cheeks or near the mouth, and a dermatologist can take care of their removal. For broadcast purposes, tattoos and piercings are still generally not acceptable.

What are the characteristics of your hair?

People want full-bodied, shiny, healthy hair that will remain in good condition and retain its color for a lifetime. This cannot be achieved in reality, however. About a year after birth a child usually has a full head of hair that remains full until the late teens or mid-twenties. Men, particularly those with fair hair, often experience substantial hair loss early in life. However, hair loss, which is believed to be hereditary, may occur in anyone. Women, who are fortunate in having less vulnerability to hair loss, may have deterioration and thinning exacerbated by various chemicals and treatments.

Hair has many characteristics including color, luster, thickness of strands, abundance, and manageability. Because so many people experience early hair loss, numerous remedies are available, and more research is under way to improve the prospects for having and keeping hair. A practical solution for performers is hair products: extensions, wigs, toupees, falls, and other hairpieces. Women have made substantial use of these products in the past, and men also use them. Male celebrities have depended on hairpieces for centuries. Though they may be self-conscious about it, more men in public life find that wearing a hairpiece is desirable, even though it may not deceive everyone. The point is that performers—whether male or female—must have the courage to decide for themselves whether their hair looks good enough for the role they wish to have in media. If a sportscaster looks better with a toupee, then he should wear one; if he looks better without it and feels comfortable, then he should go for the natural look.

Hair coloring, perms, and adornment for both men and women have become common because more men and women want to retain a youthful appearance for as long as possible. Nowhere is this more evident than among those who assume leadership roles in media. Women and men are advised to discuss their hair with professionals at salons.

CHOOSING THE RIGHT IMAGE FOR YOURSELF

After an analysis of your look, what are your overriding characteristics? Do they add up to the image you prefer? Is this image right for your professional future? Don't be hasty in making this judgment. Let us say, for instance, you are a man who has a more rounded face, a larger build, and a ready smile. Though you may think that the ideal is a chiseled-jaw anchor, you can build on your personal image of a likeable how-to show host or comic. Consequently, everything you do and develop for television supports this friendly, open, person-next-door image. Your success and audience response demonstrate that this image is right for you, is consistent with your assets, and is admired by your viewers. You, therefore, accept this fine talent for what it is. Soon you find that this asset enables you to sell products and services, or to do sports features, or to add flare to weather reports, or to be an effective television instructor. In other words, build on the television image you have rather than lament the one you do not have.

Controlling and Improving Your Image

nce you have evaluated your look and chosen the image that is right for you, you are in a position to decide what, if anything, you need to do to improve it. Presumably your assets far outweigh your liabilities; but to be effective as a competitor with the best performers in your field, you want to improve whatever deficiencies you may have identified. Few, if any, deficiencies are insurmountable. You must find a way to overcome your less attractive qualities by altering them, by reducing their impact, or by utilizing them in an innovative way. Let reason prevail; set aside your fears. It is your life and career, so seek good advice at a time when you can do something about your concerns. Remember such a positive attitude also extends to persons who are disabled and elderly, because as years pass, they, too, will be on television in increasing numbers, and those who have inner faith and energy will benefit.

IMPROVING THE BODY

Controlling the body requires coordination between the body, mind, and spirit—an attitude that dates back to the ancient Greeks. The discussion that follows will aid those performers who wish to improve their appearance and their present physical condition. A steady, consistent approach is essential to being physically fit, according to experts. Discipline is the foundation for success.

Exercise

Improving the body physically is accomplished through exercise, which is largely a matter of forming good habits early. The need for a good physical education program, including proper diet, exists at the preschool level and continues throughout life. People typically reach their physical peak during their late teens. Once they leave high school, work, and assume responsibilities of adult life, exercise, participation in sports, and other recreations are often abandoned and it is easier to slip into physical decline. The deterioration may be caused by neglect due to the inner loss of a competitive spirit. Such neglect is unthinkable for a media performer.

Proper exercise is essential for maintaining full height. Balanced physical exercise is critical. For instance, riding a bike is good for improving the legs and hips. But exercise that develops arms and shoulders is essential, too. Keeping workouts in balance will develop the body's frame properly during growing years and maintain it afterward.

A key to working out regularly is to find what is convenient and enjoyable for you. You may prefer to work on weights or use elliptical machines at a gym or in a swimming pool or tennis court. You may have access to parks or trails near your home for running. Sports are a good way to stay in shape, as long as you make sure to develop your entire body and do not neglect any aspect. Consider developing skills in sports that may be relevant to performing in media. Many performers turn to dancing because it combines physical discipline, grace, and exercise. It increases your ability to control your movement, an important aspect of performing discussed further in Chapter 5. Other performers develop skills that may be used for fund-raising, such as golf, tennis, running, and horseback riding.

A regular exercise routine is a must. The best place to exercise is in a large room with mirrors so that you can check your form from every viewpoint. Allot a certain amount of time for exercising and stick to it. One hour three or four days a week is minimal. This brief period is for tonal maintenance. If you want to accomplish more, such as weight loss or muscle building, you must stay longer and work harder. One New York performer spends five hours a day.

Begin your basic physical conditioning with a few stretching exercises. Talk to a trainer at your local gym or go online to find a myriad of resources, including YouTube videos and slideshows that walk you through each step. Figure 3.3 provides a few ways to get started.

FIGURE 3.3 *Stretching and general exercise links.*

- www.mayoclinic.com/health/fitness/SM00103: The Mayo clinic provides a database of stretching and strength-training guides, including a collection of fitness videos and tips on proper techniques.

- www.fitlink.com: Here you can keep a log of your exercise and build your own workouts from a list of recommended activities.

- www.youtube.com/profile?user=expertvillage&view=videos: This channel of how-to videos includes a large section of stretching videos. Try searching for "basic stretching exercises" to find some beginner videos.

After limbering up, move to those exercises that you need to do, those you like, those that will show improvement and will be rewarding. Count each movement so you can noticeably improve. Accurately record your accomplishments on a chart or in a notebook; the data will be encouraging because you can calculate your progress. A basic routine can include stretching on the floor, stationary bicycle riding or running on a treadmill, weightlifting, and performing other machine activities that will shape specific areas of your body.

Eventually any routine may become dull. To avoid boredom, enlist the assistance of a partner. Encourage each other to be enthusiastic. Or watch a newscast that you would like to see. You may get some pointers from the program, and the exercise time will go by much faster. Consider putting audio books or podcasts onto an mp3 player so that you are working out the mind and the body.

Exercise is hard work and requires consistent discipline. On a note of caution, be sure you use appropriate weights and do a routine that is appropriate for your level of ability. A professional trainer can help you. Excessive weight can cause serious damage to your muscles and joints. Increase weights only when your body is ready.

Posture

Posture is important, too. Are you like the many people who sit on the midpart of the backbone and walk with slightly drooped shoulders or a humped back? Instead, stand tall by balancing your weight on the balls of your feet and especially the joint of the big toes, pulling your shoulder blades back and down, and putting the chin forward but level. For sitting, you should slide back, trying to sit tall, holding the torso straight, and pulling the abdominal muscles in.

Nutrition

There is a relationship between weight, height, and good health. As long as you consume the proper daily nutritional requirements for your body, you need not eat additional food. The fact is, most people enjoy eating and are therefore prone to eat more calories than they need each day. In general, if you eat more calories than you burn, you will gain weight; if you burn more calories than you eat, you will lose weight. Start improving your diet immediately by limiting fast food, caffeine, and alcohol. If you are more disciplined, count calories. Most product labels are based on a 2,000-calorie diet, so a rough count of how many calories you are eating can be calculated in your head. Consuming 1,400 to 2,000 calories a day will enable you to adjust your weight. Some restaurants have begun to list calories on menus. The difficulty is that most performers who have the desire to control their weight lack the discipline. Try recording your food intake and exercise, either by writing it down in a notebook or using the online tracker at www. mypyramidtracker.gov.

In general, broadcast journalists, hosts, and feature reporters are trim. Aside from diets, several products allow for reproportioning the body. For example, undergarments can slim the body, while padding adds the illusion of weight gain. Of course, these items are concealed by clothing. The most important thing, however, is to both appear and be healthy.[1]

CHANGING YOUR HEIGHT

The illusion of height can be achieved in various ways. As much as two inches can be added to height by using lifts inside specially designed shoes. High-heeled shoes accomplish the same purpose, and boots are suitable for both men and women. Figure 3.4 includes some additional suggestions for helping you to seem taller.

Unusually tall persons should stand their full height and make the most of it. Do not stoop or keep the head down. However, dropping the waistline and wearing lower heels, patterns, and longer coats may help to reduce the illusion of height. The director can help a great deal by means of clever camera angles. Overall height denotes power, and that is a good thing.

MAINTAINING YOUR COLOR AND COMPLEXION

Regardless of the color of your skin, you will look best in natural sunlight or artificial white light. Whether you are performing out in the field or are indoors, stand in the area where there is a lot of white light. You will be better defined, look livelier, and be more prominent. Do not stand in semi-shadow, which may create a dull image. Keeping your eyes closed temporarily before going on-camera may help if sunlight bothers

---

FIGURE 3.4 *How to appear taller.*

1. Make maximum use of your current height by perfecting your posture. Stretch and strengthen the spine through exercise, pull up your ribcage, and hold your head high. Practice with a book on your head. This old technique aids balance and awareness of height.

2. Comb and style your hair in front of a full-length mirror, adding proportion and balance to your entire body.

3. Wear the same color clothing to lengthen the line from head to toe. Look for clothing that elongates the figure. Long legs create a sense of tallness.

4. Keep accessories simple and diminutive in proportion to your entire ensemble. Do not break up the long line of a suit or dress with horizontal lines or belts.

them. During the few minutes on-camera, you must be in the whitest light possible.

However, keep in mind that the sun is a danger to everyone because of its harmful rays. Fair-skinned performers are especially vulnerable to brown spots and sometimes skin cancer. Avoid the sun and tanning beds; lotions with sunscreens should be verified for their effectiveness and whether they will quickly wash off. Serious sunburns are possible even in the shade. Persons who have been sunburned may have sun damage beneath the skin for the rest of their lives. The sun may also cause premature aging, wrinkles, and blotches.[2]

Aside from color, the greatest concern is skin clarity. The skin must be free of blemishes. Few faces and bodies are free of them, but performers need to make extra effort to keep the best complexion possible. Cleanliness practiced from an early age is important in protecting skin. Some specialists recommend washing your face with cold water to remove the dirt, then deeper cleansing with hot water and mild soap to open the pores. Patting your face rather than wiping it helps the muscles to keep it firmer longer. A washing technique that pulls the muscles downward is not good for any part of the body. Finally, splashing on cold water to close the pores is recommended.

Avoid products that dry or irritate your skin. Substantial acne may leave scars. Breakouts may be caused by allergies related to common foods, animal hair, dust, pollen, and even sunlight, grass, and your own perspiration. If like many performers you are subject to skin allergies, using hypoallergenic products may minimize risks of irritation to the skin. Often simply changing to a milder soap may be the answer. Allergies may also be aggravated by nervous tension and the strain of media work. Reducing stress benefits your face and your entire body. Retaining water in your skin also plays a very important part in keeping a youthful look. Make sure to use oil-free moisturizers, drink plenty of water, and splash water on your face before a performance in dry weather.

Some performers may need to use soaps with scrubbing qualities or medical ingredients. Minor blemishes can be treated with over-the-counter medicines. Look for products that contain benzoyl peroxide or salicylic acid to fight acne, and retinol to reduce wrinkles. More major problems may require a trip to the dermatologist, who can prescribe an individualized plan of action. Pimples should not be squeezed because this may spread infection. Dark skin is particularly slow to heal and tends to scar. Keep hands away from the face on and off camera.

Acne is common in both sexes during later adolescent years and sometimes into adulthood. Numerous allergies can create red, bumpy, swollen, and crusty areas on all skin types. Look for food or contact dermatitis as possible causes of minor infections. If the condition is serious, then consult a medical specialist, because much can be done to reduce or eliminate these conditions.

USING MAKEUP

For performers, great attention to personal appearance is necessary because of time spent on camera. Makeup is any cosmetic used to enhance or alter your look. The objectives of basic facial makeup are to keep the healthy color you already have, to cover up any unsightly areas, and to reduce shine and perspiration. The rule of thumb is to apply makeup that will reach these goals. Assuming you are healthy and your body is in good condition, you won't need much makeup. Both men and women may find it beneficial to have face and hair charted by a professional makeup artist. It is worth the consultation fee.

Most television professionals have their own makeup supplies, but they rely on studio makeup artists to create the proper effect. Television lights tend to drain energy from a performer's face, especially the pink hues in fair-skinned persons. To reestablish these tones, the makeup artist will apply a base that is either the same color as the performer's skin or one or two shades darker. The makeup artist may need to experiment with several before choosing the right one. A youthful person tends to look darker and redder, and an older person looks paler. Naturally tanned skin may need only a foundation that matches it and allows easy cover-up of discolored areas and blemishes. For oily skin, a matching foundation may dry up the oil and produce a matte finish. Do not highlight the face with a white powder. Buy one to three water-based foundations of good quality (often called **pancake**): one matching and one or two somewhat darker than the normal skin color. They must be durable under hot lights, smooth after application, blend with the complexion, easy to apply, and render a non-reflective, matte look. A sure sign of a careless performer who has lost the competitive edge is neglecting makeup and assuming the public is willing to overlook facial imperfections.

A basic makeup kit includes preparations manufactured by an established theatrical supplier. These items are commonly kept in a small bag or metal box: the three different kinds of water-based foundations (as mentioned, the one that matches the skin, and two variations), brown or black eyebrow pencil and sharpener, soft brushes in a few different widths, a small mirror, mild soap, cold cream, washcloth and towel, and tissues or cotton balls.[4] Women should add their mascara, any false eyelashes, various eyeshadows, shades of blush, and lipsticks.

Makeup for men

In applying makeup for typical use on men, a water-based foundation is evenly spread over the face and ears and under the jawline and chin. Usually no makeup is applied to the neck because it is near to or touches a man's clothing. Difficult blemishes get two or three coats of foundation. No makeup is applied to the mouth, and much of the foundation is thinned out around naturally colorful areas like the eyes, brows, and lashes. While beards may be minimized, the hairline may be darkened in hairline strokes by the careful use of an eyebrow pencil on fair-haired men.

Makeup for women

Women should identify their most attractive facial assets and accentuate them with cosmetics. Eyes, mouth, and bone structure are emphasized by adding and shading various colors of foundation, blush, and eyeshadow. Mascara, false lashes, lipstick, and eyebrow pencil do most of the work. Fashion dictates the color of eyeshadows and blushers for the cheeks. Experimentation results in the right amount of makeup without calling attention to it.

Keep in mind that light colors appear to advance, and dark colors seem to recede on television. To make eyes recede, for example, use a dark eyeshadow. To emphasize cheekbones, apply a light foundation above the bone and a darker blusher underneath it. Do not apply blusher to the cheeks closer than the midpoint of the eye. Lips should be outlined in a desirable, but reasonable, shape in a somewhat darker shade before adding lipstick. For a fuller look to the lips, top the main coat with a lighter hue or gloss.

Makeup for HDTV

High definition television (HDTV) allows viewers to see vivid colors and extensive detail on everything ranging from landscapes to performers' faces. Because of the move to HDTV, many performers and makeup artists have had to change the way they apply makeup and even change the makeup itself. Blemishes have to be better concealed, and some kinds of makeup appear chalky or overly fake through an HD lens. Some performers find that applying less makeup works better for HDTV.

One of the biggest differences in makeup for HD is the use of an airbrush to apply makeup, especially foundation. The brush distributes the makeup in tiny dots. This provides a smoother, more matte finish and eliminates smudges or fingerprints that can come from hand application.

Products are being created and labeled especially as HD makeup. Some experts say that these products can make the difference in looking one's best on HD cameras, whereas others say it is just a new way of marketing makeup. If the studio or organization provides a makeup artist, he or she will most likely decide on the right products to use.[5] If you are responsible for your own makeup and will be spending significant time on camera for HDTV, consider buying a basic HD makeup kit and comparing the look with your normal performing look.

STYLING HAIR

Good skin, natural-looking makeup, and clean hair that balances your features round out your facial assets. If your hair is ample, manageable, of good color, and silky in texture, you will probably depend on it greatly to enhance your media image. If you have difficult hair to work with, you may need to wear a full or partial hairpiece.

Wigs have been available and popular with both sexes for centuries. The key to a good modern hairpiece is how well it blends into the natural hair. A finely crafted hairpiece, made of real hair and carefully styled, is essential to the image of many of the world's leaders and media performers. Performers have them because of insufficient hair, the convenience of multistyles and quick changes, and to avoid using harsh chemicals on their own hair. Young men who experience premature hair loss should seriously consider a medical or cosmetic remedy, for a man does not want to look older than he is for the rest of his professional life.

Hairstyles throughout the world are similar. Although some trends influence youths, particularly for festive occasions, hairstyles for both sexes in media are conservative. Newscasters keep their hair rather short. Few men on the air in news have long hair. Some men try permanents for body and curls, but they eventually settle for straight hair, combed back and parted. As they get older, many men in media dye their hair.

Female journalists are quite conservative in hairstyles, too. A plain hairstyle is easier to maintain. Once she has found a really attractive hairstyle, she uses it consistently. Typically, a woman's hair has some curl or wave. It is combed straight back and tied or allowed to fall to shoulder length. Fussy, long hair, or exotic, frequently changed styles tend to deny the serious image that most female performers want to establish. Female performers tend to be consistent with a good hairstyle, and it becomes part of their image. When a more complex hairstyle is required, hairpieces usually meet the demand.

Hair and makeup have long been relied on for enhancing the appearance of those who use them. On the other hand, some resist the use of these aids because they are supposedly unnatural. Some men are particularly reluctant to use cosmetic products. These aids are used to improve a performer's image. Tastefully designed and carefully applied, these aids will, in the long run, benefit a performer in news and information.

CHOOSING THE RIGHT CLOTHING

The purposes of clothing in media are to provide essential covering; to lend aesthetic attractiveness, distinction, or personal satisfaction for a performer; and to mask unattractive features of the body or face. "You are what you wear" is a widely held view on clothing. For most performers in media, conservative attire is best. Medium colors as converted from a **grayscale** are best; that is, colors that correlate to the middle range on a scale that runs from black to white. For men, an understated medium-colored suit, shirt with wrinkleless collar, hand-tied tie, socks that match the trousers, and dark shoes are fine (Figure 3.5). Generally, men with dark hair tend to look best in blue or gray suits, and those men who have blond or brown hair look better in brown suits or in other warm colors.[6]

FIGURE

3.5 *Typical clothing for a male performer.*

Correct fit. No wrinkles at collar.

Jacket or blazer for sportswear. Avoid checks and stripes. Buttoned or unbuttoned.

Revealed cuff.

Trousers vary in length.

Polished shoes.

Suit should be of contemporary tailoring (cuff, coat length, lapel width, trousers).

Tie requires tight, crisp knot. Use correct size.

Single-breasted suits are easier to wear than double-breasted.

Long coats for tall men; long line is slimming.

Trousers should be darker than coat.

Socks should match pants.

For women, a simple dress or pantsuit, in a midrange (gray scale) flattering color is ideal (see Figure 3.6). The shirt usually should have sleeves and a plain neckline not cut too low. Skirts can be pencil or A-line and fall at whatever is the preferred length, though never too short. For women who have light skin, medium to dark clothing tends to set off the face. For women with dark skin, medium-colored clothing is better.

The clothes should fit smoothly without wrinkles. Plain fabrics have a conservative look, and accessories can easily be added. Although patterns should be avoided, a fine-striped suit or a subtly flowered blouse may work out quite well. They may be remembered by the public, too. A performer tends to work toward a vertical look by wearing vertical stripes and designs, height-increasing shoes, and solid colors. A performer who wishes to

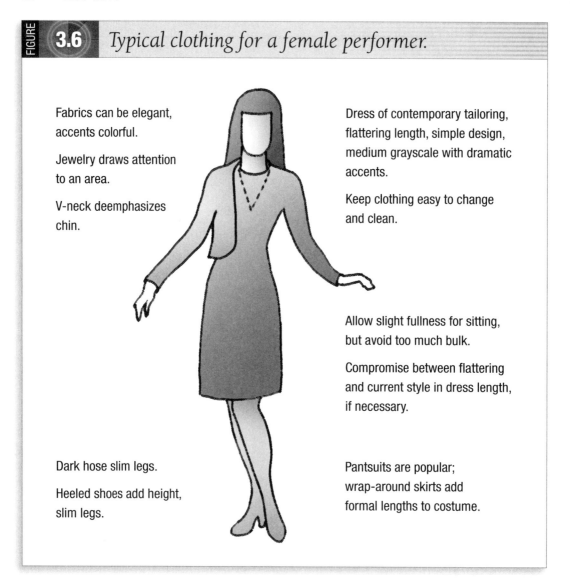

FIGURE 3.6 *Typical clothing for a female performer.*

Fabrics can be elegant, accents colorful.

Jewelry draws attention to an area.

V-neck deemphasizes chin.

Dress of contemporary tailoring, flattering length, simple design, medium grayscale with dramatic accents.

Keep clothing easy to change and clean.

Allow slight fullness for sitting, but avoid too much bulk.

Compromise between flattering and current style in dress length, if necessary.

Dark hose slim legs.

Heeled shoes add height, slim legs.

Pantsuits are popular; wrap-around skirts add formal lengths to costume.

lengthen the body line should concentrate on the center panel in the attire, using dark retiring colors at the sides. In effect, this is what most performers do somewhat subconsciously. For example, a man wears a dark suit with a light shirt, which provides the attention-getting vertical panel.

Colors and accessories

White and light colors are dominant. Light pastels may look white. (Color quality on-camera depends on the ability of the engineers working behind the scenes and the capability of the equipment.) Do not wear white socks unless you want viewers to watch your ankles while you are conducting an interview. Dark pants with a lighter jacket will slim a man, and a dark skirt with a lighter blouse will benefit a woman. Color television is the occasion to wear colorful clothes; however, let the guests do that. Remain neutral. Accessories usually call attention to themselves and should be worn with care.

Mainly for electronic reasons concerning the scanning patterns of cameras, avoid complex patterns, plaids, checks, some stripes, and shiny jewelry. Engineers prefer that performers stay away from shades of blue and green that may be earmarked for electronic inserts during the program, such as pictures beside or behind the newscaster. However, newer television equipment is eliminating these restrictions. High contrasts such as a white shirt against a very dark complexion may result in a loss of facial definition, as an engineer must balance the high-contrast white shirt against the dark face.

What to avoid

Do not use your clothing as an advertisement, unless you do so purposefully. News policy usually prohibits bias of any kind. Ordinarily, clothes with words or symbols send messages that a news and information reporter may not intend. The fabrics should not rustle or make noise when you move. Cotton or soft weaves may prove better than corduroy or silk. Avoid large buttons and other hard surfaces if they get in the way of body microphones. Also avoid bright shoes, mismatched or loud socks, and bare ankles. An exception is if your objective is to show off the latest fashions and such a demonstration is consistent with your message and image, as it is for some talk show hosts. If that's the case, then these clothing extremes are appropriate.

Clothing in the studio

Wardrobe consultants are frequently used by news anchors and hosts who appear daily. For others, many books and magazines are available on the subject. Eventually, both men and women find a lot of planning is needed to buy the right clothes and to rotate them. Most performers want attractive clothing that is easy to wear and maintain, and looks presentable under many different conditions. Reporters often provide their own clothing and may receive a clothing allowance for doing so.

It is obvious that if you are on-camera frequently, you do not want to wear the same outfit every day. Determine what few things you have as the nucleus of your wardrobe and add to it carefully and inexpensively. Many discount stores and consignment shops sell jackets and accessories that can help you get started. Rotate your clothing on a schedule so that you are less inclined to repeat your favorite items. Some stations allow anchors to acknowledge clothing stores for the loan of some clothes. Men have a better chance of getting away with a conservative collection of a few dark, well fitting suits than women, who probably need a different dress or suit every day. Women are more likely to receive comments on their clothes and how they wear them. Temperature on location and in studios may vary a great deal all year; therefore, keep a versatile jacket permanently at the studio.

Clothes as an illusion

A major use of clothing is to add or reduce weight by means of illusion. To shed pounds a performer wears clothes that hug the larger parts of the body, but not too tightly, such as skirts and blouses that do not have excess material on the sides. Softly woven fabrics, a simple uncluttered look from shoulder to hem, dark hose, V-necklines, upswept hairstyles, hemlines that fall a little lower, vertical designs and patterns, dark to medium colors, and long narrow lapels on blouses, jackets, and coats all contribute to a slimming effect. A heavy performer should avoid flat shoes and flat hairstyles, horizontal stripes and patterns, gathers, pleats and large patch pockets, white or light solid colors, accessories like sashes and belts, hems above the knee, rough-textured fabrics such as tweeds, bulky wools, shiny fabrics, doubled-breasted coats with wide lapels, turtleneck sweaters, and slim and tight straight skirts. An opposite approach to most of these suggestions will add weight for the slender person.

CONSIDERING MEDICAL OPTIONS

Improving your look may require orthodontic, optometric, or surgical procedures. Many medical options are available to consider. They are designed to enhance your appearance and are generally safe, although no reputable medical practitioner will guarantee absolute results. Once again, survey your assets, current status, and professional objectives. If, after making a serious study, you identify certain problems that need correcting, seek professional advice on remedies and costs. You owe it to yourself to set aside whatever fear and apprehensions you have in order to thoroughly investigate your options.

One of the most common concerns is orthodontic. Your teeth should be attractive, white, and even so that you can depend on a pleasant smile. Proper dental work can make a remarkable transformation in your appearance. Teeth can be straightened, repaired, capped, replaced, and generally made to seem perfect. Depending on the extent of the work you require, the cost will vary greatly, but this lifelong investment in your teeth and smile will be worth it.

Another frequent medical consideration has to do with your eyes. As a television performer, you must be able to read a prompter or cue cards ten or more feet away from your position on the set. If your eyes need assistance to do this, consider the options, including contact lenses, laser surgery, or glasses. Contact lenses, available in many formats and colors, may allow you to see properly without interfering with your appearance. Glasses, unfortunately, have drawbacks for television performers. Glare from lights reflected in the lenses, shadows from rims and temples, and glasses slipping out of position are some of them. Laser surgery and nonglare lenses such as contact lenses aren't for everyone, so seek competent professional advice. Proper eye care demands in-depth study and is critical to your future.

Further medical options deal with surgical alterations to your face and body. Cosmetic surgery has become more popular as improved techniques, better results, and lower costs have made it a desirable option for some.

FIGURE

3.7   *The pros and cons of cosmetic surgery.*

All of these, plus your own personal beliefs and feelings, must be thoughtfully weighed before you make a final decision.

PROS

1. Personal image can improve.

2. The procedures, carried out by a highly competent medical staff, are relatively safe, are becoming more affordably priced, and are readily available.

3. It is a long-term career investment.

4. It can increase your self-confidence.

5. Why spend an entire lifetime wanting a smaller nose, larger chin, or whatever, when you can have your wish while you are young and when it will do you the most good? In later life, you may choose to have a facelift, if that is a benefit to you, your career, and your personal measure of self-worth.

CONS

1. The procedure may not make a significant difference in your dominant image.

2. It may be painful and risky.

3. Expectations of the results can be unrealistic.

4. Recovery time can be long.

5. It may not be affordable.

Again, thorough investigation of what can be realistically accomplished and what values cosmetic surgery will provide for you is essential for proper decision making. Bear in mind that many procedures can be safely completed in outpatient office visits.[7] Figure 3.7 explores the principal reasons people choose to have or not have cosmetic surgery.

Sex Appeal

ex appeal is important to anyone who appears on camera. News and information specialists, such as entertainers, must consider maximizing their attractive characteristics, including sex appeal. Information programs, including most newscasts, are a mixture of journalism and show business. Few anchors in either large or small markets are unattractive. They wear makeup, have their hair styled, wear different clothing each day, are lighted perfectly, and look confident. Most anchors look youthful if not young, such as CNN's silver-haired Anderson Cooper.

Although physical attraction heads the list when it comes to sexual appeal, action, disposition, and style reinforce the public's perception of an information specialist. Because television can intensify or modify a performer's sex appeal, newscasters and entertainers can make a positive contribution to viewers through their own example. Rather than displaying overt sexuality, the performer may interpret sex as vitality, wholesomeness, and positive self-worth. Another characteristic of sex appeal is power. Risk taking, dangerous activities, and nonconformity have their admirers also. The zeal for preserving a healthy, active, youthful look is shared by many people, especially performers, who often manage to stay active for decades, never retiring even though they tend to slow down. Such positive respect for one's life creates the perception of sexual appeal. This kind of sexual appeal may maintain a career performer well into his or her mature years on television. Often, as media performers gain wealth they find they want to share it (and sometimes must for income tax purposes). Such generosity may be considered sexy.

Though good looks are important, they are not enough. Sex appeal implies a pleasant personality, and in reporters an inoffensive, conservative appearance and manner. Television personalities to some extent are created, even those in news and information. They want to appear to be intelligent, mature, good looking, and articulate on a range of subjects. They want to seem to be very likable.

Of course, off-camera these individuals are human beings, too. They have their bad moments, as so many reporter biographies reveal. But professional performers realize that suggestive appearance, movement, or innuendo is inappropriate and even potentially damaging to their careers. Some news contracts go so far as to prohibit appearances in public that management considers contrary to the television news image. For instance, a performer during off hours may not be allowed to take part in controversial plays or demonstrations and may not engage in any activities that could bring unfavorable attention. Such activities, even though not personally harmful or illegal, may nevertheless seem inconsistent with the leadership responsibility of a newscaster. Certain restrictions imposed upon a performer's personal life are a price that is paid for high visibility.

Is conservative sexy? In news it probably is.

Maturation

 s a performer becomes older, many factors influence the skin. Sun, loss of natural oils, facial movements, and methods of applying makeup may damage the skin. Dryness is often a major problem. Facial movement is a principal cause of wrinkles. Wrinkling the brows and laughing permanently crease the face. These habits are difficult to change. Two medical remedies that have become very popular are collagen and Botox injections. These remedies may be temporary or have side effects. They may be expensive, too. The key to retaining clear skin is the amount of time you are able to devote to cleaning, moisturizing, and protecting it. In a competitive business environment that promotes and thrives on a youth culture, strive to maintain a youthful look as long as possible. This maintenance extends to the entire body, and so numerous approaches to keep body muscles taut continue to be popular well beyond average retirement years. In addition to health clubs, body massage businesses have increased. The former requires you to be an active participant; the latter enables you to relax while someone else does the physical work to relieve your stress. The gym and the spa have their place. And so does a dermatologist. Good advice on how to take care of yourself for on-camera work may require visiting all of them.[8]

Summary

hat the public sees of you and your work constitutes your image, and image is everything. Sheer brevity gives the public limited perceptions of individuals. The way you seem on the monitor screen is the way you are to your viewers. Those who are watching have little else to go on when assessing you as a performer. What they see or hear you say is all they know about you or your work. First impressions are enormously important.

Thus, you should do everything you can to make certain whatever is presented is the image you want projected. This is not always easy to do, for what is produced may be a group effort, and your best efforts may be jeopardized by someone else. Therefore it is important to make sure you have done your own personal best to take care of your appearance. Keep faith in yourself and what you are doing. Then you will probably be pleased with the outcome.

CHAPTER 3 *exercises*

1. Take a head shot, a right profile, and a left profile. The photographs should be large enough so that you can analyze them. Analyze your features using the guide in Figure 3.1.

2. Take a front, side, and back photograph or your entire body. First assume a normal position; then shoot a second set of pictures standing up straight. Do not wear bulky clothes or high-heeled shoes. Compare the differences.

3. As a class, take turns standing before the other students so that they can write down their dominant first impressions. Ask the teacher to collect these impressions and give them to you. Think of this exercise as getting "fan mail." Do not speak or act up in any way; you do not want to influence the outcome. Use their comments to guide your analysis of your image and consider areas of improvement.

4. At this point the teacher may be willing to make comments about your appearance so that he or she can identify the main things you should work on during the semester, such as toning your muscles. A teacher can identify what you need to improve, and perhaps you may get professional help beyond what the teacher provides.

5. Finally, write out your image analysis and define your goals in changing your appearance, if necessary.

Notes

1. "Healthy Weight: It's Not a Diet, It's a Lifestyle." The Centers for Disease Control and Prevention offers links and calculators, including one that helps you determine your Body Mass Index: www.cdc.gov/nccdphp/dnpa/healthyweight/index.htm.

2. Joe and Teresa Graedon, "Sunscreen Research Surprises Scientists," *Houston Chronicle* (July 14, 2008), p. E-3. Authors suggest consumers look for sunscreens with zinc or titanium to provide broad ultraviolet protection.

3. "Save Your Skin, The Ultimate Guide to Preventing Aging," *Details* (September 2007), pp. 222–230.

4. Claudia Feldman, "Magic in a Bottle," *Houston Chronicle* (February 10, 2008), pp. G1, G9.

5. Lynne S. Gross and James C. Foust, "Makeup," *Video Production Disciplines and Techniques,* 10th ed. (Scottsdale, AZ: Holcomb Hathaway Publishers, 2009).

6. "The Essential: The Perfect Gray Suit," *Details* (April), pp. 94+; "Summersize It," *GQ* (June 2008), p. 154+; "From the Waist Down," *Details* (August 2008), pp. 144+; "The Suited Man—Your Guide to Pulling It All Together," *GQ* (November 2007), p. 76.

7. "Who Gets What Cut," *Newsweek* (July 7–14, 2008), p. 60. Americans had over 1.9 million cosmetic surgery procedures in 2007, including 74,000 male nose procedures; 347,500 female breast, and 21,311 male breast procedures; 205,764 female eyelid surgeries; 13,393 male hair transplants; and about 4,000 female buttocks procedures; Lynn Cook, "Plastic Surgery Is Becoming a Guy Thing," *Houston Chronicle* (June 17, 2008), pp. 1, A6.

8. Sean Kennedy, "The Age of the Silver Fox," *The Advocate* (August 12, 2008), pp. 32–41; Joy Sewing, "Don't Wash That Gray Away," *Houston Chronicle* (July 27, 2008), p. G-1.

Other Sources

Aucoin, Kevin. *Face Forward.* New York: Little Brown & Co., 2000.

Berg, Rona. *Beauty, The New Basics.* New York: Workman Publishing, 2001.

Details, a monthly men's style magazine. New York: Conde Nast Publications.

Gentlemen's Quarterly (GQ), a monthly men's style magazine. New York: 4 Times Square, 10036. On newsstands.

"The Importance of Beauty," *20/20,* ABC Television Network. Producers: Janet Klein, Steve Brand, Shari Finkelstein. Anchors: John Stossel, Lynn Shearer, 2002.

Sepe, Frank. *The Truth. The Only Fitness Book You'll Ever Need.* Carlsbad, CA: Hay House, 2003. Fitness for men and women.

Voice

INTRODUCTION

In a visual medium such as television, it's easy to focus more on what you see and less on what you hear. However, the vocal part of a presentation is an essential component of your overall performance. Using your voice to your best advantage includes knowing the characteristics you can control and understanding the physical elements and the environmental conditions that affect your voice. Characteristics range from voice types to pronunciation and pitch; physical aspects include voice quality and breath control. Knowing about objects in your environment, such as microphones and their various pick-up patterns, will also enable you to make the best use of your vocal talents.

Voice: Connecting to the Audience

n audience must hear well. It wants to hear every word or sound without undue strain and frustration. Sometimes a performer mumbles, slurs sounds, or speaks inaudibly; sometimes extraneous noise (static or electronic interference, overriding background) keeps the audience from hearing what is said. Some 911 calls and news reports from overseas present this problem. Sometimes the volume is insufficient on the microphone. Whatever the problem, it must be corrected so that the audience can hear well.

After the impact of a performer's initial appearance has passed, audience members are focused essentially as listeners. What will the performer say? How will the performer say it? The performer then has to inform, alarm, caress, tease, shock, amuse, embarrass, excite, and/or frighten listeners with, among other things, the voice. A performer's voice communicates by overtly and consciously moving the audience to respond, to understand, and to enjoy what the performer is saying. A good performer knows how to influence the audience and enjoys the challenge.[1]

Experts from various fields have concluded that the voice is the most efficient way of communicating. It carries information about the personality, mood, and present state of functioning. No two voices are apparently alike, and this belief has given rise to the electronic printing or charting of voice characteristics, as seen on a number of television crime programs. Voices are very sensitive to the performer's entire physical condition. In the main, a voice depends on vigorous internal energy, generated from good health, a certain amount of personal daring or abandon while performing, self-confidence, and a joy derived from sharing news and information with viewers.

Bringing Out the Best in Your Voice

o ascertain audio characteristics of a performer, it is necessary to examine the capabilities and limitations of the voice. Performers strive for perfection even though it isn't attainable. Performers with a professional attitude strive for voice improvement and are willing to invest a great deal of time toward this achievement. After much hard work, performers are likely to find that once the obvious irregularities are corrected, the less obvious ones are much more difficult to define and isolate. A speech coach or someone with a keen ear and training in voice can listen for subtle irregularities and help performers correct them. Some suggestions for improving voice problems are included in this chapter, but personal voice problems must be brought to the attention of a voice specialist.

PRACTICE AND CONDITIONING

As a performer, you should practice voice prodigiously. Good vocal communication requires rehearsal, and the amount of practice depends upon the degree of perfection you wish to attain. Read copy a few times through to be sure you understood it thoroughly. Then read it aloud several times to be certain that each syllable flows easily and clearly so that the listener will understand the message instantly. Rehearsal must continue until you can look up from the copy or away from notes to allow proper eye contact with the viewer or other performers. Try to read ahead two or three words with your eyes. Some performers require much rehearsal, others are "quick studies," but it makes no difference so long as the final performance is flawless. Nothing else matters to the viewers but how the voice sounds on the air. To have that "good air sound," according to one news director, you must feel your job is important, and if it is important to you, it will be important to listeners.

It is necessary to condition the voice so that it can communicate effortlessly and tirelessly through media. This means that as a performer, you must be physically conditioned. Because your voice is often a reflection of your general welfare and attitude, your voice may be the first indication of fatigue. When you are tired, your ability to produce low and high sounds (**range**) shortens; the **timbre** or quality of each tone decreases. Eventually, a few shrill middle to high tones are all that can carry whatever communication is necessary. Even these tones fray until a hoarse quality develops, and this yields to a vocalized whisper. Finally, there is no voice at all. Deterioration of your voice may come from incorrect placement of the tones in your throat—too high or too low. Excessive shouting, such as at football games, and disease, ranging from colds to cancers, cause organic or functional disorders. Lack of hydration can also cause problems. Atypically, some performers are fortunate enough to be able to talk indefinitely without noticeable fatigue. One former radio student used two voices: one for normal conversation (low key, personal) and the other on the air (energized, fast, bright). His on-air voice would last for hours and always sounded the same.

AVOIDING TENSION AND FATIGUE

Relaxation, a state of physical and mental rest, is key to a full, rich voice. Often relaxation is not possible because of tension and/or fatigue. Relaxation is largely a state of mind. If as a performer you believe that listeners are friendly, that they want to see the program, and if you know from experience what to expect and like what you are doing, your voice will convey a relaxed tone. Some performers are much better at being relaxed than others because they have greater self-confidence. Others are less confident and worry about how they will be received. Worry causes tension in the muscles of the entire body, particularly the throat. Tight muscles reduce the vibrations in the cartilage and bones, limiting the richness of tone the performer can get from the voice. A tense voice is often harsh and strident and may salivate more, have less breath supply and control, or quiver. In addition, a tense voice may squeak, shift pitch unexpectedly, or cough uncontrollably. Fatigue is the other extreme. The muscles simply do not function precisely, so words are poorly articulated. Some voices tend to shift to higher pitch and are thin when the performer is tired.

Characteristics of Voice

TYPES OF VOICES

Most voices are a pleasant combination of various sonorous qualities. Some dominant, clearly definable, and notably less attractive voice qualities are nasal, breathy, thin, harsh or strident, and hoarse. At times nearly everyone's **vocal quality** depends upon these characteristics for expression, but it can be grating to hear those qualities constantly. Voices having these qualities in the extreme are probably the result of organic or functional disorder. Keep in mind that while the following qualities may be suitable for entertainment, they are not suitable for presenting news or information, which calls for clear, pleasant voices.

Performer ideal

Voices vary, and society associates certain qualities with the voices of successful and appealing performers. The public expects a male's voice to skew low, giving it a pleasant strength and resonance. A female's voice is usually lighter and equally resonant. These voices are the ideal for performers, especially those in news.

Nasal

Nasal quality occurs either by allowing air to escape through the nose or by preventing air from doing so. The former is referred to as **nasality,** which can be produced for example by a cleft palate; the latter is **denasality,** which can be caused by a common cold.

Breathy

A **breathy** quality is popular with some female performers. Breathiness can produce an effective seductive utterance stronger than a whisper. The iconic Marilyn Monroe was very skillful at adding a breathy quality to her voice, projecting intimacy with mellifluous tones through manipulation of the mouth and lips. Breathiness is achieved by letting an abnormal amount of breath escape through the mouth with each utterance.

Thin

A **thin** voice has insufficient nuances, thereby reducing the full, rich qualities associated with a resonant voice. Comedians may use such a voice for comic effect, such as when a man pretends to sound like a woman. The thin voice is particularly noted in women and men who for years have pitched their voices too high, and in effect have developed the high range only during maturation. This characteristic may be picked up by children who imitate their mothers' or sisters' voices.

Harsh/strident

A **harsh** voice is caused by lack of nuances from primary and secondary vibrations in an entire pitch range, resulting in a rough, irritating, and genuinely unpleasant quality. A similar-sounding **strident** voice is produced largely by hard-driving strain and tension. The resonators in the throat and neck are tense.

Hoarse

A **hoarse** quality is common and can be useful in some situations. This sort of frog-in-the-throat to foghorn utterance can be comic, or in a mature woman, seductive. The truly hoarse voice may be caused by excessive shouting, laryngitis, polyps on the vocal cords, and perhaps allergies. If a hoarse voice is sufficiently audible and if its range is not impossibly limited, its unique quality can be fascinating to listen to and thus memorable for the public. Clint Eastwood has made a career out of screen characters with hoarse voices.

TIMBRE

The resonant quality generated from the entire vocal mechanism in an individual is called *timbre*. Timbre includes all of the nuances and subtle reinforcement an air stream receives from vibrating bones and cartilage and from the size, shape, and strength of associated muscles. No two voices are quite alike, because the throat, chest, and mouth are not alike in any two individuals, although family members may sound similar. A voice depends on organic construction as well as function. Terms such as *mellow, harsh,* and *shrill* are efforts to classify vocal timbre. Although they are inexact, they recognize that we hear distinct differences in voices. The reproduction of a single utterance is rather complex, for each vibration produces other vibrations, some in symphony with the first vibration, some not in phase with it. Those in phase are said to be in *harmony;* those that are not are **dissonant.** These complex factors suggest why a human voice is unique. Unless a voice is altered surgically, timbre cannot be changed. It is comparable to a fingerprint and can be electronically charted.

RESONANCE

Every sound you produce is a nonsense syllable that takes on meaning only if it can be consistently recognized and repeated. **Resonance** is the vibration of the vocal folds or "cords" and their surrounding environment of bones and cartilage that produces sound waves. These bones and cartilage include the skull bones, nose, nasal sinuses, windpipe, chest bone, and ribs. Adjustable resonators can change in size, shape, and tenseness. These are the mouth, the pharynx or soft palate at the back of the mouth, and the larynx. Vocal folds are left relaxed and open for breathing, producing no vibration, but they are tightened and vibrate during speech-producing voiced sounds such as "da," "ga," or "va." In contrast, so-called unvoiced sounds such as "f," "t," or "p" restrict the airstream at the teeth (**fricative**) or lips (**plosive**), but no vibration of the vocal mechanism is required to form the sound.

Practice the exercises in Try It Out 4.A for improving your resonance, but do not strain or force your voice.

 try it out   4.A   **EXERCISES TO INCREASE RESONANCE**

1. Strive for the complete relaxation of your throat by yawning several times.

2. Hum with your lips closed until you can feel your entire head vibrating.

3. Vocalize by sustaining each vowel sound for several seconds, maintaining the same pitch.

PHONATION

Phonation is the precise production of a phoneme or sound. Phonation may be thought of in terms of **articulation,** any sound made in forming words clearly, and **pronunciation,** the accepted way of saying words using emphasis and intonation. For performers to have facility in any language, they must learn its sounds precisely.

Articulation

Articulation is vital to phonation. *Articulation* is a performer's ability to produce sounds with precision by changing the movement of articulators (lips, mouth). Some performers are easily adaptable to languages and enjoy languages; they may absorb them quickly and hear the nuances accurately. Hosts of classical music programs on radio tend to be very adept, for example. However, some performers may be less convincing when articulating the sounds of other languages.

The accuracy of speech is reduced by laziness that restricts the precision with which the tongue, teeth, and lips respond to each other. The result is that the speaker may be difficult to hear and understand, especially if there is competition from other speakers or other sources of

General American Speech: The Issue of Correctness

The objective in media has been to use General American Speech, which is not English or British speech. Every language has numerous variations; however, performers who are in or depend on American media quickly learn standard speech. In most cases regional, ethnic, and racial speech patterns can be eliminated or at least minimized to the extent that they are imperceptible to most listeners. Traditionally, news personnel have trained their voices so that they have universal acceptance throughout the United States. Non-career performers, such as politicians or advocates, on the other hand, may retain some accent to preserve a specific image.

Those performers who elect not to aim for General American Speech may have found that their peculiar speech pattern is more consistent and desirable for their personality, even though they serve the general public. For example, a performer from New Orleans may retain his Southern regional dialect. Perhaps he has a cooking program that specializes in gumbo and Creole cooking. It has been said that President Lyndon B. Johnson purposefully spoke with a distinct Texas dialect when he was in Texas but used standard American speech when addressing a national audience.

Current trends in media suggest that dialects enrich programs, so there has been less effort to eliminate accents from newscasts and other information programs. The term *accent* usually refers to an emphasis on a syllable that may be natural to one language but out of place in another language. The variation was illustrated several years ago in a song that says, "You put the accent on the wrong syl·la´·ble (not syl´·la·ble) and you sing a tropical song." Here a Spanish influence is put on the English language.

The standard of correctness in speech has come under more scrutiny as more diverse groups have found roles in the media. Whereas in the past Southern, Midwestern, and Eastern speech patterns have been dominant, now African American, Latino, and Asian words and speech patterns, especially in music, have influenced pronunciation. Foreign pronunciation may be either Anglicized or given its correct foreign pronunciation. A media performer with fluency in more than one language has an obvious advantage.

The best approach for the novice or young professional in media is to learn standard or General American Speech and to depend on widely recognized pronunciation for all English words, names, and phrases. Those performers who want to keep their dialects and accents should learn to change between them and General American Speech.

noise in the room. Impediments to good articulation may range from inactive use of articulators (resulting in mumbling) to overactive use of them (resulting in mouthing words) in which instance the lips are moved excessively. Conscious effort by the performer can eliminate or greatly improve these problems.

Soothing sounds usually mean pleasure; jarring sounds usually indicate displeasure. Language is derived from assigning meaning to vocal sounds.

Meaning and the techniques for producing sounds are transferred through imitation. A child imitates the speech of parents, relatives, friends, and teachers. So, your speech is the result of imitating those around you. If the models you have imitated all your life have been excellent, then your speech will be excellent, assuming there is no pathological interference. Environments with models who are poorly educated or have regional dialects, or both, are two common deterrents to standard speech. It is possible to improve and correct speech by watching and listening to performers who have an appealing resonance and working to imitate them.

 try it out   4.B   ARTICULATION WORD PRACTICE

Vowels: beet, bit, bait, bet, bat, bath, bomb, wash, bought, boat, book, bird, bitter, sun, sofa.

Diphthongs: bite, how, toy, using, fuse, say.

Consonants: poor, boor, time, dime, kite, guide, few, view, thigh, thy, sing, zing, shock, Jacques, chest, jest, how, when, mom, noun, sing, love, watch, yellow, run.

 try it out   4.C   ARTICULATION SENTENCE PRACTICE

To improve your articulation while reading sentences, repeat these classic nonsense exercises. These tongue twisters can be fun and improve your articulation at the same time.

- How much wood would a woodchuck chuck in the woods if a woodchuck would chuck wood? If you were a woodchuck and would chuck wood, would you chuck wood like a woodchuck or would you chuck wood differently? No doubt some woodchucks chuck more wood than other woodchucks.

- Peter Piper picked a peck of pickled peppers. How many peppers did Peter Piper pick, if Peter Piper picked a peck of pickled peppers?

- A big black bug bit a big black bear.

Pronunciation

If articulation refers to the sounds that produce parts of words, *pronunciation* is the enunciation of the entire word. Aside from certain regional dialects, the principal conflict in the United States has been between a preference for long "a" or short "a" sounds in such words as "tomahto—tomato" or long "e" or short "e" as in "been—ben." Media performers tend to say "ayther" rather than "either." The longer "a" and "e" sounds probably came from theater speech that emphasized the necessity for clarity when the voice was projected into huge auditoriums before the days of microphones. Some people associate these sounds with culture, higher levels of education, and sophistication. So there is some conflict, though modest, in standard speech pronunciation. Performers should choose their preferences and consistently repeat them.

Professional commercial announcers, newscasters, politicians, and others who presume to represent large segments of the population and who wish to communicate with their viewers use the most generally accepted form of the language. Pronunciation guides published by networks and wire services help to acquaint performers with national standards of pronunciation. For example, Voice of America, http://names.voa.gov, contains audio files for pronouncing the names of international figures, and www.howjsay. com gives audio pronunciations of common words.

Regional dialects, racial dialects, and international languages influence a performer's speech. Local names, phrases, and other references may be different from the standard but are essential for effective communication.

Errors in pronunciation are heard frequently on media information programs, which are often ad-libbed as opposed to using memorized scripts. Errors typically occur when performers do not learn how to pronounce a word correctly in the first place. Are you guilty of any of the errors in Figure 4.1?

INTERPRETATION

Modulation of the voice can occur through mental demands placed on it, called **interpretation**. Interpretation is based on logical and emotional responses generated in a performer's mind when a passage is recited or read. Every utterance is interpreted in some way, whether colorfully or flatly. For instance, the sound "o" can be interpreted in various ways with different meanings: "o" means understanding, "o" means surprise, "o" means dejection, "o" means emotional satisfaction, "o" means the last gasp after a fatal blow, "o" means "I'm thinking." Interpretation of this vowel varies in accordance with inflection, or the willful or subliminal raising or lowering of pitch and volume in response to the text. Interpretation depends on several variables, including pitch, range, volume, timing, variety, and style. Interpretation is a subtle and complex art of carefully selecting those elements that will communicate impact on viewers. The more you know of life, the better educated you are, and the more experience you have, the greater ability you will have in creating those nuances. As a performer, you will bring new insight to audiences largely through interpretation.

4.1 *Common pronunciation mistakes.*

Sound substitutions: git for get, sinator for senator, min for men, jist for just, becuz for because, pressperation for perspiration, Illinoise for Illinois, pitcher for picture, whur for where, witch for which, wear for where, watt for what, madder for matter, baddle for battle, pilla for pillow, coworse for coerce, liberry for library, groshers for grocers, intertainment for entertainment, mintal for mental.

Sound omissions: han for hand, son for song, slep for slept, goin for going, trus for trust, whi for white, chile for child, spect for expect, feel for field, an for and, playin for playing, memry for memory, hunred for hundred, lil for little, spose for suppose, mir for mirror, tempeture for temperature, genlmen for gentlemen, hep for help, zackly for exactly, las for last.

Sound additions: Acrost for across, cain't for can't, pom for poem, athaletics for athletics, meilk for milk, mis chee vi ous for mis chie vous.

Slurred additions: discs, doncha for don't you, valyabul for valuable, wanna for want to, harya for how are you, howjado for how do you do.

Misplaced accents: de´-bate for de-bate´, com-par´-a-ble for com´-par-a-ble, the-a´-ter for the´-a-ter, in-crease´ vs. in´-crease (the former should indicate the verb form, the latter the noun), re´-fill vs. re-fill´ (the former should indicate the noun form, the latter the verb), a-li´-as for a´-li-as, dis´-close for dis-close´, in-fa´-mous for in´-fa-mous.

Pitch

Pitch is determined by the frequency of the sound wave you utter when you speak. The degree of pleasantness with which that wave is perceived by listeners is its timbre. The objective of speech lessons and electronic equipment is to change or modulate the frequency so that perception of it is optimal. Every voice is capable of producing a range of frequencies from high to low, some voices having greater range than others. Ideally, these sounds are produced without strain or irritation to the throat. Almost everyone finds a comfortable speaking range and with practice can maintain it naturally. However, because pitch can be influenced through imitation, a voice can be the victim of abnormal placement. Remember, if children continually imitate their mothers' high-pitched voice while growing up, even though it is unnatural to them, they may develop high, thin voices. This is caused by abnormal placement. A boy has a chance to redefine his voice as he matures, and though a girl's voice may change less noticeably, it can be improved through training and practice.

Your singing range correlates with your speaking range, but as Lynn Wells mentions in *The Articulate Voice*, there is a difference between singing and speaking. "If you attempt exercises to determine pitch range or to work toward extending your pitch range, take care to speak pitch changes rather than sing those changes."[2] The exercises at the end of this chapter include tips for checking your range and pitch. You may notice that a range exists beyond the highest note you can comfortably produce. This artificial range of high-pitched sound is called **falsetto.** It may have no value in your work, but you should know what it is.

Your pitch may be influenced by a grating or fraying that dissipates the sound, especially when your voice is tired. A relaxed voice in a rested body of high energy will enable you to produce the best normal sounds. Pitch can be enhanced when it is reinforced by favorable acoustic conditions, such as speaking or singing in a shower. In this instance, the frequencies are reinforced by bouncing off the walls, adding richness to the basic sound. While you cannot go around with your head in a shower stall, you can use electronic equipment, such as a proper microphone, to enhance your voice. Interpretation requires a substantial collection of high-quality frequencies that the voice can produce on demand.

Range

Range is the extent of a performer's vocal ability. When the term is applied to interpretation, *range* considers pitch from the lowest sound produced through high falsetto sounds; volume from barely audible to deafening yells at pep rallies; timing or the precision with which material is delivered as some words, phrases, and passages are slowed or speeded up; variety or the flare for the unusual or dramatic in delivery; and style, or the way performers present themselves. The sum of these variations, which are merely hinted at here, constitutes a performer's range. The greater the range, the more variations the voice has, and the more useful it is.

Volume

Increases or decreases in the **volume** or loudness of a person's voice give it force, emphasis, and sufficient strength to be heard and understood. Generally, performers use only enough volume to do the job, because they learn to conserve their abilities without reducing the quality of the performance. A news anchor may keep viewer interest by increasing the loudness of her voice during a police chase; a weathercaster may modulate his voice to suggest the relative severity of an approaching storm. Both performers graduate volume in accordance with the perceived drama of the moment.

The objective is to have the volume sufficiently soft so that it can be heard comfortably without straining at the low end, and loud enough so that it is stirring at the high end. Use of automatic equipment, known as limiters, keeps volume within prescribed ranges beyond which over-modulation or distortion would occur. For live appearances (often recorded for later replay) high volume may be called for. A performer uses volume variations as an interpretative tool, with louder and quieter volumes appropriate at various times. Raised volume, short of shouting, is the most common way to tell an audience to pay special attention. Continuous, excessive volume can harm vocal cords. In some forms of cheerleading, for example, the vocal cords bang together savagely until a tissue buildup eventually causes a callous to form, frequently causing hoarseness.

Timing

The concepts of timing, time, and rate can be confusing. **Time** refers to how long it takes a performer to deliver a syllable, word, or sentence. For aesthetic purposes, **timing** refers to a performer sensing precisely when to utter a sound, such as on the beat, after a laugh, or before an action, and precisely when to pause, for pausing can add emphasis to a message.

Mechanically speaking, a performer delivers lines—the spoken words or dialogue—timed to the second so that the commercial, newscast, or documentary will end appropriately. This may mean speeding up or slowing down the **rate** or pace at which the words are delivered. On average about 120 to 140 words are spoken in a minute of copy. Many performers read slightly faster or slower, but all must finish on time or "on the nose." Consider how rapidly you read copy, maintaining accuracy and clarity in the delivery. On average, a 60-second story is about 140–160 words; a 30-second story is 55–85 words; a 20-second story is 44–55 words. The famous 10-second sound bite is about 12 words. Have you developed a feeling for the time it takes to read several lines of material aloud without looking at your watch? Strive to develop an innate sense of timing that enables you to deliver material to the second without looking at your watch. After all, broadcasts are usually timed to the second. Train yourself to read with timed precision.

Variety

Variety is the use of the voice in an unexpected way: a change of pitch (raising pitch at the end of a sentence instead of lowering it), a change of time (slowly reading a line that ordinarily would be read rapidly), a shift in volume (emphasizing phrases through loudness), or a change of style (giving an audience the unexpected, such as reading something in a comical way that most would expect to be read in a somber tone). Variety draws upon all of the tones available to an interpreter. It can be fun, because the clever performer brings new excitement to material. Variety should be motivated and not just mechanical or arbitrary. When a coach asks for variety in a reading, a novice typically responds, "Do you want it louder?" The coach answers, "No, say it differently." The performer must use imagination to express the line in an original way. Read the copy differently bringing a new meaning to an idea, or, in other words, by reinterpreting copy through the inflection in your voice. This ability shows you have imagination for media work.

Style

If you ask members of your family to recite "Mary had a little lamb," each will say the verse differently. One might be enthusiastic, one shy, one bored. Each will read it with a personal *style*. **Style** is the unique way a performer presents material. A performer's dominant style might be described with such terms as *innocent, friendly, aloof, crisp, relaxed, artificial, neurotic,* or *bizarre.* These terms are attempts to differentiate one performer from another. Media performers define who they are by means of vocal expression.

Media personalities develop a manner of presenting material that is individual to them. Some read the news as though it were part of a long narrative with moments of optimism and despair; some read copy with humor and warmth; some read it in a slightly critical or scolding tone; some read it with an intelligent, reflective, and philosophical flare; some read in a chatty, flighty, and sensational manner. Others are conversational and sentimental, and still others have a knack for the grave, dramatic, and urgent.

Typically, when material is being read, a reader begins at a high energy level, called the **attack,** that tends to burst on the scene without being out of context, progressing at a somewhat rapid rate, rising to a vocal crescendo, tagging the final line, pausing, then cuing the next segment of the program (or a commercial). The performer's final pose is then retained until the next segment is on the air. As a performer, you must not break your gaze, pose, or position, or add any gestures (such as sniffing) or remarks that are unexpected or not in the script. Using expletives can result in suspension or termination.

Styles vary noticeably in weather and sports reporting. Some read the weather news as a simple fact, some tell it in a more comedic style with wit, some are folksy and include information about recreational activities and meetings, and some go for flight information and meteorological detail. Why is one weathercaster preferred to another? Since the information is basically the same, the answer is in the person's style. A few sportscasters have magnified their own characteristics to become personalities covering the sports scene. A dapper dresser spins complex yarns about selected events with the finesse of a connoisseur of fine wines. These performers are usually good storytellers and personalities in their own right.

Voice Analysis

 o assess your voice, record it and play it back. You may not like what you hear; you may be highly critical of it. This is a common reaction. Regardless, the main concern is whether you have a voice you can develop. You want a voice consistent with your image and sufficiently flexible to meet your expanding career goals. As discussed previously, the main characteristics of a voice are quality, resonance, and phonation. Of equal importance is the way the voice is used; that is, the thought process behind speech, called interpretation. Let us, therefore, define and analyze your voice and later discuss the complex task of developing it. As you listen to your voice, carefully note its main attributes. What is the overall sound of your voice? Is this sound consistent with your appearance? Do listeners seem to understand you easily? What aspects of your voice need development? Again, do not make premature judgments or be overly critical. Instead, let the following discussion guide your analysis.

Try to describe your voice accurately using the guidelines in Figure 4.2. Do not be overly critical. Your views will change as your voice improves.

Improving Your Voice

 oices are very sensitive to a performer's entire physical condition. As mentioned, a voice depends on vigorous, internal energy generated by good health, a desire to perform, an ability to relax into the job, and the pleasure derived from performing for others.

FIGURE 4.2   *Guidelines for assessing your voice.*

Ask yourself the following questions to assess your voice:

- What is the dominant quality of your voice? Is it pleasant? Unpleasant?

- Do you sound confident, or do you come across as uncertain?

- Is your voice consistent with your media appearance?

- Does your voice tend to be nasal? Breathy? Thin? Harsh? Strident? Hoarse?

- Do you have trouble speaking clearly? Can others understand you easily? Is the problem articulation or the way you form sounds? Or is the problem pronunciation due to inaccuracies in your understanding of words and grammar?

- Have you considered the many ways in which you can bring new energy, life, and excitement to reading and reciting old material?

- Have you tried to vary the pitch, volume, timing, or style in preparing copy?

Now look in a mirror as you recite lines from a narration, a feature story, or a newscast. What effect does the combination of your voice and appearance have? Is it the dominant image and sound you want?

RELAXATION AND PREPARATION

Relaxation is one key to a full, rich voice, and often relaxation begins with a good night's sleep. Worry causes tension in the muscles of the entire body, particularly the throat. Performers often worry over whether their performance will be successful. You cannot predict whether you will be successful; uncertainty goes with the occupation. Assess whether your worries are caused from a failure to prepare adequately for your performance. Do you really know your material? Did you pre-read your material? Did you memorize or semi-memorize your lines? If you have difficulty reading notes, cue cards, or scripts, you may stumble when reading. This hints that you are ill prepared. Some stumbles are bound to happen, especially when you are learning. It is important for performers to focus on a smooth recovery when this occurs. Try It Out 4.D includes simple exercises to help you relax before a performance.

 try it out 4.D | **EXERCISES FOR RELAXING PRIOR TO A PERFORMANCE**

1. Inhale deeply. Hold the air as long as you can. Slowly exhale. The result may be a reduction in tension.

2. Push the tips of your fingers on one hand against those of the other hand. This may have a stabilizing effect.

3. Bend forward at the waist and roll the torso in a circular movement to the left, back, right, and front, stretching as much as you can. Repeat the exercise in the opposite direction. This limbering-up exercise is relaxing.

4. Run in place. This may use up and redirect excess energy.

5. Think of relaxing in a quiet place, perhaps with soft music playing.

6. Stretch your arms toward the ceiling as you lift up on your toes on a one-two count.

7. Jump up and down like a rag doll to relax muscles.

8. Repeat these exercises, keeping in mind that you are not competing with anyone. You are relaxing your body and mind. Remember, being nervous is common.

BREATH CONTROL

All human beings produce sound in the same way, by inhaling an air supply and by controlling it when it is exhaled. The air supply is taken into the lungs, then it is released out of a tube in the throat called the **trachea.** The airstream is shaped or modulated as it passes soft surfaces such as vocal folds and muscles (such as the tongue), and hard surfaces such as bone and cartilage. Figure 4.3 is a diagram of the body's breathing structure.

FIGURE 4.3 Physiology of breathing and voice.

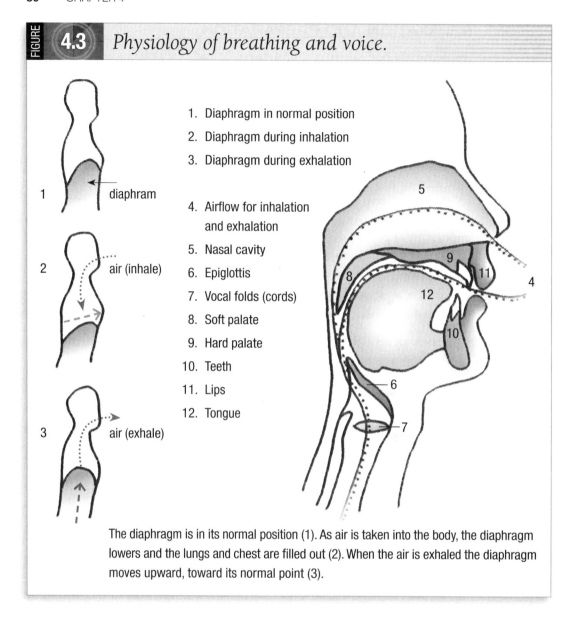

1. Diaphragm in normal position
2. Diaphragm during inhalation
3. Diaphragm during exhalation

4. Airflow for inhalation and exhalation
5. Nasal cavity
6. Epiglottis
7. Vocal folds (cords)
8. Soft palate
9. Hard palate
10. Teeth
11. Lips
12. Tongue

1 — diaphram
2 — air (inhale)
3 — air (exhale)

The diaphragm is in its normal position (1). As air is taken into the body, the diaphragm lowers and the lungs and chest are filled out (2). When the air is exhaled the diaphragm moves upward, toward its normal point (3).

The objective in controlling your air supply is to inhale a great amount of air and release it at will. The greater the amount of air you can draw into your body, the longer you can speak without taking a breath, if the release of the air is properly controlled. By standing erect, you elongate the torso and should be able to speak effortlessly for some time. To do this, breathe in, hold the air supply, and then breathe out slowly. This should help adjust your position, which should be straight but not uncomfortably so. The body may be thought of as a large balloon: if any portion of the balloon is restricted, it will hold less air. If you place your hands at the waist with fingers almost touching in front of you and thumbs to the rear and breathe deeply, you can feel your fingers being pulled apart as the body is inflated.

When inhaling, think of where the breath is going. When a person inhales, the uppermost part of the body is filled first; that is, the upper trunk, to roughly the clavicle or collarbone. Panting is an example of air exhaled from this uppermost cavity. More commonly, air is taken into the upper lungs for normal breathing and speaking; this is the thoracic or chest cavity. Lungs are quite expandable and the lower region is used if an effort is made to relax the **diaphragm** sufficiently to fill the lower lungs. The diaphragm acts like a bellows and helps to create the partial vacuum that draws air into the body and pushes the air out again on command with assistance from the intercostal muscles and the rib cage. Inhaling should be quick, quiet, and as complete as possible. It should be reserved for ends of paragraphs, lines, or phrases. Only amateurs, smokers, and those with upper respiratory problems gulp air within words or phrases or exhaust themselves in their delivery.

Breathing is not merely a matter of getting air *into* the body. It is more importantly getting air out. On expulsion, the air supply, shaped as a stream, is released conservatively so that the performer inhales less frequently and uses the air more efficiently. You must learn to control inhalation, retention, and exhalation of breath. The principal muscle controlling these activities is the diaphragm, located between the chest and the abdomen. An erect torso can take in the same amount of air whether standing, sitting, or lying, but the air supply is more difficult to control in the latter positions. One breath control exercise is to practice enunciating vowels within a few inches of a lighted candle without having the flame flicker. Another is practicing writing copy that can be spoken with a minimum of inhalations. A third is to time yourself while sustaining a note or sound. Breath control takes daily practice. Try It Out 4.E provides exercises for improving breathing, and Figure 4.4 includes two scripts to use for practice.

 try it out   4.E   **EXERCISES TO IMPROVE BREATHING**

1. Practice enunciating vowels within a few inches of a lighted candle but without having the flame flicker. If the flame flickers, you are using too much of your air supply.

2. Take a deep breath and read aloud long paragraphs from newscasts or documentaries, allowing a minimum of additional inhalation.

3. Sustain a note or sound for as long as you can. Time yourself so that you can sustain the sound for longer and longer periods.

4. Prepare to read 20 seconds of news copy written for broadcast in front of your class. After performing, ask for comments from your instructor and the other students.

FIGURE **4.4** *Practice scripts for breath control.*

```
6-110    1 indonesia earthquak  (vic)
============================================
TAKE VO ANIMATED MAP    ((VIC VO MAP))
FULL
ART IS MAKING THIS
MORNING - INDONESIA
QUAKE MAP
*PILOTMOS L3 MAP
ANIMATE                    EARLY THIS
5.8 EARTHQUAKE             MORNING /. AN EARTHQUAKE
                           SHOOK INDONESIA.//
                             THE U-S GEOLOGICAL
                           SURVEY ESTIMATES THE
                           MAGNITUDE WAS 5-POINT-8./
                             IT HIT ABOUT 155 MILES
                           NORTHEAST OF JAKARTA.//
ONCAM                      (VIC OC)   (sǔ-'na-mē)
                             A TSUNAMI/ALERT WAS
                           ISSUED AT FIRST.. BUT WAS
                           CANCELED HALF AN HOUR
                           LATER. //
                             SO FAR THERE ARE NO
                           REPORTS OF DAMAGE OR
                           INJURIES. //
```

Note the markings that indicate breathing points (/ = brief breath, // = full breath).

INTERPRETATIVE CONTROL

The degree of vigor, brightness, energy, nuance, and meaning in a phrase depends on the brain's mental control over various parts of the body. This is called **interpretation.** A performer continuously hears: "Think what you are saying while you are saying it." This mental activity contributes so much that is involuntary that without it, a performer's message may be totally ignored or dismissed as boring. Mental control largely governs interpretation, which in turn conveys what the story means to the performer. A delightful exercise in conveying meaning through the mind is to have

FIGURE **4.4** *Practice scripts, continued.*

```
9-03     1 la porte chemical r   (VA)
==========================================================
TAKE LIVE PIC OR BACK
UP VO
METRO FEED FROM 7AM
THIS MORNING
*PILOTMOS BREAKING       ((VO))
NEWS 2LINE                 CHEMICALS HAVE BEEN
BREAKING NEWS            LEAKING OUT OF A RAIL
CHEMICAL RELEASE         CAR/... SINCE ABOUT 3-30
LA PORTE                 THIS MORNING.//
                           WE'RE TOLD THEY ARE
                         USED TO MAKE PESTICIDES./
                           THE LEAK... HAS FORCED
                         FAIRMONT PARKWAY...
                         BETWEEN HIGHWAY 146 AND
                         BAY AREA BOULEVARD TO
                         SHUT DOWN.//
                           AND RIGHT NOW...
                         THERE'S A "SHELTER IN
                         PLACE ORDER" FOR
                         BUSINESSES IN THAT AREA.//
```

Note the markings that indicate breathing points (/ = brief breath, // = full breath).

a conversation limited to a single syllable such as "ah" or "mm." Your imagination can quickly conjure up 10 to 20 meanings with discernible inflections. Some performers imagine they are communicating the sense of a story to one viewer at a time. The result should be a conversation that is personal, even though millions may be watching. The English language is highly dependent on inflection and interpretation. All performers must be well aware of the importance of this mental dimension to delivery and learn to use it effectively. The techniques for interpretation in Figure 4.5 may be helpful.

4.5 *Interpretation techniques.*

1. If you have a live audience, such as your classmates, prepare your viewers by pausing slightly before you speak.

2. Your first words or action, known as the attack, should be strong in volume and decisive, though not necessarily loud or overly intense.

3. Learn to deemphasize words of no consequence, such as "a" and "the." Both should be pronounced with a short vowel rather than a long one, giving them less attention than nouns and verbs.

4. Collect a few professional news and documentary scripts, such as the ones in Figure 4.4. Practice reading them aloud, changing the emphasis in order to add better understanding and variety for the listener.

5. Deliver the last line in a report, story, or scene with slightly greater volume and intensity. This is the "tag" line and tells the viewer the story is ending.

LANGUAGE CONTROL

Language control concerns your ability to articulate, enunciate, and pronounce words properly. It also has to do with phrasing and grouping words to facilitate the listener's understanding. An intensive study of language is essential for one who aspires to a leadership position in media. Because much of performing, especially reporting, is ad-libbed, you must depend on your knowledge of language to avoid mistakes. When you are on-camera all by yourself, you will be glad you have had a strong education. Those performers who are not proficient in language find themselves apologizing for their errors on the air. Such errors are heard on networks and local stations. How many times have you heard newscasters stumble over copy? Perhaps they do not speak clearly enough to be understood. A word is slurred, the ending is cut off, the "i's" sound like "a's" and the "t's" like "d's." Perhaps the performer simply does not know how to pronounce the words correctly. Names of persons and locations are particularly troublesome. Perhaps the announcer is poorly trained in English grammar. For example, one sportscaster in a major television market said he felt "badly" (instead of bad) three times while reading one paragraph on the air. (He wouldn't say he felt "goodly," would he?)

A common problem is the misuse of the adverbs "hopefully," "reportedly," and "allegedly." Avoid these words. You are not in the business of cheering on the home team or pulling for a stranger's recovery. And you either know or you don't know the circumstances of the story you are covering. When you know, quote the source; otherwise do not allege something may be true.[3]

Language Control on Public Airwaves

challenge arising in English usage comes from the need to be "politically correct." This is an attempt to reduce, if not eliminate, stereotypical, often hurtful, references and comments about groups of people. Over the past several decades persons have come forward to complain about verbal or visual mistreatment, and the public has agreed that individuals or groups should not be offended over the public airways. Among those groups are the elderly, those with disabilities, those of certain racial or sexual orientation, and some veteran groups. There are no absolute rules except perhaps the one that begins "Do unto others . . ." In media, remarks that are shared with the public are supposed to be acceptable to all listeners so that no one feels discriminated against or hurt. In private gatherings or in some forms of entertainment programming, what's accepted may vary. But in the context we are discussing, if there is a possibility that a remark will hurt someone, keep it off the air.

Language control also involves taking care with the words you use on air when describing certain people and groups. See the box above.

How do you know whether you are having difficulties with language control? Try It Out 4.F outlines exercises for articulation, enunciation, and pronunciation.

▶ *try it out*   4.F   **ASSESS YOUR LANGUAGE CONTROL**

1. Record five minutes of television copy. Two days later, after you have forgotten it, play it back while sitting about 20 feet away. Write down every word or syllable that is not absolutely clear and analyze why you could not understand it. Ask a friend to do the same thing: write down every word that is unintelligible. The list that results will suggest how proficient you are in reading aloud. A good announcer is able to read rapidly when called upon to do so, without making an error. These performers can deliver messages flawlessly under the duress of extreme conditions.

2. Make a list of common English words that contain vowels, consonants, and diphthongs. Record your list. Compare your speech with that of local media leaders.

3. Limber up the muscles around your lips, tongue, jaw, and soft palate by stretching your lips, whistling, blowing, extending your tongue, and moving your jaw in various directions. These exercises should help improve your articulation.

4. Obtain a good, recently published dictionary or consult a reputable online dictionary. Whenever you encounter a word that gives you trouble, look up the pronunciation. Begin with "athlete" and "theater," two commonly mispronounced words.

5. Record a recognized newscaster, whose voice you admire, as a model for your troublesome words. The words serve as models for you to imitate. Compare your pronunciation with the models. Carefully break down each word into syllables. Try to reconstruct the word. Listen to the model again. Repeat the correct form until you have it firmly in your mind. Do not be impatient. This may take a long time.

Amplification

mplification is the magnification of the voice so that the audience can hear it better. This can be done through voice projection or the use of microphones.

VOICE PROJECTION

Projecting your voice is not merely a matter of shouting or increasing the volume, although this sometimes accomplishes the goal. Projecting requires that the performer think where the voice should reach, and through thinking help to send it there. This technique is effective in an auditorium where the performer can project or think the message to the back of the house or balcony, and can elongate certain words as one might in a theater so that they will carry the distance.

Usually projection is not necessary beyond a minimum distance, for the tiniest murmur can be amplified with the right equipment. For practical purposes, however, you should project your voice about seven to ten feet, or the working distance from a television camera. Such projection will give your voice energy. Amplification enables the voice to range from the softest to the loudest volume levels (**level,** in audio terms, refers to the electronic reading of a sound on a volume units meter), and these levels can be electronically reinforced and extended so that a performer's voice will sound even better than the performer may sound in a live appearance. For most news and information circumstances, maintaining good sound quality in a studio is not difficult. On-location shooting is where many sound problems may arise. Background noise may override the performer's voice, the relationship of the performer to the microphone may reduce sound quality, and of course, the potential for faulty equipment always requires duplicate microphones, cable, and other sound equipment. Remote shooting may be so hazardous that the voice may have to be rerecorded over the video back in the studio, called dubbing or **looping.** This may be the only way to provide quality.

USE OF MICROPHONES

Microphones as equipment are discussed further in Chapter 7; however, it is important to understand when and how microphones can be used to amplify your voice.

The objective in using a microphone is to provide a clear, noiseless reproduction of the voice and related sounds. In reality, audio for news and entertainment can range from booming high quality to virtually inaudible moments. Usually this is intentional, but sometimes it is accidental. In difficult circumstances, such as criminal investigations, unanticipated natural disasters, or amateur recordings, poor audio quality may result. Events in progress (wars, earthquakes) may preclude the use of sophisticated equipment as reporters at the scene or in transit feed audio live via radio signals, cell phones, or computers to news programs. However, these circumstances are comparatively infrequent with today's technology and transportation.

Keep in mind that a microphone is relatively delicate and expensive. You can test it by simply speaking into it, using the same volume and pitch of the voice that you intend to use on the air, and maintaining an appropriate distance from the mike. Tapping, whistling, blowing, or yelling into a microphone for testing purposes not only is unnecessary but may permanently damage the instrument. During a voice or **level check,** the engineer will adjust the level of the microphone on the console so that every performer's voice blends with the rest of the program. If you are at a loss for words when an engineer asks for a level check, simply read the script or count in the voice you would use on the air. The engineer will let you know when the audio level has been properly adjusted. Do not stop or start sporadically. The suggestions in Figure 4.6 may prove helpful.

FIGURE 4.6 *Suggestions for using microphones properly.*

1. If you have a microphone clipped on your collar or clothing, be sure that your clothing or jewelry doesn't brush across it and create extraneous noise.

2. If you must use a microphone with a cable, be sure to have sufficient cable to move about comfortably.

3. If you are working with a microphone stand, practice in advance removing the microphone from the stand to hold it. Do not hit the stand.

4. Do not play with a microphone's cable because its internal wires break easily.

5. If the microphone is overhead, be aware of its location and range so that you do not drift out of its beam.

6. If you are wearing a wireless mike, make sure you turn it on before you go on-camera, and off when you are on breaks or off the set.

Summary

The vocal abilities you display during a performance are as important as your material, your appearance, and your overall look. As with other facets of your performance, there is work you can do to develop your voice if it is unsatisfactory to you. Physiological and emotional components of your voice—relaxation, fatigue, and tension—affect the underlying physical states where good vocal delivery begins. Each performer's voice is different, and because of that your voice may be better suited to entertainment or news delivery. Timbre, articulation, pronunciation, interpretation, pitch, range, and volume are technical components of your vocal delivery that combine with volume, timing, and variety to create the sum total of your vocal style. Breath control, interpretative control, language control, and voice projection are all tools that you must employ to become an adept performer who makes the most of a vocal performance. Developing good habits of practice and conditioning will enable you to bring out the best in your voice.

CHAPTER 4 *exercises*

1. Read the same news or feature story twice and record it both times. The first time, read it while smiling. The second time, read it but do not smile. Listen to the stories—can you hear the difference?

2. This time, pair up with someone and each read the stories with your backs turned to one another. Can you tell which story was read with a smile and which one was not?

3. To check your pitch and range, go to a piano and strike middle C, then imitate the notes in speech or musical sounds, going higher and lower. Your range is the extent to which you can imitate these notes with a clear sound of good quality. Listeners can easily tell what sounds are comfortably made without straining.

4. Breath control takes daily practice. One exercise is to read aloud the children's poem "The House That Jack Built," which is provided below. Read each paragraph on one breath. Because the verses get progressively longer, you will find it increasingly difficult to finish a verse without stopping to breathe.

THE HOUSE THAT JACK BUILT

1. This is the house that Jack built. (*Breathe*)

2. This is the malt
   that lay in the house that Jack built. (*Breathe*)

3. This is the rat,
   That ate the malt
   That lay in the house that Jack built. (*Breathe*)

4. This is the cat,
    That killed the rat,
    That ate the malt
    That lay in the house that Jack built. (*Breathe*)

5. This is the dog,
    That worried the cat,
    That killed the rat,
    That ate the malt
    That lay in the house that Jack built. (*Breathe*)

6. This is the cow with the crumpled horn,
    That tossed the dog,
    That worried the cat,
    That killed the rat,
    That ate the malt
    That lay in the house that Jack built. (*Breathe*)

7. This is the maiden all forlorn,
    That milked the cow with the crumpled horn,
    That tossed the dog,
    That worried the cat,
    That killed the rat,
    That ate the malt
    That lay in the house that Jack built. (*Breathe*)

8. This is the man all tattered and torn,
    That kissed the maiden all forlorn,
    That milked the cow with the crumpled horn,
    That tossed the dog,
    That worried the cat,
    That killed the rat,
    That ate the malt
    That lay in the house that Jack built. (*Breathe*)

9. This is the priest all shaven and shorn,
    That married the man all tattered and torn,
    That kissed the maiden all forlorn,
    That milked the cow with the crumpled horn,
    That tossed the dog,
    That worried the cat,
    That killed the rat,
    That ate the malt
    That lay in the house that Jack built. (*Breathe*)

10. This is the cock that crowed in the morn,
    That waked the priest all shaven and shorn,
    That married the man all tattered and torn,
    That kissed the maiden all forlorn,
    That milked the cow with the crumpled horn,
    That tossed the dog,
    That worried the cat,

That killed the rat,

That ate the malt

That lay in the house that Jack built. (*Breathe*)

11. This is the farmer sowing his corn,

    That kept the cock that crowed in the morn,

    That waked the priest all shaven and shorn,

    That married the man all tattered and torn,

    That kissed the maiden all forlorn,

    That milked the cow with the crumpled horn,

    That tossed the dog,

    That worried the cat,

    That killed the rat,

    That ate the malt

    That lay in the house that Jack built. (*Breathe*)

Notes

1. Many news directors will first *listen* to an on-air job candidate's resume tape to determine whether the person has the right voice. Only then will the director *watch* the tape.
2. Lynn K. Wells, *The Articulate Voice* (Boston: Pearson Education Group, 2004), p. 52.
3. Stuart Hyde has an interesting discussion about these commonly used words in *Television and Radio Announcing* (Boston: Houghton Mifflin, 1998), pp. 149–151.

Other Sources

Entertainer's Secret. For Dry Throat and Hoarse Voice. Throat Relief. KILT Corp., Carmel, IN 46032.

Gross, Lynne S., and James C. Foust. *Video Production: Disciplines and Techniques*. 10th ed. Scottsdale, AZ: Holcomb Hathaway, 2009.

Hagerman, William L. *Broadcast Announcing*. Englewood Cliffs, NJ: Prentice Hall, 1993.

Hyde, Stuart. *Television and Radio Announcing*. Boston: Houghton Mifflin, 1998.

"One on One. Classic Television Interviews." CBS Television, 1993. Produced by the Museum of Television & Radio. Executive Producers: Robert M. Batscha, Peter W. Kunhardt.

Schmidt, Wallace V., and Roger N. Conaway. *Results-Oriented Interviewing Principles, Practices, and Procedures*. Boston: Allyn & Bacon, 1999.

Utterback, Ann. *Broadcast Voice Handbook: How to Give Meaning and Style to Each Word You Speak*. Chicago: Bonus Books, 1991.

Wells, Lynn K. *The Articulate Voice: An Introduction to Voice and Diction*. Boston: Pearson Education Group, 2004.

Movement

INTRODUCTION

This chapter focuses on movement, beginning with developing a foundation based on concentration and relaxation. Once you master the ability to concentrate while simultaneously being relaxed, the movements required of you should follow easily—standing, sitting, walking, and gestures. From the simplest, smallest nuance in your facial expression to the largest gesture, your movement is a communication tool. Most of what we communicate to others is communicated through nonverbal cues, and these must not be overlooked.

The Study of Movement

performer in visual media is defined as much by movement as by voice. Research indicates that nonverbal cues are more than four times as effective as language cues in transmitting attitudes. One study found that body language accounts for as much as 93 percent of one person's message to another.[1]

Anthropologist Ray L. Birdwhistell coined the term *kinesics* in the early 1950s to include the study of all body movement of communicative value.[3] During the ensuing years, a substantial body of research has suggested that no body movements have meaning in isolation and that performers should focus all their movements on the message. Dr. Cody Sweet[2] identified eight types of nonverbal communication (see Figure 5.1).

Movement is more important and complex than most performers realize. Our discussion of movement includes a look at the moving figure, reasons for movement, characteristics of movement, the elimination of involuntary movement, and aspects of nonverbal communication. Concentration and relaxation are prerequisite to these considerations.

Controlling Movement Through Concentration and Relaxation

By applying concentration and relaxation, you will be able to keep your movement under control in order to convey subtle messages. For instance, if you pick up an art object in a demonstration, the arm movement should be clear. How you hold it shows the importance you attach to the object. You may touch it reverently or casually, depending on whether you think of the item as priceless or as a prop. Close observation through the tele-

---

FIGURE 5.1 *Nonverbal communications.*

1. Body language conveyed by gestures and postures
2. Voice tones
3. Physical appearance
4. Clothing
5. Touch and touching
6. Use of space
7. Surroundings
8. Time and timing

vision camera lens magnifies your movements. Are they stable, hesitant, insecure, over-eager? No matter how you move, it has meaning. Similarly, in an interview you can convey warmth, friendliness, intimacy, and concern by being in close proximity to your guest and relating to your director what you plan to do and the level of familiarity you want to convey to your guest and the public.

CONCENTRATION

Concentration aids a performer in controlling movement and in focusing attention on the message without interference from unrelated activities and stress. Concentration allows performers to become completely absorbed in what they are doing to the exclusion of everything else, the opposite of multitasking. Some performers are much better at concentrating than others.

The loss of concentration in a performance frequently causes forgetfulness, stammering, the delivery of the wrong line, or losing one's place on a prompter. "Quiet on the set" is not a casual request; it is essential during a program or a recording to avoid unwanted noise that may contribute to a performer's loss of concentration. Crew members whispering in the background can distract a performer. Concentration can be broken, too, if items such as scripts are misplaced or furniture is rearranged, thereby disrupting the performer's anticipated routine. Expert performers ad-lib around unexpected changes without notice by the viewers. Broadcast performers must play to the audience, whether it consists of one person at home or thousands, by maintaining confidence in themselves and the material and concentrating on what is being said or done each moment.

Try It Out 5.A provides simple exercises that can bring your mind into focus and boost your ability to concentrate.

 try it out 5.A **CONCENTRATION EXERCISES**

1. *Rewind:* Think of a familiar story such as a tall tale or myth, or a movie you've seen recently. Now try to retell the story in your head, starting at the end and working toward the beginning. Retelling a story backward requires concentration.

2. *Slow-motion concentration:* Pick a movement you commonly use in your performance, such as sitting down in a chair or picking up an object, or an everyday continuing movement such as washing dishes or setting the table. Perform this action in slow motion, concentrating on making every second of the movement clear and exact.

RELAXATION

Relaxation is as necessary to movement as it is for voice control. As a performer, you must learn to relax. Relaxation is not easy because of the personal strain that usually accompanies a performance in front of the camera or an audience. Tension can become very intense, and it's crucial to channel this energy into the performance, released in just the right amounts to ensure a swift pace for the program. Relaxation enables you to knowingly control the voice and body.

Exercises to achieve relaxation are based on controlling tension. For example, tense and then release the body while breathing deeply, and accompany this physical procedure by clearing your mind of all thoughts not directly related to the immediate task. If your mind is without stress, the body will relax. The mysteries of relaxing for the purpose of mental and physical control have been studied for centuries by those who practice yoga. A few simple exercises, shown in Try It Out 5.B, may help you to relieve tension and control the voice and body.

 try it out | 5.B | **RELAXATION EXERCISES FOR PERFORMERS**

Breathe deeply while practicing each of these exercises. Think only of relaxing in a favorite quiet place. Close your eyes and play soft music if that helps you.

1. Assume a basic stance with your feet together and your hands relaxed at your sides. Be at least an arm's length from anyone else.

2. Drop your chin to your chest and slowly rotate your head in a circle. Inhale for one complete cycle and exhale for another.

3. Raise your right shoulder as high as you can then lower it as far as possible. Repeat the exercise with your left shoulder.

4. Sit on the floor with legs apart. Bend from the waist, extending the fingers as far as you can in the direction of the right foot, then the left.

5. Lie down on the floor and relax. Lift each limb, stiffen it, and relax it.

Repeat each exercise several times. Do not hurry. Gradually build your stretching capability. The objective is to relax. You are not competing with anyone. You are relaxing your own mind and body.

The Smile

In performance, perhaps the most important movement is the smile (assuming a smile is appropriate to the occasion). Smiling varies from a minimal smile to fully parted lips exposing much of the mouth. Remember that a smile is not restricted to the mouth. It's important that your eyes and the rest of your face convey the essence of the smile, also. If your mouth "smiles" and your eyes do not, the smile will not appear genuine.

A smile is a sign to a viewer that the performer and the program are under control, even under difficult circumstances. Although a pleasant smile does not always arise automatically, as a performer, you should strive to develop a smile that appears natural and genuinely expressive. Try the following steps:

1. Record yourself or look in a mirror to establish a smile you like by observing different poses. Be sure your eyes are smiling, too—they should convey the same emotion your mouth is expressing.

2. Practice the position and facial aspects of that smile until it can be duplicated on command.

3. Display the smile whenever it is called for.

Having the confidence that your smile is attractive and amiable will aid your performance. Even when the smile may not be motivated because of the stresses you are experiencing, you will shield your uneasiness from the viewers.

The Moving Body

Movement begins and ends in a firm position: standing, sitting, kneeling, or lying. The body is in a pose that seems natural, yet it is not. If a performer were to sit in a totally natural and relaxed pose on-camera like he sits at home, he would probably look like a lump of clay. Such relaxation may be appropriate for a conversation with friends, but it makes for a poor on-camera appearance. In most circumstances you cannot be so relaxed that you slump, droop your head, cave in your chest, or stick out your stomach. Instead you must stand and sit in a state of heightened naturalness with muscles only slightly at ease. However, a taut military stance is too rigid for most on-camera situations; a straight body held in somewhat easy posture is preferable. Relaxation is achieved when you have control over your body and its movement.

Surprisingly, performers move relatively little on-camera, in part because the camera moves, too. The principal action takes place in the center of the screen, and that action must be instantly understood by viewers. In a studio only a relatively small space is lighted and miked for showing on-camera. Movement must be subtle. Action that is important to the presentation is often shown in close-up, which means the performer has far less distance in which to move than onstage.

In any case, movement on-camera always is or should be motivated. If there is no reason for moving, then do not move. There are two kinds of movements: those that reinforce the message, such as walking through high water and looking into the camera, and those that do not, such as looking down at your notes. Reinforcing movements animate, interpret, clarify, and add emphasis and style to the performance. Meaningless movements blur the message you are attempting to convey and distract the viewer's attention. The rule is: movement dominates message. Sometimes movements call so much attention to themselves that the viewer loses the main intention of the message. For instance, if you jiggle your foot on camera, viewers will pay attention to that movement and wonder why you are doing it. The message is lost. For that reason, it is generally assumed that you should remain still until there is a reason to move.

The best way to check your movement is to make a short practice video. The recording should show you sitting, getting up, walking to the center of a lighted area, saying a few words as if you are hosting a program, using a few gestures, and returning to your chair. Another common situation is sitting at a desk reading a newscast or conducting an interview. Recording these activities will allow you to analyze your movements. Watch the video carefully, noticing your principal movements. Do you have energetic, natural movement? Are you conveying unwanted, unnecessary, or negative messages by means of movement? Share the video with a coach or other objective outsider, for you may not be an objective judge of how you look to others.

POSITION

Central to on-camera work is the moving performer and the corollary, the moving camera. As a rule, the camera moves more often and farther than the performer; therefore, you should understand that for much of the time you will be essentially static or motionless. **On-camera** means you are actively in the scene and are probably in camera view. You are **off-camera** whenever you are out of view, even though you may be a participant in the scene.

Whether moving or not, you should be aware of your body position in relation to the camera. An **open position** allows the lens to easily reveal the face and the body, as illustrated in position 1 in Figure 5.1. As you move toward a profile, shown in position 2 in Figure 5.1, you close your position so that it is more difficult to be seen by viewers. The director can get the best shots of performers if they face or **cheat** toward the camera. Cheating creates the illusion of speaking to another performer while still facing the camera. For example, anchors banter and turn toward each other between stories, and during stories they return to make **direct contact** with viewers by looking directly into the camera lens as much as possible. Or, during an interview, the interviewer and the guest face each other as in normal conversation, but both may slightly favor the camera lens. The director will move the cameras in order to capture the best shots of the participants.

FIGURE 5.1 *On-camera positions.*

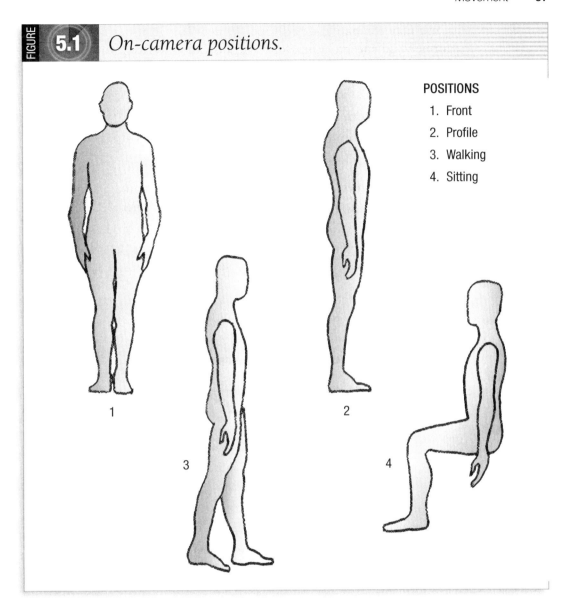

POSITIONS
1. Front
2. Profile
3. Walking
4. Sitting

At other times, such as recording a sitcom, a performer may avoid the lens and look at the other persons on the set, in which case the viewers become observers. Even during such times, performers still need to enhance audience contact by keeping them involved. As a performer walks, opens a door, or hands someone an object, she does it with the limb farthest from the camera so that the position is still open to the camera.

A closed position reduces the director's and the viewers' chance to observe the performer. If, for example, an interviewer looks directly at the interviewee, at the back of the set, or off-camera, or if he crosses the leg nearest to the camera over the farther one, he is restricting access to the camera operator, resulting in a closed position.

You may compare the performer–camera lens relationship to the basic performer–audience positions onstage. Instead of relating to an in-person audience, the performer relates to the audience through the camera:

- directly facing the lens (audience)
- one-quarter turn right or left away from the lens
- three-quarter turn from the lens
- full back to the lens

These performer–camera relationships are illustrated in Figure 5.2, along with various facial positions in relation to the camera.

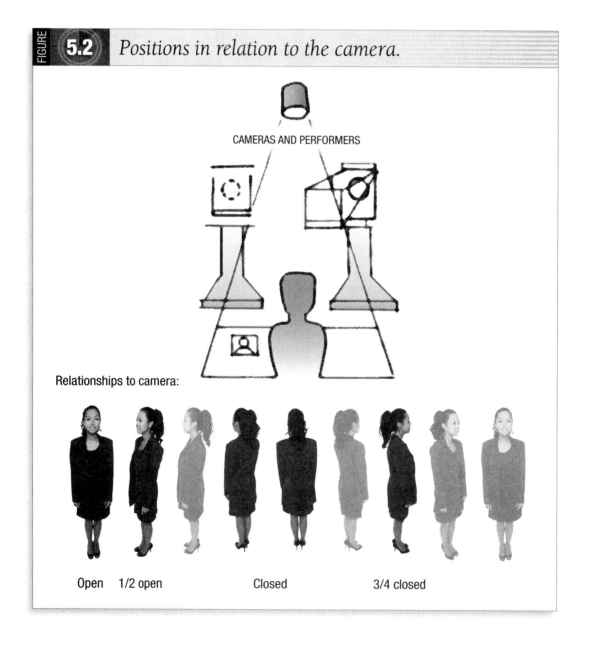

FIGURE 5.2 *Positions in relation to the camera.*

CAMERAS AND PERFORMERS

Relationships to camera:

Open   1/2 open   Closed   3/4 closed

NATURAL MOVEMENT

Natural movement is the appearance of being at ease, warm, and friendly, on-camera and on-microphone. Naturalness in a performer varies with age, experience, and self-confidence. Children move naturally and without regard for social conduct. But as people grow older, they may become aware of social restraints that impose or restrict certain movements and gestures. Performers then become conscious of the way they move. Self-consciousness may hinder the natural ease with which a performer moves. Many aspiring performers must be taught how to move so that they appear natural, yet graceful, before the camera lens or an audience.

Everyday movements may be quite difficult on-camera: walking across a room, sitting in a chair, moving a hand. You may find that your first awareness of movement occurs when you appear before a group. Suddenly, you are pulled from anonymity and are singled out by being in the spotlight. Fear strikes, and you may be temporarily paralyzed or "frozen." You are focusing on yourself, your performance, and your appearance rather than on your ability to serve the public by providing information important to their lives. Get over focusing on yourself and the "freeze" will thaw. You cannot move with confidence and grace until you learn how to be natural in front of viewers.

POSTURE

A performer often hears the expression "Stand tall" or "Stand your full height." This suggests that you should stand as though a string is attached to the center of the top of your head, and presumably a pull on this string could lift you skyward. So it should be with your posture as you perform. The body should be aligned and balanced so that a line from the forehead to the feet would divide the body equally, with half of the weight on either side of the line and the hands and arms hanging relaxed at the sides, as illustrated in Figure 5.1. The tilt of the head should allow the eyes to look directly forward. The shoulders should be level, the chest capable of taking in a good air supply, and the stomach held flat. The upper torso should appear to be directly over the hips; the buttocks should be tucked in. The body should be supported by straight legs, and the feet should point directly forward.

Proper alignment of the figure depends on a backbone that is essentially straight, allowing for a slight curve inward at the lower back. Your posture can be quickly checked by standing next to a perpendicular surface such as a wall. What parts of your body protrude? Many people lead with the head, or thrust it forward when walking. The chest may be sunken, the stomach and buttocks may protrude, the legs may be bowed, and the feet may point outward. As you look at your posture in a mirror or on a recording, observe these potential problems. If they exist, retraining at the conscious and subconscious levels may be necessary. Of course, some physiological problems may prevent an individual from achieving perfect posture.

BASIC MOVEMENTS

Everything you do should be rehearsed until it is exactly right. For now, go through the following movements before a mirror or have them recorded, or both. Figure 5.3 lists some common errors to watch for. Remember, if you are role-playing, movement that would ordinarily be considered an error could be correct. Once you take your work seriously, you will strive toward perfection just like a professional in any field.

Standing

Standing in place means you are exactly on the **mark,** a designation made in tape or chalk on the floor of the studio. Your posture is correct and natural looking. No other movement distracts from the message. Frequently performers tire and break stance by shifting their feet, drifting away from the marks, and gradually out of optimum light level. Avoid this and other common movements such as twisting, swaying, and leading while standing.

Sitting

To sit down gracefully, feel for the chair or seat with your leg. Lower your body onto the chair while the thigh muscles keep your back straight. As you prepare to get up, don't anticipate the rise by moving forward. Stand back up using your leg muscles, keeping your back straight. While sitting, legs may be crossed at the ankles or knees so that your body position remains open toward the camera. Position long legs as inconspicuously as possible by keeping them crossed low and together. If the leg nearest the camera is crossed higher up over the other leg, the screen will show a large hip and a partly concealed body, an unattractive sitting position for both men and women.

Walking

In walking, the secret is to move the weight with ease. To begin, lift your body and keep your weight on the balls of your feet. Start moving with the leg farthest

FIGURE 5.3 *Common movement errors.*

DO YOU MAKE THESE COMMON MOVEMENT ERRORS?

- Fidgeting or moving slightly out of position while standing. This is known as drifting.
- Swinging your arms, stooping, or moving your feet like dead weights when walking.
- Sitting down with a thud, and then collapsing in a sprawled position.
- Swinging your arms when you walk, wait, or talk to another person.

from the camera, and point the toes straight ahead and not outward or inward, which may result in a waddling effect. Move legs from the hip in an easy rhythm with relaxed and flexible knees. Take moderate steps, letting the ball of the foot touch the floor a fraction ahead of the heel. Do not swing your arms.

Hands

Hands should be an integrated part of body movement and personality. They may feel like dead weights at your sides whenever there is no motivation for moving them. You must find a comfortable position for your hands and remember it when they have nothing to do. Practice moving smoothly into the hand positions in Try It Out 5.C.

 try it out   5.C   **COMMON HAND POSITIONS**

1. Hands at the sides.

2. Hands folded in front.

3. Hands folded in back.

4. Hands on hips.

5. One hand at the side and the other clasping a wrist or arm.

6. Arms folded in front with hands buried.

7. Arms folded with one hand resting against the face.

8. Hands or thumbs in pockets.

Motivation, which is discussed in a later section, is key to using your hands naturally and effectively. Performers may use props such as scripts or microphones to practice. As a performer, you may need to hold books, photographs, food, or other such items. Hold these objects in a predetermined and lighted position for perhaps five seconds for the camera. You must hold an item long enough for the viewer to know what it is and to study it, if necessary. Only steady hands can do this effectively.

ANIMATION

In one sense, animation simply refers to movement of the face and body; in another sense, animation gives life or a quality to a movement by making it more interesting, exciting, and impressive. Such movement has been formalized in an art form practiced for centuries called **pantomime**. Pantomime is communicating ideas, emotions, and narratives by means of body expression without words. A few basic principles of pantomime are provided in Figure 5.4.

Pantomime principles.

1. The chest is the key to all body action. It inflates the figure, making it seem long, impressive, and worthy of attention.

2. Positive emotions are expressed through an expanded body. Hold chest and head high. Keep movement free but conservative.

3. Expression in the face precedes action; thought is first detected in the eyes and then flows through the body.

4. All action must be definite in thought, execution, and motivation.

5. Negative emotions are expressed by a contracted chest, restricted gestures, tenseness, and drawn features. Avoid this kind of body action.

BALANCE

Animating a static pose requires balance if you are to have easy, fluid movement, instant bodily response, and quick changes of direction. Establishing your balance will give you emotional as well as physical stability. The exercises in Try It Out 5.D will help you perfect your balance.

 try it out   5.D | **BALANCE EXERCISES**

1. Assume an erect stance. March in place, gradually raising your knees higher and higher, or brush the right foot forward and backward several times, then the left foot.

2. Kneel on the right foot and then the left, moving the entire body up and down several times.

3. Squat on the floor, extending your arms forward. Slowly rise, adjusting your feet to a secure stance. Once standing, note the position of your feet and body in a mirror. If the stance is attractive as well as balanced and comfortable, remember it, for it can be used as your basic standing position.

4. Practice moving from this position by taking a few steps in various directions.

5. Walk directly to a chair and sit in it. Practice moving around the set until you are absolutely secure in your movements, efficient in their direction, and smooth in every gesture.

Motivation in Movement

ecause unnecessary movement wastes energy and may blur the message being conveyed, a performer moves mainly for one or more of the following six reasons:

1. to define purpose
2. to catch attention
3. to tell a story
4. to convey emotion
5. to delineate character
6. to explain relationships

DEFINE PURPOSE

Movement should have purpose. Movements such as moving your head up and down to indicate agreement, turning to wave goodbye, pointing to a chart, and holding an object for a demonstration are integral to constructing the visual message. A host moves from the shadows into a pool of light in the center of the studio floor in order to be seen. He knows why he is moving. In this case, the movement is for technical reasons. More often, however, action is generated from the material, such as commands in the script.

CATCH ATTENTION

Movement catches attention—even the smallest movement will draw a viewer's attention. In general, movements are obvious and intentional. You want the viewer to follow your action so that the message is understood or your ability is appreciated. Movement can be used for capturing attention, focusing attention, or redirecting attention. To illustrate: a meteorologist stands to the right of a weather screen. She points to a cold front with her right hand (capturing attention). She moves her right hand past various locations, calling attention to areas where rain may fall (focusing attention). She points to a second front that may meet the first front (redirecting). How distracting it would be if during the presentation she wiped her nose, looked off-set away from the weather board, or stumbled. That may seem absurd, but some performers have equally distracting movements that immediately draw viewers' attention away from the message and to the distraction.

TELL A STORY

Performers tell brief stories, whether they are presenting a news report or answering questions. Movement can be used to tell or enhance a story. For instance, an investigative reporter walks deliberately up to the door of a school bus. He opens it and dramatically shows how dirty it has become while sitting idle. As the shot widens to show 20 buses in disuse, viewers begin to understand his point. Then he is shown walking into a repair shop where two mechanics are working on one bus. The performer builds suspense—what will happen? He stands naturally, talking to the mechanics, asking them when the bus will be repaired. They are unsure. Viewers begin feeling disgust for the situation. Then the shot cuts to children waiting at bus stops, and the performer steps into view, asking, "Does your child need a ride?" A cut to a new shot shows him in static, seated comfort as he interviews a school administrator. This contrasts the shot with the dirty buses and emphasizes the failure to serve the kids.

Such stories are frequently released during Sweeps Week, a system used by Nielsen Media Research to measure audience viewing. These are stories that affect families and communities. The movement of the performer gets the story across to viewers and may anger them and motivate them to action.

CONVEY EMOTION

Professionals strive to control their emotions. When a football player throws a ball onto the ground with force and glee, when a political candidate raises her arms in victory, when a relative wipes his eyes while recounting the death of a child killed in an accident, emotion is expressed. These examples are probably spontaneous and uncontrolled, but to career performers, these same events are reported with practiced control. Seldom does a news reporter reveal personal emotions, even when reporting about a colleague's death in a war zone, but a reporter may use emotion as a persuasive tool. For example, a fund-raising drive showing children who are disabled struggling to walk or hugging promoters is a primary use of movement to influence emotion.

When movement that conveys emotion is morally or ethically justified remains debatable; it has become commonplace in many newscasts. Those performers who use emotional movement are often seen on public affairs programs where opposing views are expressed; this use is inappropriate in news. Non-career performers may use movement to create emotional response.

DELINEATE CHARACTER

Movement delineates character, which usually refers to whom a performer is portraying or the image she wants to get across to the audience. One worthwhile exercise in a performance class is to ask each student to walk across a room, a distance of 15 feet or so. Then the instructor asks the class to analyze what it saw:

- What is the person like?
- Is the person ambitious, fun, dynamic, nervous, or friendly?
- What were the position of the head, the eye level?

- Did the arms swing too much?
- Was the walk straight?

From these questions a class learns to observe carefully and to notice that every person is a different "character." Careful study enables performers to improve their images.

EXPLAIN RELATIONSHIPS

Movement should explain a performer's relationships. In a newsroom the placement of the reporters around, next to, or near the anchor explains their relationship. Typically, the anchor is in the center position and turns right or left to acknowledge the sportscaster, weathercaster, and contributing reporters. The main person, however, is the anchor. Politicians, entertainers, and community spokespersons usually sit to the side. Such decorum is adhered to on talk shows where guests move over one space at a time to yield to the newest guest the chair next to the host. In the telecast of a message at a political convention, the politician is the star. The supporting persons cluster around him. The star is in the center, featured players are recognized nearby, and supporting contributors are at the ends. Guests move toward or away from each other to demonstrate attitudes through spatial relationships.

Characteristics of Movement

very movement can be defined and studied in terms of direction, strength, speed, duration, timing, and grace. No movement should signal anticipated action to the viewers, but certain movements may cue the director. As mentioned earlier, perhaps the most important movement in television is the movement of the mouth. If the lips are extended broadly, curved slightly upward (direction), with sureness (strength) and quickness, and held for a few moments (duration) after a remark or significant action (timing), and this is done with ease (grace), it is usually interpreted as a friendly smile. The smile aptly illustrates characteristics of movement, which can be readily applied to broader actions.

DIRECTION

Direction refers to "in place" activity, movement away from where the performer is located. In-place movement includes face or body gestures, but it is usually thought of as repositioning the entire body. Direction on television has to do with the relationship of the performer to the camera. A performer moves up or down, horizontally or vertically, depending on where she is compared to the camera. Typically, a performer moves into or out of camera view and moves toward the camera or away from it. Once the movement of a scene is determined by the director, called **blocking,** the performer knows where to move during the production. If the performer moves from one place to another, this is called a **cross.**

Conversely, performers may remain in a relatively fixed position and the camera operator can move in relation to the performer. While shooting the scene, the director moves the cameras in relation to the performer. The director may say, "Don't worry about the cameras, we'll find you." This is typical for ad-libbed shots during a discussion program or an interview. In other words, the performer is at the mercy of the director.

A third possibility is to have both the performer and the camera moving. This often happens, as in a moving shot at the courthouse where clients and lawyers are talking side by side.

Direction, therefore, refers to the moving performer in relation to a fixed camera and lens, a static performer with a moving camera, or both.

STRENGTH

Strength is the degree of power in a movement. Strength of movement is largely psychological: How motivated is the performer? What is the emotional level of action? Is the performer emphatic or uncertain? How dominant is the physical presence of the performer on the screen? Strength is especially important in athletic events, but it is important in news and entertainment, too. For example, an actor may rehearse the strength of the delivery of a movement without real physical contact, as in a fist to the jaw that misses in reality. The thrust of the move in each case is at full strength, but only the illusion of strength exists on impact. A reporter looks to put the strongest action on the screen, whether it is a powerful delivery or a strong clip. The reporter may be excluded from the story visually; however, her voice-over account will be essential.

SPEED

Speed refers to the amount of time it takes performers to move their entire body or any part of it from one place to another. Fast action can speed up a movement so much that the movement may resemble that of an old film. Normal movement is anything that appears to be equivalent to the movement seen every day, and slow speed is familiar to television viewers because of instant replay in sports. Movement should be judged in the context of the total performance. Speed can be skillfully used to lend variety to a performance. For example, as people move faster, they may speak faster, also.

DURATION

The length of a movement can play a key role in a performer's delivery. A movement can be so painfully long that the audience tires of watching it, or so short that the audience misses the movement altogether. The right length is the amount of time it takes for viewers to understand, comprehend, and appreciate the movement. For many newscasts this means playing a moment in slow motion rather than real time so that viewers can get a good look at the newsmaker and the action. The last flick of a victim's hand may be the perfect touch to end a story of disaster; a close-up of a face bowed in prayer may be the proper duration to stress a point during a televised religious program; dragging a body across a floor in slow motion may provide the psychological impact required for a statement of social reform. Today, television's most graphic images tend to be continuously repeated. For example, within a one-hour newscast viewers may see the same few seconds of a tornado many times. Repetition makes the duration of the event seem longer than it really is.

TIMING

A performer controls movement so carefully that he or she knows when to be at an exact position on the floor, when to pick up a visual, and when to turn from looking into one camera lens to looking into another. Timing must be perfect because equipment may have already started to run footage or sound that will coincide with the performer on the screen. A speaker should know when to deliver a line to get maximum laughter or to evoke sadness and respect. These judgments are collectively referred to as timing. Timing, then, is the ability to predetermine the moment you will move, or the speed with which material is paced.

GRACE

Grace is the ease of movement and its appropriateness to the total action. Moving with confidence, as though the performer has done the task many times before, and yet is fresh about doing it again, is thought of as being graceful in an ordinary way. Human beings have a natural grace in walking, standing, and sitting that is quite acceptable—if it can be preserved for media. A feature program performer who likes to get involved with show content, such as cooking or auto racing, uses fine motor skills to avoid nervousness and shaking. Gross motor skills likewise need to be practiced. Sometimes a performer experiences intense self-consciousness on-camera, which stiffens the muscles and produces a high level of nervousness that prohibits graceful movement, making him look uncomfortable. Nowhere is this awkwardness more apparent than when a novice public speaker takes predetermined, even counted, but unmotivated steps toward the audience to provide a mechanical transition during a speech. A performer's uneasiness may be eliminated by expert coaching and diligent practice. A clever coach may assure a performer that she is doing well, even though she may not be at her best on the occasion. Giving self-confidence may be the most important contribution a coach or director makes to a performance, especially if it sets the performer at ease.

Involuntary Movement

 ommon involuntary movement occurs at the subconscious level. Performers do it without realizing they are moving. Frequently these involuntary movements are caused by stress. Common distortions of the face include: frowning, grimacing, sniffing, mouthing words, pouting lips, enlarging the nostrils, squinting, blinking, turning down the corners of the mouth, biting the tongue or lips, chewing without gum, picking or scratching the face, leaving the mouth open, and licking the lips. Unattractive positions and movements of the hands include clawed, stiff fingers; heaviness of the hands; playing with hair, jewelry, paper, or pencils; tapping or shaking objects; repeated and rhythmic gestures; and wringing of hands. Distortions of the torso are wriggling shoulders and hips, muscle spasms, heaving the chest or abdomen, humping the back, stiffness in posture, and twisting or swinging in a chair. Distracting movements of the legs include swaying to and fro, foot jiggling, and locking the legs at the knees. Facial reactions such as registering disgust or disappointment may be particularly detrimental and should be kept off camera. You can work to minimize involuntary movement by following the suggestions in Figure 5.5.

Body Language and Nonverbal Communication

I n addition to conveying a message through purposeful movement, performers must also be aware of the intentional or unintentional way their bodies are communicating. Nonverbal communication is a powerful form of communication that has been studied for more than 60 years. Usually nonverbal communication is used in conjunction with verbal communication, but it usually does not draw one's attention like verbal communication does. However, some research indicates it may be the more significant of the

FIGURE 5.5 *Controlling involuntary movement.*

Control involuntary movement by

- recognizing the offending movement by seeing it on a recording or being told about it.
- rehearsing the action you will take to avoid it.
- remembering the offending movement and the action you will take against it when you are under stress.
- keeping the offending movement at the conscious level until it has been completely eliminated.

two. In his book *Nonverbal Communication: Forms and Functions,* Peter A. Andersen[4] looks at a multitude of studies in nonverbal communication and discusses their findings and importance. For our purposes these studies document what we have already learned from practice and have mentioned in earlier chapters. Andersen refers to the five codes of the body:

1. physical appearance
2. kinesics or body movement
3. eye behavior (such as eye contact)
4. interpersonal special behavior (such as putting the moves on one's object of affection)
5. tactile communication (such as touching)

These codes help to categorize topics of interest to performers. As indicated previously, controlling a performer's image is essential in making a positive impression on viewers. What viewers see in one's appearance and hear in the voice registers in their minds and may be remembered for a long time. Movement complicates what messages you send to viewers without saying a word. For example, eye movements, standing a certain distance apart, and touching may show approval or disapproval. Looking directly into the camera lens is essential to inviting viewers to like you and to listen. When a performer looks away toward a co-anchor or fellow actor, the viewer is excluded momentarily; when a guest is seated next to the host, that guest seems more important than other guests. When you touch someone, a tactile movement, that act may be judged as favorable and friendly, or distant and reserved or even inappropriate. A simple act of touching may mean something more than you intended: notice that in some situations, certain interviewees get a handshake and others get a hug. Furthermore, your type of personality may resist some of these acts, but you will need to perform them anyway if you want your image to appear friendly and receptive.

Of course, these nonverbal relationships occur in everyday life; however, when they appear on television or in the media, nonverbal movement is under much more scrutiny—it is up close and personal. At times, work on television may seem like acting; you must appear to be believable and hospitable even though you do not like the guest or agree with his point of view. Sometimes it will be difficult to control your verbal and nonverbal responses that are not at your conscious level, though, as discussed in the previous section, there are steps to take to gain more control. But to retain your image as an open and receptive person, you may have to closely examine your nonverbal communication skills. It is amusing to see that celebrities seem to know each other; but during the ensuing conversation, viewers may learn the host and guest met in the greenroom before the program. Extraordinary nonverbal movements, such as jumping on a sofa during a talk show or walking on a desk in a moment of comedy, may draw a great deal of favorable or unfavorable attention that exceeds expectations. For a performer, two of the most important nonverbal movements you need to practice are walking into the spotlight and smiling. Nearly every host does this, so you need to do it well.

By contrast, anchors and field reporters are shown instantly in rather static positions. Usually they are in comfortable circumstances, but even if they are not, the performers make do and continue their reports smoothly. Short anchors have been known to sit on thick books to level the anchor positions so that the performers seem to be of the same size when in fact they vary greatly. A reporter at a remote location may need to have supplies that will keep him cool despite hot weather or warm in cold weather. Reporters need to be remarkably resilient and flexible in adverse conditions.

Nonverbal Communication on the World Stage

The easy access to videos of performances in other countries and cultures has led to changes in the way performers move and communicate. Performers have to deal with new sets of nonverbal requirements in communication, including appearance of face and body, details of expressions through gestures and eyes, and relationships of proximity and touching. In addition, various subtleties of weather and clothing may have to be addressed. With the prominence of the Internet, these nonverbal forms of communication are extended to the world stage with a myriad of cultural differences. An example is the greeting between men of kissing each cheek. Many men wear long or short skirts; both men and women wear minimal bathing suits, and so do their offspring. Certain gestures that mean nothing in one culture may be offensive in another. Some of these obvious differences are changing as cultures become more aware of each other. Therein lies one of the most important aspects of what performers do as communicators: they change their behavior through verbal and nonverbal communication to connect with their widening audience.

It is really remarkable to see the growth of uniformity in some aspects of nonverbal communication because of the distribution of visual media. Whereas verbal communication may need translation, nonverbal communication, especially through music, is having an enormous impact, particularly among people in Europe, the Americas, and Asia. Haircuts for world leaders are strikingly similar, with relatively few men having facial hair, unless it is customary, such as across northern Africa and the Middle East. American advertising and international conglomerates have a great deal to do with what appear to be widely acceptable and marketable nonverbal images that directly apply to employment and social acceptance. In an increasingly connected world, it is important for performers to be aware of how their movements and actions are communicating with not only their local audience but a global one as well.

Summary

Most of what you communicate is transmitted nonverbally, and the most powerful nonverbal message is a smile. With so much to take into consideration, such as your appearance, your voice, and your material, concern about your movements may have been the last thought to occur to you. But it is important to realize that any movement on a small screen will be exaggerated. And, since we use movement naturally when we speak, it is your task to translate that movement naturally into your performance. Standing, sitting, walking, and moving your hands are movements you do every day. But now you need to rethink each of those movements and study how you use them on-camera. Each movement must have a motivation: to define purpose, to catch attention, to tell a story, to convey emotion, to delineate character, or to explain relationships. Each individual movement has attributes, too: direction (to camera), strength, speed, duration, timing, and grace. First-time performers are often surprised when they see themselves on camera—having never been made aware that they squint when they speak, nervously fumble with keys in their pocket, or move their head so much. Try the relaxation and balance exercises included in this chapter to help you achieve the goal of incorporating natural movement into your performance.

CHAPTER 5 *exercises*

1. Do the relaxation exercises listed earlier in the chapter as a class or on your own. Remember that these simple exercises are no substitute for a workout at a health facility. Like acting classes, a physical exercise program should accompany a television performance class.

2. Get in a circle, preferably before a mirror, for at least a brief workout, consisting of limbering up your head, shoulders, arms, torso, legs, hips, and ankles.

3. Standing your full height, walk around the room several times, practicing being aware of your movement but looking natural. Check your feet to be certain you are walking directly ahead. Put a book on your head to check your balance and to be sure you are walking gracefully.

4. Stand in one place an arm's length from your neighbor. Try to squat down while maintaining your balance. Stand, back up, and then take a few steps in each direction, purposefully shifting your weight. You are trying to maintain your poise and balance so that your limbs do not feel like lead. Repeat these exercises.

Notes

1. M. Argyle, V. Salter, H. Nicholson, M. Williams, and P. Burgess, "The Communications of Inferior and Superior Attitudes by Verbal and Nonverbal Signals," *British Journal of Social and Clinical Psychology,* vol. 9 (September 1970): 230.
2. Dr. Cody Sweet, Nonverbal Communications, Mount Prospect, Illinois.
3. Ray L. Birdwhistell, *Introduction to Kinesics* (Louisville: University of Louisville Press, 1952), p. 3.
4. Peter A. Andersen, *Nonverbal Communication. Forms and Functions* (Mountain View, CA: Mayfield Publishing Company, 1999).

Other Sources

Booth-Butterfield, Melanie. *Interpersonal Essentials.* Boston: Pearson Education, Allyn & Bacon, 2002.

Cornett, Claudia. *Comprehension First.* Scottsdale, AZ: Holcomb Hathaway, 2010.

Fast, Julius. *Body Language.* New York: Simon & Schuster, 1970.

Remland, Martin, and Kay Neal. *Nonverbal Communication in Everyday Life.* Boston: Houghton Mifflin, 2004.

Succeeding as a Performer

INTRODUCTION

You may have dreamed of performing on television since you were young. You may have practiced, made personal and financial sacrifices in order to learn the necessary skills, and consistently worked hard to achieve that goal. However, there are some key areas that all performers must master before they can truly succeed. Even if you seek the limelight with so much intensity you cannot conceive of yourself becoming nervous, you might just find the opposite when faced with a highly pressured situation or a tight deadline. Stress is a fact of life for most performers; awareness of it and having a plan to combat it will undoubtedly contribute to your success and extend your career. Good mental and physical health is essential to the life of a performer. The objective is to gain experience and exercise complete control over your mind and body. To accomplish this you must have discipline, which includes a positive attitude concerning your self-worth, ambition to be a competitor, mental concentration, control over nervousness and stress, a reputation for dependability, physical discipline, and longevity.

Attitude Makes the Difference

escribe it as a wish—drive, yearning, obsession, or calling—this is the attitude you must have to succeed. You choose the ultimate personal principles you live by. For example, you may strive to seek truth, to be honest, to serve the needs of others, and to appreciate and respect your talent. To be successful in your goals, you know within yourself you must be highly disciplined. For instance, you know that arriving late for class or a job is unacceptable. It did not happen because the freeway was crowded; it is crowded every day. It happened because you overslept, moved too slowly, did not have your things laid out the night before, or did not allow enough time for the unexpected. Recognize that you are late through your own lack of planning, and forgo the excuses. You are a competitor; you need to take on the attitude that you can outperform the competition.

Few performers succeed by accident. Despite obstacles, biographies of successful performers show a deep, intrinsic desire to appear before the public and to mobilize all assets toward that goal. Sometimes this desire is labeled as having a positive attitude or simply believing in oneself. This self-confidence may not be easy. After all, performing professionally is a gamble, and discouraging data and testimonials abound. Disregard the advice of some people who have no experience in the field and who may express their own fears that the field will be disappointing, a conclusion often based on hearsay and half-truths.

A dedicated performer depends instead on a positive attitude. With drive, good training, and opportunity, real performers know deep inside that they can be a success. If you are a dedicated performer, you will practice until you know the work is good enough to show the public. You won't have to be coaxed to practice, even though there is neither applause nor money for such solitary work. Don't waste time wishing for airtime; instead, practice writing and speaking until the result is interesting and expressive. The true performer makes no excuses for a weak show. If you have difficulty pronouncing certain words aloud, use a pronunciation guide and practice until the troublesome words blend into the rest of your vocabulary, flowing with your delivery as smoothly as more familiar terms.

Belief in yourself, desire for perfection, and self-assertion in practicing your talent contribute to an attitude that builds success. Lacking the right attitude automatically portends defeat, even though you may be very attractive, have a wonderful voice, and have been told you have natural aptitude for the work. Performing is very difficult. To reach your goal, you must have a dominant attitude that refuses defeat on the way to success.

Be Ambitious

mbition is your desire to reach a specific goal. The general goal, of course, is to be a successful performer. But you must further refine your ambition to define the degree of fame and fortune you are striving for. Do you want international fame or is local recognition more desirable? Is great wealth important or is an economically comfortable life sufficient? Define your ambition, because to obtain your goal, whatever it is, you must pay a price in terms of hard work and sacrifice. For example, national newscasters fly a lot—often more than 100,000 miles a year. Many are away from home and family for long periods. A major network news anchor once said he was home only one month during his first year with the network. In addition, their lives are under constant scrutiny by competitors and others who thrive on exposing their professional or personal mistakes. By contrast, working at a local station may result in a program of your own, with local recognition, a reasonable salary, the opportunity to be at home, and rewarding feedback from members of the community. You must weigh your values and priorities when you seek work as a performer.

Some individuals are more ambitious than others. The most ambitious contenders are obsessed—whether they are national figures or working locally, these performers are incredibly driven toward professional accomplishments. Be aware of such competition. A second group consists of those who have an ability to succeed at whatever they do. If circumstances permit them to become performers, then they are successful at that, but they are also confident they would do well in and enjoy other occupations. A third large group of performers is made up of specialists in subject matter. They may not be distinguished as performers. In fact, comments such as "How did they get on TV?" may be asked of them. The answer is, they are respected for knowing the field. Expertise in a specialty may lead to anything from occasional appearances on a show to a feature series.

Media performing, whether in broadcasting, on cable television, or via the Internet, presents a wide range of opportunities; therefore, you should consider the nature of a media career in the context of enhancing your life. Measure ambition and costs against the values you hope to receive, including an increased sense of self-worth, community contribution, salary, and related benefits. Take all factors into account.

Concentrate

oncentration simply means paying attention to what you are doing to the exclusion of everything else. Distractions abound in television studios, but you must focus your performance without becoming distracted by interference from nonrelated activities and stress. Concentration enables you to become absorbed in your contribution to the program. Some performers are much better at concentrating than others; some people say they can concentrate while multitasking, while others require absolute silence, as mentioned previously. Test this theory for yourself: Try reading a section of this book with the television on and with music playing. Then read another section with the TV and music off. Were you able to easily recall what you read during both situations? Now imagine you are on a television set trying to memorize your lines. Last-minute changes have been added. You have to deliver them fluently. Can you do it?

Broadcast and video production often begins with the words, "Quiet on the set." These words focus attention, stop unwanted noise, and assist performers in concentration. After quiet is called for, no one fools around and keeps his or her job for long. Stopping and starting cost time, and time is money. The loss of concentration may cause forgetfulness, stammering, the delivery of the wrong line, or losing your place on a cue card. Concentration can be broken if props are misplaced or furniture is rearranged, thereby disrupting the performer's anticipated routine, or if crew members are whispering in the shadowy areas of the studio. If crew members are noisy, bring that to the attention of the floor manager or director, if necessary. Expert performers ad-lib around unexpected changes without viewers noticing it, but a wise performer checks all props and equipment before the program.

Of course, most news organizations have been in business for years, and few new performers are invited into the group of seasoned performers. Those who have worked together for a long time and know each other well will take shortcuts, have inside jokes, and infuse humor that the public will not see. Newcomers should expect that. A television program may be shot before a small crew or a capacity-filled stadium, so the potential for losing concentration is great. Play to the audience, whether it is one person at home or thousands, by maintaining self-confidence, believing in the material, and focusing on what is being said and what action is taking place each moment.

Be Dependable

ependability sometimes is more highly prized in a performer than unusual or exceptional talent. Of course, both talent and dependability are desirable, and a station manager does not want to have to choose between them. However, a dependable person who is competent, but perhaps not so highly gifted, may last longer than a more talented but undependable colleague. Dependability means getting work in on time and being prepared. The key to dependability is commitment. A performer, regardless of illness, bad weather, family disaster, personal pleasure, or unexpected circumstances, shows up on the job because of dependability. Such a commitment is part of a performer's discipline. If you are a dependable performer, you are prepared for all eventualities, and this is possible only if you can anticipate any conditions that may arise. Dependability further means that while a producer depends on you, you depend on yourself to get the job done, even though you may gratefully accept the assistance of staff and crew. The person in the spotlight is the one who usually takes the credit or the blame for the quality of the program.

Use Your Imagination

long with talent, it is essential that you have an imagination for the work. An active, vibrant imagination is part of your intuitive ability. Imagination springs from your innermost self. It is that creative urge within you that seeks the truth and ways to present it to the public; it is like an overflowing well of ideas. Imagination can be encouraged, stimulated, challenged, prodded, or suppressed, depending on the working conditions or learning environment to which it is exposed. A good teacher or coach will let you articulate whatever ideas you have, however daring, and whenever possible will help you see those ideas materialize into productions. All top-notch performers have the imagination to dream; a few find the means to make those dreams come true.

For example, one performer did precisely what she was told on-camera. She had her visuals in order and her script memorized. She produced her part of the program thoroughly. To all present, it appeared she should do well in media, but she lacked a central requirement—imagination. She depended on her producers and directors to tell her what to do and how to do it. The director came up with clever ideas for her to use, but that is not enough. If you are a talented performer, you will come up with ideas of your own. You must fuse your past and current experiences to form new, original, and exciting concepts, themes, or perspectives that will result in features and programs. You must use your imagination, envisioning ideas that can be used to create successful programs.

A stunning example of applying imagination to opportunity occurred in 1973, when two young reporters for the *Washington Post* began to follow what at first appeared to be a routine political story and subsequently became the Watergate story. Richard M. Nixon seemed secure in his reelection when five men were arrested for breaking into the Democratic National Committee headquarters, located in the Watergate office complex in Washington, D.C. Esteemed anchor Walter Cronkite believed that he helped keep the story from the back pages of the paper by reporting it on the CBS news. From newspaper to television to book to movie, the Watergate story that led to the resignation of a president was one of the great stories of the twentieth century. This example shows how talented reporters may develop a story with great impact and spanning many media—important work in a democracy. With few facts to begin with and minimal cooperation from government officials, the reporters continued to investigate, using their imaginations to piece together the important puzzle.

Use Your Charisma

harisma is the ability of a performer to intellectually and/or emotionally reach, stimulate, or fascinate another person and, through media, perhaps millions of people. Some performers display charisma in intimate settings; some before crowds. Performers convey their charisma by their presentation. Newscasters, for instance, are speaking to multitudes, and they may enhance their presentation with videos, slides, music, or other expensive devices.

Charisma is charm: a spell that is believable, at least during the performance and often afterward, accounting for the tendency of the public to associate a celebrity's role as a performer with his or her personal life. This communication shared between the performer and the audience is charisma.

People who have charisma are those about whom the public wants to know, whether they are loved or hated. Charisma is innate; a performer is born with it. True, the characteristics of charisma can be enhanced through training and clever marketing, but basically it is a natural personality trait. A charismatic performer distills this power and exhibits it under optimum circumstances in an acceptable, pleasurable way so that the public is continually intrigued. Even if the public becomes disenchanted, sooner or later a performer with charisma is likely to return to public favor.

Television enhances charisma, refining and amplifying qualities that bring a performer to public attention. Every performer has certain qualities an audience likes to watch, be it romantic adolescence, the heroics of an average citizen, staunch independence, or aloof charm. The performer seeks to exude such qualities and cause the public to crave them.

Performers cannot acquire charisma and they cannot give it away. The public is willing to watch some news personalities but not others. Those performers who seem to attract audiences do so because they exude irresistible magnetism or charisma. Whether emotionally or intellectually appealing, a performer instinctively relates to the audience in an enticing manner, assertively and purposefully arousing the audience.

One example of a charismatic anchor is Fox News Channel's Shepard Smith. Attractive and articulate, Smith's talent is style. He uses his main camera as a subjective camera. He looks directly into it as if talking directly to a viewer who is in the studio with him. His delivery is fast and conversational. "You decide," he says to viewers. He uses common phrases—"What's up, man?" and "One heck of a foot race."—and blurts out opinions the viewer may be thinking when a teen resists a crook: "You beat up that guy pretty good. . . . I'm glad you took him down." If an error occurs, Smith corrects it on the air: "Roll it back," he gestures to repeat a line, and he openly checks his BlackBerry for a breaking story. Besides being informal and chatty, he is funny, emotional, and dramatic, with interpretative emphasis and pauses that make him compelling to watch.[1]

Have Physical Discipline

As discussed in Chapter 3, physical activity and control over your body are important to creating a successful, consistent image. Regular exercise instills consciousness of your body that tends to prevent you from becoming either overweight or underweight. Regular exercise and a healthy diet reinforce consistency in your performance, and exercise does wonders in reducing stress and nervousness. Many performers exercise before they go in front of the cameras to reduce tension and to limber up. Every performer should be in an exercise program that is enjoyable and effective. If you give good health a high priority in your life, you will also moderate or eliminate the use of tobacco, drugs, alcohol, and excesses that are debilitating.

Get Through Nervousness

When it comes from excitement and joy, nervousness is good; however, it can also be a major deterrent to your success as a performer. Nervousness can be so severe that it prohibits you from doing acceptable work; it may even jeopardize your health. Nervousness has many causes, but fear of failure is its underlying foundation. Your fear may stem from insecurity about your look or voice, your material, or your mastery of it. Nervousness may occur when you begin a new project. If you could be fully confident that everything will go well, you would probably be less nervous before the cameras. Part of being a performer, however, is the risk, the unexpected—you might fail, or you might dazzle. Thus some nervousness is healthy, at least the kind generated from genuine excitement. Meanwhile, good performers strive to work with confidence and concentrate on doing it well. Those performers who have conquered their nerves are usually quite experienced; they have been through disasters and have survived. Yet, even experienced performers often reveal how nervous they are. For this reason, some performers prefer television and film to live work because they know scenes can be reshot until they are perfect.

Nervousness tightens your entire body, including your face, throat, and physique, so you need to fight to control it. The crew will encourage you to relax, but you are the one in the spotlight, not the crew. Nevertheless, if you are to be a good performer, you must confront your tendency toward nervousness and develop techniques that stimulate relaxation, such as those in Chapter 5. Relaxation is not easy to achieve, but it enables you to consciously control your voice and body.

Determine whether you get nervous before, during, or after a performance. Are you afraid of making mistakes before the camera? What is the cause of your emotional instability? Once you think you know, try the suggestions given in the following section. If the stress seems impossible to handle, consider consulting a psychologist.

Fight Stress

ou may be someone with moderate "performer's stress."

Performer's stress can be handled in several ways, including by

- analyzing and changing the way you think about stress.
- using a speaker's stress hierarchy.
- creating pictures in your mind of your favorite peaceful place.

The best way to start is to be prepared for your performance. Having adequately practiced will put you more at ease. Don't be late to the studio or location. Wear attractive clothes you have worn before, and make sure you wear comfortable shoes.

Remember, as you think about your audience, you are the one who has the courage to speak out. Whether your audience consists of a few friends or thousands of people you can't see beyond the camera or microphone, remind yourself that of all of those people, you are the one with the fortitude and opportunity to present your message in a unique way. Your words are a true gift. Do not let anything or anyone keep you from using your media gifts for the benefit of other people.

THINK IT THROUGH

Along with breathing techniques, which are provided in Chapter 4, you can reduce stress by analyzing why you have the stress and what you can do about it. Following are helpful suggestions for thinking through your stress.

1. Stress is usually caused by excessive or extraneous emotion. Reduce emotion by logically evaluating the cause of it. For instance, are you angry because your employer gave you an assignment you do not like? Evaluate where the emotion is coming from and thereby put a fresh perspective on it. Instead of thinking about how the assignment makes you angry, think of how good it will feel once you complete it.

2. Rationalize the problem by thinking about the objective. An example of rationalizing may be: "My words on this subject are really important

and I want people to hear them said the way I want to say them. I can't let anything stop that."

3. Plan work to correspond with a realistic schedule, and pace it with cycles of natural energy. Avoid times when you are overworked or physically run down. Try to think ahead, and plan the time it takes to prepare for your on-air presentation, including practice time. Are you tired? Athletes get a good night's sleep before they perform and you should, too.

4. Eliminate stress that may be unrelated to your presentation. Instead, it may be caused by some disassociated argument. Think about all of your reasons for stress. This may be what you need to rid yourself of the tension you are feeling. Finally, remember that a small amount of stress provides the energy and excitement that you need for your on-air presentation.

USE A STRESS HIERARCHY

Stress is intangible; you cannot touch it. You can only feel stress, which makes it harder to deal with. Stress, like fear, may come from many sources, such as an experience that did not go well. Perhaps you lost a job over a poor performance and were overcome with shame. If so, you need to attack this negative feeling. By working through a stress hierarchy, you make stress visible and are more able to address your fears. This method will take time, but it works. On a sheet of paper write "Stress Hierarchy." Then, write down the problems, such as speaking on media, you are trying to eliminate. Maybe you feel stress when you are asked to speak in person, or when your work is going to be on-camera. List every detail, even such things as being teased by friends about your new celebrity status. The list may be long, but the number is not important. The fact that you have recognized things that are stressful is what counts.

Next prioritize your list of anxieties, beginning with the least stressful items. By making a list you have made tangible what is otherwise intangible. Now your fears are easier to work with. As you look at what you have written down, you may see that most of your stresses are not frightening at all. So, cross them off your list.

Reprioritize the remaining list. Eventually, you will have a hierarchy of the main anxieties you need to work through. This may take some time; therefore, do not be impatient with yourself. Keep the list available until you are no longer frightened by it and instead are comfortable with it. Remember, life is stressful—it's the journey that counts. Strive to keep most of your life orderly.

Figure 6.1 provides a sample of what a performer may put down on a stress hierarchy.

HAVE A MOMENT OF QUIET

Transporting your mind and body to a quiet place allows you to calm down and remove yourself, at least mentally, from a stressful situation.

FIGURE 6.1   *A sample stress hierarchy.*

1st list: Problems I'm trying to eliminate

- I am not confident in how well I write my material.
- Sometimes I have a hard time memorizing my material.
- I need to practice more, but I don't feel like I have time.
- I get nervous sometimes when I know I'm live on-camera.
- Some of my friends get upset that I'm spending a lot of time at the studio.
- I'm worried that my outfits bunch up when I'm on-camera.
- I need to go to bed earlier, but sometimes I get distracted by going online.
- I'm not sure if I'm ready to move across the country for a job.

2nd list: The problems ordered from least stressful to most stressful, with not-as-frightening fears crossed off

1. ~~I'm worried that my outfits bunch up when I'm on-camera.~~
2. ~~I need to go to bed earlier, but sometimes I get distracted by going online.~~
3. I'm not sure if I'm ready to move across the country for a job.
4. ~~Some of my friends get upset that I'm spending a lot of time at the studio.~~
5. ~~I am not confident in how well I write my material.~~
6. Sometimes I have a hard time memorizing my material.
7. I need to practice more, but I don't feel like I have time.
8. I get nervous sometimes when I know I'm live on-camera.

3rd list: The order in which I'm going to deal with my stresses

1. I'm going to learn to relax more when I'm live on-camera.
2. I'm going to look at my schedule and see if I can add in some more hours of practice each week.
3. I'm going to use part of that extra practice time to work on my memorization skills.
4. I'm going to talk to some of my professors or mentors to see how they handled moving for a job.

First, find somewhere you can be alone. Close your eyes and relax by going back to a place where you recall your happiest moments. Once you have found that place in your memory, make it real. Think about how it looks, smells, and sounds. Can you touch it? Can you imagine it so completely that you can put yourself there? Practice this exercise until you can escape to your special place to relieve your stress. Then, when you walk in to make your presentation, you will feel rested, look relaxed, and be ready to go.

Maintain Your Credibility

o both career performers and non-career performers, credibility is essential. Corporate heads, government officials, financial advisers, and journalists must maintain the public trust if they are to be effective. The bond of trust that the public once extended to many professions and businesses has weakened in recent years and now applies to specific individuals. A performer who has public trust is extremely valuable and may become a highly paid spokesperson.

The basis of a credible image on television is in the look, the voice, the manner, and the message that convey honesty and rationality. Credibility presupposes at least a modicum of intelligent judgment. Sometimes, a performer can be rather unsophisticated in language, appearance, or manner, and yet be believed by viewers. To the public, trust in an individual and trust in his or her media image may be different, but not inseparable.

What performers must do to create and maintain credibility depends on their field and their image. Politicians must move gracefully, smoothly, and swiftly, as though they were eager to meet as many people as they can. Though warm and energetic, they may or may not go in for physical upkeep (such as cosmetic surgery or diets), but they usually try to keep fit and often boast about it. Politicians learn to smile on cue and to shake hands aggressively. On the other hand, a journalist earns credibility from reporting from city hall in the hot sun after sitting all day waiting to summarize a trial and announce its results. Investigative reporters of major issues who bring wrongdoing to public attention are critical to freedom in a democracy. Those correspondents embedded with troops in war zones, perhaps to be shot at or captured, deserve admiration and gratitude.

Maintaining credibility as a media performer has become very difficult because media celebrities of every type are scrutinized to extremes. Intimate details about the lives of public figures—true, false, or alleged—are examined. Many famous performers cannot endure the scrutiny when bad decisions made at some point in their lives are revealed. So credibility may be fleeting. A wholesome model's role as a spokesperson for a reputable organization may vanish overnight, if he is discovered to be less perfect, and perhaps more human, than his publicity has claimed him to be.

Achieve Professional Longevity

 omeone may say, "Her job doesn't seem so hard. I can do as well as she does." But this comparison may not be true. It may disregard the fact that the performer being questioned endured good times and bad, high and low salary, criticism and praise, and adroitly kept on the good side of management. Such a person is a disciplined professional in that she has stuck to the business, and as in most businesses, opportunity usually arrives if one is not too impatient.

Audiences are capricious; they can quickly change what they want. Often they simply want a change, so performers find work in media unstable. One day a performer is a hit and the recipient of several awards, but before the ceremonies are over, his or her program is canceled. A popular sportscaster learned his contract was terminated while he was playing in a charity golf tournament. Once again, you must draw upon your abiding discipline as a performer, believing that tomorrow or soon after another opportunity will come along. Trends and styles in media are usually short-lived and constantly changing. Program ideas spiral forth, tending to repeat material, formats, and public concerns every few years. It is crucial to be ahead of the trends, anticipate changes, and strive for improvement and freshness. Staff turnover, new program formats, new sponsors, and new voices and faces are a few of the reasons a new opportunity to perform will open up, and someone with persistence, who is well-liked and known to management, often gets the nod. So to help avoid disappointment, always be looking for the next job, do not get too comfortable in your hometown, be upbeat and pleasant, and do not argue contract problems in the press.

Summary

 successful career as a performer comprises many facets. Each of the components described in this chapter contributes to the attainment of that goal. Some are more abstract and may be simply a part of your personality and intellectual makeup—such as ambition and charisma. Other components are more tangible and attainable, with some effort from you.

A performer who is mindful of these aspects will experience personal growth and achieve results as an outcome of the choices made every day. Have a positive attitude and value your self-worth. Be dependable, imaginative, and physically disciplined. Work through your nervousness; fight stress and learn to manage it. Use the stress hierarchy process to identify and write your anxieties down on paper, eliminating those fears that really are not frightening after all, and then prioritize the list. Work on eliminating those factors from your life. Find a quiet place, even if it is only possible to find a quiet place in your thoughts, to help relieve stress, too.

Be vigilant about safeguarding your credibility, which, in turn, will contribute to the staying power of your work. If your goal is to enjoy professional longevity in this career, be mentally prepared to address each of these facets every day.

1. This alternative exercise for stress relief may be helpful:

   a. Write the word "Stress," with a capital "S." Under the word write a small letter "s." Write "removing this 's' equals 'solution.'" The sooner you find the reasons that you feel upset, the better a performer you will be. The word still says "Stres," even though you have eliminated the small "s."

   b. Next, under the small "s" write the letter "e." Removing the "e," which stands for "emotion," gives you more information to work out the problem, for you need to evaluate how you are feeling. For instance, are you angry because someone else got the assignment you wanted? Evaluate where the emotion is coming from so that you can work with it.

   c. Third, move the "r," which stands for "rationalizing" your problem. Try to think about it objectively. An example of rationalizing may be: "I know this subject well and I will demonstrate that in my report."

   d. Now the word "Stress" is down to the letters "Sts." It does not say "Stress" anymore. The fourth letter you eliminate is the "t." This letter stands for "time and tired." Think ahead, and plan the time it takes to prepare for the presentation, including practice time. Arrive early enough to prepare your news copy. In short, give yourself ample time to present yourself and your work well.

   e. Fifth, the capital "S" is eliminated by remembering your stress may be unrelated to your on-air appearance. Instead, it may be caused by some disassociated argument you had.

   f. Think about all of your reasons for stress. This revelation may be what you need to rid yourself of the tension you are feeling.

   g. Finally, you still have to deal with the last of the three "s's." But you do not get rid of it. You can manage this amount of stress. It provides the energy and excitement for your presentation. At this point carefully go over the exercise you have just completed. Analyze everything that can lead to the solution of your stress. The word "Stress" should no longer scare you. You have it under control.

2. To improve your imagination, you might try the following:

   a. Remember that your thoughts may be very valuable someday, although you may not be able to use them immediately. Keep a journal or create a blog to track your ideas and to increase your creative writing skills.

b. Keep a notebook and video camera that you continually fill with ideas and images, no matter how crude or incomplete they may seem at the time.

c. Visit an art gallery, exhibition, or lecture. Write down three new ideas that you learned from it. Pick one element of the show or presentation and write out how you would present that part in a different way.

d. Actively seek out a new experience or activity. Write up your experience in your journal or blog, or as one of the formats from Chapter 2.

e. Improvise games and make up stories that relate to media.

f. Make traveling a personal priority. There is no substitute for actually visiting New York and Los Angeles. Try using sites such as www.budgettravel.about.com to find out how to travel cheaply and look at www.couchsurfing.com or at hostels to decrease the cost of accommodations.

g. Learn a second language. An entire world of millions of people opens up to you if you can communicate in a second language. Spanish, Chinese, Arabic, or French will enable you to cover most of the world.

NOTES

1. David Barron, "Fox's Flock, Shepard Smith Is Anchor of Choice," *Houston Chronicle* (January 7, 2008), pp. E1, E6. The University of Mississippi graduate worked at the campus television station. Smith anchors *Studio B with Shepard Smith* and *The FOX Report with Shepard Smith*, which has been number one in its time period for five years.

OTHER SOURCES

Bourne, Edmund J. *The Anxiety and Phobia Workbook*. Oakland, CA: New Harbinger Publications, 2005.

Lyles, Terry. *Good Stress: Living Younger Longer*. Deerfield Beach, FL: Health Communications, 2008.

Mind and Body. Athletic Contests in Ancient Greece. Athens, Greece: Ministry of Culture—The National Hellenic Committee I.C.O.M., 1989.

Roizen, Michael F., M.D., and Mehmet C. Oz, M.D. *You Staying Young*. New York: Free Press/Simon & Schuster, 2007.

"Walter Cronkite," *American Experience*, PBS/Thirteen/WNET/New York, 2005. Executive Producer: Susan Lacy. "El Sistema," *60 Minutes*, CBS Television Network, 2008. Reporter: Bob Simon. Features Gustavo Dudimel, conductor. Producer: Harry R. Radliffe. Inspirational feature about saving children's lives by engaging them in Venezuela's Simon Bolivar National Youth Orchestra. *60 Minutes* rated sixth place in June 2008 with 8.7 million viewers. No other feature news series ranked in the top twenty network television programs.

The Television Studio

INTRODUCTION

Television is a team sport. In order to show one person on the television screen, it takes a group of people with specialized skill sets to make it happen. Each member of the team has a role to play, with the same goal—to make the performers and the organization they represent look their very best. A thorough understanding of each of those jobs will come with time, but only if you make an effort to understand how each task contributes to the final product. Each person is important to your performance, and they will have more respect for you if you become an engaged part of the team. It is important to feel comfortable in a studio setting, and this begins with being familiar with the equipment, the people, and the procedures that make up life in the studio.

The Professional Studio

To a performer, a **studio** is a place where the performer can appear live, be recorded, and/or be transmitted under controlled conditions. A television or film studio is mostly space surrounded by lighting instruments, scenery, properties, and equipment that will transmit and record pictures and sounds. A performer's primary function is to work with the microphones, cameras, staff, crew, and possibly a live studio audience, while simultaneously communicating news, information, and features to a vast unseen public.

Paradoxically, as a performer standing in a pool of light amid the paraphernalia of a large studio (some are mammoth), you may find the experience lonely, frightening, and frustrating. You learn that it is difficult getting instructions outside your lighted area. Studios are often cold. Your instructions are often changed at the last minute. The live audience is impatient. The pressure is on you, and you have no place to hide. Regardless, when you step before the microphone and into the light, you must fulfill the efforts and indeed the hopes of the **producer** (the executive who arranges the business aspects of a production), the **director** (the principal person responsible for the artistic development of a production and its presentation on-air), **production staff** (the behind-the-scenes crew that takes care of sound, lighting, recording, and countless tasks), financial backers, and the public. Figure 7.1 has some suggestions to help a new performer feel more at ease in front of

FIGURE 7.1 *Suggestions for beginning performers in the studio.*

1. Know where the camera lens is and how to look *directly* into the lens.
2. Try to relax, but some tension is good.
3. Don't adjust your clothes, hair, or makeup 30 seconds before the program because you saw something out of place on the monitor.
4. Polish your shoes, press your suit, learn to tie a tie. Avoid a skirt that is too short when you are sitting.
5. Keep both feet on the floor.
6. Avoid smacking your lips and bouncing your head when cued.
7. Don't play with your hair, swing your feet, or tap your fingers on the table or desk; in other words, don't move unless you are motivated.
8. Avoid looking at your script or notes, and memorize your opening and closing.
9. Pronounce your guest's name correctly.
10. Keep your chin down so that your eyes will open up. Stand and sit in the hot white light.
11. Don't forget to pace your delivery; breathe naturally; be friendly; and smile.
12. Remember to concentrate; think what you are saying as you say it. Have fun.

FIGURE

7.2   *Possible crew members on a studio production.*

PRODUCER
- organizes the production
- handles logistics, funding, and legal issues

DIRECTOR
- supervises the shots
- leads the crew during rehearsals and recording

ASSOCIATE DIRECTOR
- assists the director
- notes script and timing changes and communicates them to the crew

FLOOR DIRECTOR
- directs the setup, use, and cleanup of the studio
- oversees blocking and staging

TECHNICAL DIRECTOR
- controls the switcher and the monitors
- works next to the director in the control room and executes the director's cues

LIGHTING DIRECTOR
- coordinates the use and positions of lights on the set
- creates any needed lighting effects

CAMERA OPERATOR
- sets up the shots according to the director's instructions
- operates the cameras during the production

AUDIO ENGINEER
- controls the sound for the studio, including microphones, music, and sound effects
- cues the audio during the production

GRAPHICS OPERATOR
- creates the visuals used in the production
- readies and cues the visuals during the shoot

VIDEO OPERATOR
- handles the recording of the production
- cues any prerecorded material to play during the program

EDITOR
- works with the final shots to create the finished product
- prepares prerecorded material

the studio cameras, and Figure 7.2 lists some of the crew members you may be working with.

Your job is to make the studio a comfortable working environment for yourself. Be aware of the placement of the microphones as well as the lighted areas that have been carefully designated on the studio floor in chalk or masking tape. These areas include precise places where you must stand in position or "on your marks." By walking through these areas you enable camera operators to take properly aligned shots so you will look your best. Being off your marks, even slightly, can make a substantial difference in the light level or composition of the shot. You may resent being so restricted in movement, but the less there is to light and mike, the better quality the lighting and audio may be. A typical studio does not have enough sound equipment or lighting instruments to cover the entire floor.

Specialists adjust for the many subtleties television requires. For instance, if the cameras do not match (an engineer's responsibility), you may look great on one camera but too dark on the other; if the light level drops below a camera's minimum (a lighting designer or electrician's responsibility), you may be in deep shadow or transmit the wrong color; if the microphone is not in the right place (a sound operator's responsibility), you may sound as if you were speaking from another part of the studio.

Television programs may be classified as live, meaning they are on the air while they are actually being performed; live-on-tape, meaning they are recorded without editing; or recorded, meaning they are probably edited. Each method has its advantages. The material in live programs may be perishable and have little replay value. Live-on-tape programs have spontaneity, good for audience participation shows such as public discussions or sports programs, with little editing required. The content of these programs may be replayed in various time zones and still seem fresh when they go into possible later syndication. An edited program is extremely popular with performers, because the content is close to being artistically and technically perfect, and it will be replayed perhaps for years. Frequently, the only live portions of a newscast are of those who anchor it. To be competitive, however, a feature performer's work must be perfect, and good editing makes that possible. The only limits are money and time. The performer's company may not be able to purchase enough studio time to reach perfection, but with attention to details it can come very close. Studio time is expensive because it contains high-end equipment and a highly trained staff of artists and technicians.

The Equipment

erformers stay out of the studio until they are summoned from the waiting area, called the **greenroom.** This warning that rehearsal or recording is about to begin is the **call.** A studio can be a dangerous place because of all the complex equipment and wiring. When called, performers must do their job precisely as told and then leave the studio. Most of a performer's time is actually spent outside the studio, preparing scripts in an office. The complex work of production will be discussed as it relates to you.

TELEVISION CAMERAS

A television camera looks like a box mounted on a cylinder or tripod. Depending on where you work, cameras may be big and clumsy or very small. Cameras function at the performer's eye level most of the time. The internal workings of a camera are often adjusted by focusing it on a chart of electronic color bars or on an in-studio color chart. If the flesh tones look natural, the rest of the television picture is probably acceptable. Engineering adjustments begin an hour or more before recording or air time. Instruments in the **control room** (an area off the studio floor where the audio and visual controls are used and where the production staff works during the program) indicate to an engineer when the cameras are ready for operation. You may not be interested in these technical adjustments, but they are absolutely necessary if you are to look your best to the public. So, any adjustments that require your presence or your accompanying visuals are well worth the time and inconvenience.

Cameras, their mounts, and their lenses move according to simple commands from the director or camera operators. The principal commands for moving both the camera and its mount are **dolly,** which means moving toward or back from the performer or object; **truck,** which moves the camera mount right or left; and **arc,** which means moving the camera mount right or left in a curve relative to the subject. **Crane up** or **down** elevates a camera filming overhead. Many cameras may be handheld or on wires, especially for sports, but those on pedestals move up or down hydraulically on the command **pedestal up** or **down.** The principal commands for moving the camera itself, without moving its mount, are **pan,** which moves the camera horizontally right or left; and **tilt,** which moves it vertically up or down. The variable focus zoom lens is on most television cameras. These lenses have a sweeping capability, from a wide shot covering a panoramic view to a close-up of detailed action. Expensive shows may use robotic cameras, also.

At the back of a television camera, sometimes on the studio floor, and in the control room are **monitors,** or tiny television receivers that allow the director, camera operators, and engineers to adjust focus, lighting, composition, and the field of view. Because of the complex nature of television, a director has to be careful that the content of the program does not get lost in the difficult technical process of getting it on the air. You can help directors, without imposing on their authority, by calling attention to the objects the viewers must see and when they must see them in your presentation.

Working on-camera

The camera shows everything in its field of view. Whether you are scratching your leg, adjusting your microphone, or frowning, the camera will show it, perhaps to thousands of people. And with high resolution digital cameras, every detail of your face, body, and movement will be scrutinized. You must assume you are on the air all of the time during the airing or recording of a program. Never do or say anything that should not be aired.

No matter how many camera lenses are visible, a camera has only one lens that is **hot,** that is, on the air. Be aware of which camera lens is hot. You may or may not be asked to look directly into it. Often cameras have tiny **tally lights** that indicate they are on the air.

Audience connection through the camera

The performer's point of view changes according to the relationship he or she has with viewers, at times being indirect and at other times direct. Performers who wish to address an audience directly look into the on-air lens, just as though they are speaking to a close friend. Newscasters, politicians, teachers, and clergy frequently look into the on-air lens. Any other position, such as glancing down to read a script, is disruptive, distracting, and sometimes breaks communication completely. To some extent, an audience accepts reading from notes because of the tradition of lecturing and public speaking from notes. However, the illusion of fluid conversation, either ad-libbed or read from prompters without interruption, improves direct communication between the performer and the audience. This means looking directly into the camera lens and, when necessary, discreetly shifting your gaze from one camera to another. For example, begin by looking into Camera One, then down at the script, and up into Camera Two. Peripheral vision enables you to see the floor director wave you from one camera to another camera.

If a performer is addressing someone on the set, the television audience acts as an observer of the scene. If the performer is leading a group discussion, the performer interacts with the group and ignores the cameras. A performer who has to conclude the discussion may look into the camera lens and speak directly to the viewers. If the performer has a solitary role, such as narrating a documentary or hosting, he or she will focus on a point about 10 feet off the floor and in a direct line with the performer's brightest light, the **key light.** This light illuminates the performer's face. Although the light should not be uncomfortable, it may make a performer's eyes water. However, slight watering will make the eyes sparkle. Some performers use eyedrops to get the same effect.

MICROPHONES

A performer must be familiar with a microphone's frequency, range, coverage, size, placement, and use. The term **presence,** in terms of a microphone, is the degree of clarity of a sound. Ideally, this sound is what an audience would hear if it were in the same room with the performer and listening under optimum conditions.

Types of microphones

Each microphone has its own characteristics. The **pickup** refers to the range from where the mike can get a sound signal. The principal microphones a performer uses are listed below:

1. the **dynamic** or pressure microphone, which tends to favor the high frequencies
2. the **ribbon,** which favors the low frequencies
3. the **condenser,** which gives the truest frequency response

The dynamic microphone is the least expensive and most rugged. It comes in various models. It is **omnidirectional,** meaning that it picks up sounds from everywhere, whether the performer wants these sounds or not. The ribbon microphone is much more selective, having a narrow beam extending outward in a **bidirectional** (two-direction) pattern. The condenser microphone is often used on complex productions, partly because its omnidirectional pickup can be made unidirectional (one direction). In addition, some microphones pick up sound in a heart-shaped pattern known as **cardioid.** See Figure 7.3.

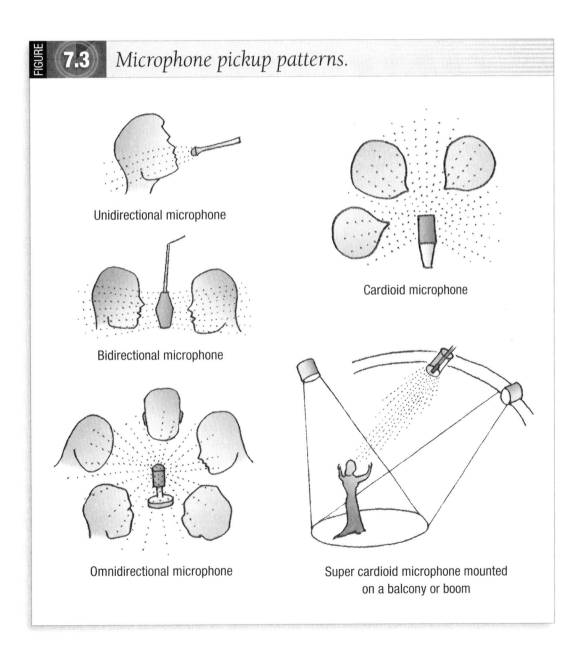

FIGURE **7.3** *Microphone pickup patterns.*

Unidirectional microphone

Bidirectional microphone

Omnidirectional microphone

Cardioid microphone

Super cardioid microphone mounted on a balcony or boom

A performer works four to eight inches from a dynamic microphone and speaks across the surface of it, depending on how much he or she wants low frequencies to register. The closer a performer gets to the mike, the better the low frequencies will register, but breathing and plosives in the English language will begin to be heard as "popping" sounds. Condenser and cardioid microphones also use the pressure principle. However, when a mike's pickup patterns is uni- or bidirectional, it may be used like a ribbon microphone. Some newer microphones look like small circular screens and a performer speaks directly into them.

Sizes of microphones

The smallest microphones are the lavalieres. They are the size of a tie tack and may be clipped to a suit or dress. Though tiny, these microphones are usually noticeable, especially on a dress. Handheld microphones are about six inches in length and can be mounted on stands or in brackets suspended from overhead booms. A super version of the cardioid, about 18 inches long and casting a rather narrow pickup beam about 10 to 15 feet, is a shotgun, which is mounted on the balcony of a theater and aimed in the direction of a performer onstage.

Wireless microphones attached discreetly to the head or back have a transmitter attached to a belt. These microphones enable performers to work within a 25-foot radius of a larger receiver-transmitter off the set, thus relieving the performer of an unattractive microphone cable. However, frequency and range are limited. Much improvement continues to be made in microphones—fidelity continues to improve as size diminishes.

Working with microphones in the studio

The performer's relationship with a microphone is primarily one of placement. Typically, microphones are of sufficient frequency range to capture and reproduce the full range of human sounds. An engineer will control the performer's volume with the understanding that the performer will articulate clearly and project adequately no matter where the microphone is located. Even so, the difficulty of volume control is illustrated by the number of anchors and reporters who seem to shout at the viewers.

In the studio, news performers, community experts, politicians, and public relations representatives sit or stand in relatively static positions. They walk very little. Assuming that the microphone is to be hidden or minimized in this limited staging, performers learn to work with whatever is provided. Movement by the performer can be difficult to accommodate with a microphone. The solution may be a microphone with a long cable, a wireless microphone, or an overhead boom microphone. Whatever the situation, you as a performer must be prepared to relate to it effectively.

Most situations require alertness but little real movement. If you are sitting behind a desk, a wireless microphone may be used. A mike mounted to a short stand placed on the desk slightly to one side, as seen on *The Late*

Show with David Letterman on CBS, is also an option. In this case your main concern is to know the shape of the beam of the mike and to be certain you speak into it. Occasionally the mike is suspended overhead and at a 45-degree angle in front of you on a long pole called a boom. The problems are the same. The advantage is that you keep your head up with a boom-mounted mike, while you tend to lower your head to speak into the desk mike, which keeps your eyes open.

You may be called upon to use several microphones, moving from one type to another during the progress of the program. With this staging your basic concerns stay the same, they just come faster; therefore, your goal is to learn to move from one microphone to another without the viewers noticing.

The microphone of choice usually is the tiny lapel-mounted lavaliere. The lavaliere mike picks up the sound only of the person wearing it. You must keep the mike in mind because pulling on it may reposition it or create unwanted noise, or both. Performers sometimes forget to turn it on, while off-camera someone is frantically motioning to them that they cannot be heard. Do not let the cable pull on your clothes or trail behind you. Plan in advance so that you are not wildly throwing the cable around and are able to move from the anchor desk to another studio location.

If you are standing, the microphone may be in front of you on a shaft anchored in or on the floor. If so, be careful not to kick the shaft. It is probably metal and will amplify a resounding thud. The floor microphone relationship is the same as other static microphones mentioned above. Nowadays this microphone is continually raised or lowered.

In general, if you are simply speaking, one microphone, preferably unseen, should be enough. If you are a newsmaker, a battery of microphones may be necessary to accommodate each reporter with a **sound bite,** but this really is the same as one microphone to one performer. If you use a separate sound source, mike it separately. If you are part of a roundtable discussion, one good omnidirectional microphone may be adequate. If there are several mikes, just know which one is for you. If you are on a panel, a separate desk microphone will probably be required for each person. Passing a microphone around a table usually results in poor audio and video. If you are narrating in a concert hall, many microphones may be used, and you will probably have a personal microphone. Make sure you know how to operate it.

Usually, a performer, especially in a union market, does not move microphones. This is the audio operator's job. Moreover, moving a microphone may jeopardize the sound quality or the aesthetics of the shot. If you are not comfortable with a microphone, discuss this issue with the floor director or director. Testing a microphone takes only a few minutes. If you are a participant in a panel discussion, do not move the microphone(s) that may be present. Let the engineer do it. You may benefit by leaning toward it, however. In some interviews you may have a handheld microphone. Never let your guest take the microphone away from you. If you do, you have temporarily lost control of your sound source and your program.

SWITCHERS

Somewhat comparable to the audio control or **mixer** board (a panel device that has inputs and outputs for microphones) is the **switcher.** This electronic control panel consists of several buttons and levers that execute changes from shot to shot. These transitions can be instantaneous, called a **cut,** or of longer duration, called a **fade,** or of overlapping scenes, known as a **dissolve.** A variety of electronic transitions, termed **wipes,** enable the technical director or switcher operator to use various geometric configurations such as squares, circles, and bars to move from one shot to another. Additional effects can be inserted electronically, such as a tiny window that can move around on the screen. Colors, distortions, numbers, lines of type, and computerized designs are additional special effects available from an electronic device that creates words and designs, often called a **character generator** (CG). You do not have to know how this electronic video equipment operates, but you should know what effects are available so that you can use them to enhance your program.

DIGITAL RECORDING EQUIPMENT

Analog-based technology has been replaced by digital technology—digital cameras, recording, and editing. Performers should be familiar with digital equipment now that it is commonplace.

The more skillful a performer is with digital technology the better, for the same or similar equipment may shoot performances on location. Whether preplanned or spontaneous, recorded scenes are taken to the station editing bay for editing, edited at the production studio, or edited with equipment located in a live truck. Editing is another skill a performer should master. Commercial editing is largely computerized, with frame-by-frame, utterance-by-utterance electronic scanning. The potential for perfecting a performer's work is virtually limitless. A person knowledgeable enough to participate in the editing of video material will benefit greatly.

One benefit of interning or being employed by a top broadcast station is that it will accelerate your opportunity for being exposed to state-of-the-art digital equipment. For more information, see Chapter 9.

STUDIO MONITORS AND PLAYBACK

A monitor is a silent viewing screen. Often it resembles an ordinary television receiver. **Playback** is the replay of the performance. One monitor (or more) is usually positioned on the studio floor or at the news desk within easy view of the performer. In some studios, monitors are visible through a cut-out in the top of the news desk; anchors then simply look down to see the video and may listen to the audio over a headset inserted in the ear. These monitors enable the anchor to see video clips for voice-over narration, feeds from other cities, or remote units. Whenever a newscast calls for a prerecorded segment, the anchor watches it on the monitor. If an emergency occurs or if the pictures are substandard, the anchor knows what the viewer has seen and ad-libs necessary information. The anchor makes certain a monitor is within easy viewing range so that, for example, she or he can identify small objects mentioned during a demonstration. On the other hand, using the monitor as a mirror should be avoided—by the anchor and guests. The anchor should focus on the guest and the floor crew—mainly the floor manager—in order to see hand cues. Guests need to be instructed not to look at themselves in the monitor; instead, they need to focus on the interviewer.

Depending on the studio, you may be able to hear the audio playback if your anchor's mikes are off. When your anchor's mikes are on, the playback is muted. You may also be able to hear playback material through an interruptible foldback (IFB) line in the headphones that enables you to hear the producer, the control room operator, and the program output.

Chroma key walls

When standing in front of a **chroma key** wall (commonly called a bluescreen or greenscreen) so that a video source or picture may be inserted in the background (such as a weather map), the performer may be advised to avoid wearing certain shades of blue or green. Engineers reserve certain colors for keying inserts— that color is blanked out and the background image replaces it.

Projecting images

Moving and still pictures may be projected or electronically fed by a computer onto the screen for the viewers to see during the broadcast. All of the still pictures for the program may be stored on a computer called a **still store** and integrated on command. Likewise, the moving images—regardless of the original medium (film, tape, or digital)—are transferred to technology currently used by the station. The information that is added to the main presentation is usually referred to as **B-roll,** a film term referring to a secondary source.

Older analog technology and rear screen projection may continue to be in use as smaller stations seek funds for digital equipment. **Rear screen projection** (RSP), where a photographic image is cast on a screen behind a newscaster, remains popular. Another method shows an image inserted in a box behind the newscaster electronically through computer technology. Several images—primarily of people, significant events, maps, scenes, and remote telephone pickups identifying the reporter—may appear behind the performer during a single program. Much of what appears to be RSP may be produced through the switcher, in which case the performer is keyed or inserted over the background. This electronic technique is attractive for announcements, educational programs, and newscasts.

Determining the content of the RSP or electronic inserts is a production decision, but the performer may be involved in obtaining the original material, selecting what to use, and making certain that items are cleared from copyright. Memorabilia may be particularly vulnerable to damage, and RSP sometimes requires special staging. In time, however, the older techniques will be replaced. But because studios vary widely in how up-to-date they are with their technology, a performer should be acquainted with both old and new technology.

VIDEO PROMPTERS

Video prompters are mechanical devices attached adjacent to the on-air lens of television cameras that reveal the script line-by-line to the performer, shown in Figure 7.4. The lines or script are shown through a lighted prism that magnifies the type. The close proximity of the video prompter and the on-air lens or the use of a prompter that scans the lines of copy over the lens creates the illusion that the performer is speaking memorized material to the viewer. Over the years visual prompters have become indispensable to speakers. They can be used effectively as long as the camera is relatively close to the reporter (about seven feet) and the copy is easy to read. Any squinting or other signs of strain on the performer's face nullify its value, and so a video prompter works best for static situations or those within a close radius of the performer. Prompters are also built into lecture stands and desks, allowing performers to read copy from a projection of the script.

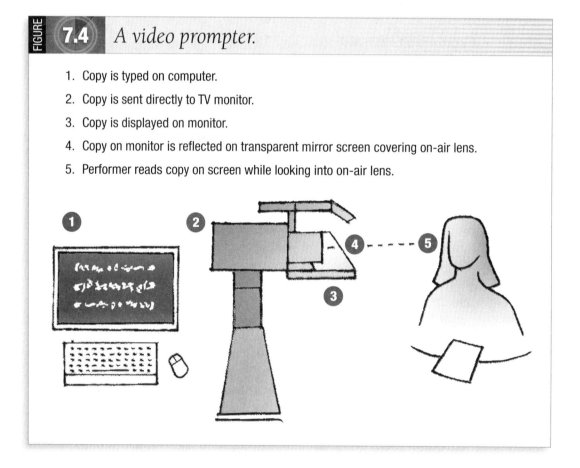

FIGURE **7.4**   *A video prompter.*

1. Copy is typed on computer.
2. Copy is sent directly to TV monitor.
3. Copy is displayed on monitor.
4. Copy on monitor is reflected on transparent mirror screen covering on-air lens.
5. Performer reads copy on screen while looking into on-air lens.

Over the years attempts have been made to develop an electronic memory. Instead of reading a prompter the performer would hear lines read over a headset. A tiny recorder and a wireless hearing device seem like a good solution. The performer's script is recorded in advance and then is replayed during the performance. In effect the performer recites what is heard over the headset, delivering lines about two words behind the dictation. Thus, a stand-up news report could have the fluency of absolute memory without actually memorizing the copy. If, however, the performer loses his or her place, a disaster could occur, damaging the reporter's reputation. So this technique has never been perfected. Also, some time is needed to record the material. The biggest problem, however, is pacing the delivery without becoming confused; so other techniques are preferred.

CUE CARDS

Cue cards, sometimes called "idiot cards," carry a performer's lines or keywords in bold letters on large sheets of cardboard or paper. They are held near the on-air lens by a production assistant, sometimes referred to as a cue card holder. Such cards are difficult because they bend easily, may be large and long, and depend upon legible printing by hand or type to be effective. The production assistant must change the cards quietly, keeping them in the right order and pointing, if possible, to each of the lines being read on the air. Like video prompters, cue cards must be close enough to the lens so that the performer can create the illusion of memory instead of obvious reading.

Many professionals are very skillful at reading cue cards, depending greatly on peripheral vision and a well-placed production assistant. Occasionally when the system fails, the performer is forced to acknowledge the cue card holder while on the air. Still, cue cards may be very helpful for some feature programs and demonstrations. Late-night comedians who appear live daily may be observed occasionally reading from cue cards.

Studio Sets and Furniture

 simple setting or **set** consists of the background and floor, scenery or furniture to make it look finished, and lighting. **Properties** (props) are items that must be manipulated during the presentation. A **cyclorama** is a drape, often made taut, or plaster wall (hard cyc), usually white, gray, or blue, that encloses much of the back of a set. Most performers look good in front of a blue cyclorama.

Furniture can be troublesome. Some things to watch for are furniture that dwarfs you, that relaxes you to the extent that you look slovenly on-camera, that is too attention getting because it is too colorful or complex in design, or that obscures you from the audience, such as a large desk. Molded plastic chairs with straight backs, shallow seats, and moderate padding and of medium grayscale color are common. These chairs should be armless so that you can get close to your guest, and they should allow both feet to touch the floor when you are seated. Chairs can be too low, too high, too deep, too bulky, too cushioned, or too hard. Consequently, stools are sometimes used. The stools should be of the right height to give you a strong vertical line. None of the chairs should swivel; if they do, you need to be careful not to move in the chair while you are on-camera.

In reference to set decoration, be certain the flowers, papers, books, sculptures, paintings, and miscellany do not call attention to themselves, nor should they appear in odd places, creating optical illusions. Plants behind performers may appear to be growing out of body parts, or during a newscast, a figure on a rear screen may be pointing into a news anchor's ear. A bowl of light-color flowers in front of dark clothing may be undesirable because the video engineer will have to calibrate the iris of the lens to the brightest part of the image—as a result, the performer and guest will appear darker than normal. In addition, metal objects may cast unattractive reflections.

Usually the above problems are the responsibility of the production staff, but you should be aware of them. Most sets are disappointing to look at—makeshift, tacky, even dirty and discolored. Do not worry about this; instead, check what the setting looks like on-camera. It will probably look fine when lighted properly. Don't worry about the space you have. Some of the finest programs are produced in almost no space.

In-Studio Preparation

 he arduous work of performing is the preparation. Well-prepared performers are secure. They know what they are doing and how to do it. This knowledge is the result of study, practice, and experience on the job. Like the proverbial iceberg, preparation is the mass and depth below the surface, and performance is its majestic peak. Preparation is a lifetime occupation of gathering ideas and experiences, selecting and discarding, assembling and combining shapes, depths, and nuances by objectively and emotionally observing life's passing parade. Preparation is an amalgamation of all that life has to offer. Everywhere performers look, there are bits and pieces of material they can apply to their presentations.

Preparation requires much time spent without praise, alone in seclusion, reading and rehearsing for hours and hours. Serious performers like to do this work; those who are not serious do not want to do it. Although a few people can get away with minimum preparation for a short time, most performers require years of study. For this reason many professionals are relatively old before they become prominent. They need time to prepare, to mature, to understand what they are doing. Such seasoning takes years, and this is often based on the sheer speculation that one will succeed, for success is never guaranteed in any occupation.

MEMORIZATION

If a performer could present a continuous flow of fascinating conversation or prepared copy without referring to notes or a prompting device, that would be ideal. Performers, such as hosts for political debates, try to do this by reading extensively, becoming familiar with the backgrounds of guests they interview and keeping up with complex issues and changes throughout the world. To use expensive media time wisely every second must be planned. Every word of a speech, a news story, or a feature must be as exact as possible, which requires an accurate memory. The substitution of a thoughtless word or phrase could destroy the idea being presented, place the station in legal jeopardy, or ruin the reputation of an innocent person. So, memory must be exact. This perfection can be obtained through exact performer recall, reshooting, and/or editing.

Memorization comes easier for some people than for others. These people are often called **quick studies.** Some performers concentrate better than others, and therefore mentally arrange ideas in the script quickly. Others have a fondness for verbal expression and language, and they hear with a finer discrimination of sounds. A few have a natural talent for memorization or may have a photographic recollection of the printed page. Most of all, skill at memorization comes with time and practice. Viewers enjoy experienced news anchors because they have absorbed memorization techniques, and when they speak they are delightful to listen to.

Know the material flawlessly. Security in memorization is absolutely essential if the performer is to relax into the delivery and reflect a deep, subtle interpretation and professional level of confidence. One technique for memorizing material is provided in Figure 7.5. More memorization hints are provided in Figure 7.6.

FIGURE 7.5 *A sample memorization technique.*

1. Grasp the major ideas first.

2. Look up the pronunciation or meaning of any difficult words, phrases, or ideas.

3. Take note of meters, rhyming, or other euphonic aids.

4. Read the material aloud several times, experimenting with inflection, reciting the material line by line, and building your recall.

5. Recite the entire piece, aloud if possible, over and over until it is verbatim.

6. Perfect your interpretation.

7. Test yourself by repeating your lines anywhere, anytime.

FIGURE **7.6** *Memorization hints.*

1. Write down difficult passages for visual re-enforcement.
2. Work with friends or a voice recorder that will feed you your cues.
3. Move according to blocking instructions while you are delivering your lines.
4. Memorize prior to bedtime, when presumably your mind is at rest and will retain the material more readily.

SCRIPTS

Most performers depend on reading a typed script or notes, preferably in a discreet manner. These scripts are typed in easy-to-read big, black, bold letters, and double- or triple-spaced. In addition, these scripts are typed with paragraph indentations, few lines to the page, and divided words or interrupted phrases. Newscasters often type their scripts so that they fill the whole page, although many in television type on only one vertical half of the page and allow the other half for director cues and notes on visuals. These cues may be essential for performances that integrate live cutaways (discussed in Chapter 8), recorded inserts, still photographs, and other visual content.

Marking scripts

Although markings on scripts are kept to a minimum, they must be clearly denoted. The markings can be used to indicate where a reporter can rest during the reading. For instance, periods, semicolons, and commas may be enlarged to indicate stops where a performer can breathe, if necessary, at the end of sentences and phrases. Words and phrases requiring special emphasis are underlined. Some inflections, such as a rise or lowering in volume or pitch, may be noted by curved lines above words or at the end of sentences. These notes are especially helpful if the performer has gotten into the habit of a monotonous delivery and wishes to break it. Continued speeches should be noted with "More," indicating that there is a carryover onto the next page. Pages are usually numbered in one upper corner and/or identified in the other corner by a keyword, known as a slug, such as "accident" or "city hall." Insofar as possible, be certain that the same type of identification is used on all copies of the script. Clear identification avoids confusion and saves a great deal of time. All abbreviations should be noted, understood, and if helpful, spelled out at least when the organization is first mentioned; for example, "FCC" written as "Federal Communications Commission." All new or foreign words should have English phonetic respellings to aid pronunciation. The final script should be clean and unconfusing, like the one in Figure 7.7.

FIGURE 7.7 *A clearly marked script.*

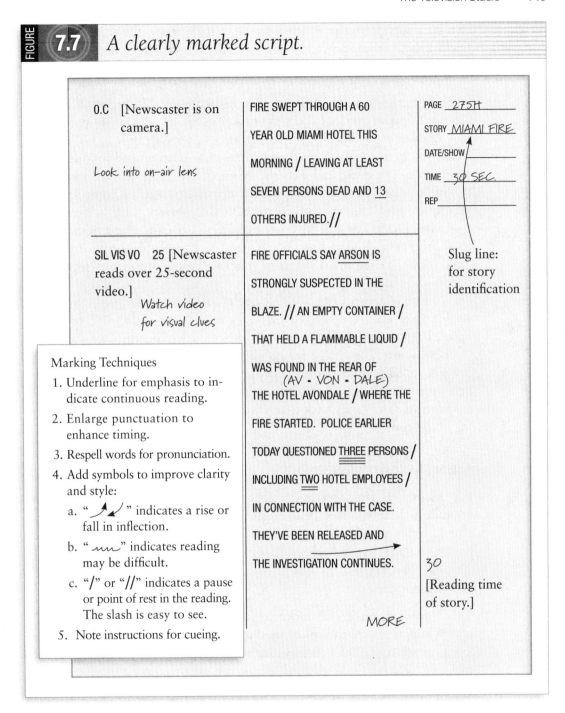

0.C [Newscaster is on camera.]

Look into on-air lens

FIRE SWEPT THROUGH A 60

YEAR OLD MIAMI HOTEL THIS

MORNING **/** LEAVING AT LEAST

SEVEN PERSONS DEAD AND 13

OTHERS INJURED.**//**

PAGE _275H_

STORY _MIAMI FIRE_

DATE/SHOW _____

TIME _30 SEC._

REP _____

SIL VIS VO 25 [Newscaster reads over 25-second video.]
Watch video for visual clues

FIRE OFFICIALS SAY ARSON IS

STRONGLY SUSPECTED IN THE

BLAZE. **//** AN EMPTY CONTAINER **/**

THAT HELD A FLAMMABLE LIQUID **/**

WAS FOUND IN THE REAR OF
(AV • VON • DALE)
THE HOTEL AVONDALE **/** WHERE THE

FIRE STARTED. POLICE EARLIER

TODAY QUESTIONED THREE PERSONS **/**

INCLUDING TWO HOTEL EMPLOYEES **/**

IN CONNECTION WITH THE CASE.

THEY'VE BEEN RELEASED AND

THE INVESTIGATION CONTINUES.

MORE

Slug line: for story identification

30
[Reading time of story.]

Marking Techniques
1. Underline for emphasis to indicate continuous reading.
2. Enlarge punctuation to enhance timing.
3. Respell words for pronunciation.
4. Add symbols to improve clarity and style:
   a. " ⌒ " indicates a rise or fall in inflection.
   b. " ‿‿ " indicates reading may be difficult.
   c. "/" or "//" indicates a pause or point of rest in the reading. The slash is easy to see.
5. Note instructions for cueing.

Reading scripts

When reading, a performer's peripheral vision allows her to see a few words in advance. This helps fluency. Football quarterbacks use peripheral vision to see the field broadly enough to enhance their game strategy. Performers should do the same. Most anchors read from a prompter and also have a paper script in front of them. If the performer moves the next unread sheet from the right over the read sheets on the left, the copy is moved inconspicuously.

You will notice a script in front of most anchors and notes on pads or cards for on-location reporters. For example, on ABC's *This Week with George Stephanopoulos* two stacks of scripts are usually highly visible.

Reading with fluency, interpretation, and style takes much practice. Reading requires instant word recognition for meaning and pronunciation. It also requires pacing, and if the viewers are to respond, the performer must be able to make clear the content and meaning of what is being read. The performer must truly communicate with the viewers. This is particularly true when journalists and government officials are expecting specific actions from the public. You can practice by reading the sample scripts in Chapter 2. Better yet, write similar scripts of your own using information from newspapers and online sources.

Common errors in reading include slurred words, halting delivery, excessive sweetness, unexpected extremes in volume, noticeable breathing, failure to look up sufficiently from the script, lack of energy, being too sober in delivery, stumbling, and an inability to read copy smoothly without rehearsal, called reading the script **cold**. If a mistake is made while reading, a performer must be able to regain composure smoothly. If an item is misread, a performer rarely goes back to re-read it unless the error changes the meaning of the content.

MENTAL OUTLINES

For discussions and interviews that have little time for preparation or are ad-libbed, the performer must cluster his thoughts on a dominant simple structure that provides coherence and direction for the subject. The principal approaches are chronological, topical, and importance.

Chronological

This approach consists of background, present status, and the future. The chronological approach is often used for interviewing guests—What are you doing now? What are you planning to do next? A simple mental outline like this technique will give the performer organization and security, and the audience direction and perspective; in other words, it gives the audience something to remember.

Topical

The performer includes items of similar classification in the topical approach. For example, in regard to discussing a film's content, a performer might organize questions around the cast, direction, and impact. A topical approach may be applied to a piece on selecting plants for an apartment by first discussing plant sizes, then discussing topics that relate to required care, and finally talking about price.

Importance

This approach begins with asking the questions of greatest significance and then discussing others of descending importance. Journalists are fond of discussing topics in their most up-to-date form, knowing that the broadcast has little or no time for background; therefore the barest background information is given to viewers to enable them to understand the report. For instance, when this approach is applied to the subject of insufficient funds for spraying to eliminate mosquitoes, the important questions are: What does this mean to human beings? What are the chances for disease? How hazardous are the diseases? What can be done? What has been done? and so forth.

Guests in the Studio

Much programming from local stations involves a guest performer, usually a non-career performer: a subject expert, a personality, or a representative of a community group. Local television's morning, home, noon, celebrity, and talk programs and the network equivalents depend heavily on guests. In such a format, the interviewer or moderator asks pertinent questions and guides the program by responding to signals from the floor director. In these cases interviewers have the principal responsibility for the program and many, in fact, serve as producers.

Contacting the guest

Although for some celebrities an interviewer/producer must work through the guest's agent, in most instances the interviewer calls the guest directly. Most people are willing, even celebrities, especially if they have a project to promote. Having general consent, the interviewer arranges a mutually satisfactory time to discuss the topic and to get somewhat acquainted. Frequently, however, broadcasting does not permit this because the number of guests is too high and time is too limited. In that event, the interviewer meets the guest just prior to the program.

Local citizens are usually quite easy to work with unless they are embroiled in controversy and believe that an interview could be harmful. In these cases the interviewer must reassure the guest, discussing the procedure for the program and the opportunities the guest will have for telling his or her own point of view. The interviewer should be as flexible as possible in regard to scheduling so that the guest cannot decline for technical reasons.

When dealing with celebrities, there are greater variations. Some celebrities are extremely responsible and willing, others are not. They are often used to being paid and flattered. Insofar as possible the interviewer should try to do both, but unpaid guests are standard for news if the guest is the main subject of a story. In general, giving any guest the "red carpet" treatment pays.

An interviewer is always slightly apprehensive about the arrival of the guest(s). Will the guest cancel? Will the guest arrive on time? Occasionally guests do cancel, and the interviewer must be prepared with alternative material, such as a piece already filmed or a feature that is purposefully prepared to stand by. Nevertheless, most guests do show up on time. Often celebrities have agents with them to arrange appointments and limousine service to expedite a tight schedule. A good agent will be certain that the guest arrives on time, although that may be mere seconds before the show. If you are particularly desirous of having someone and uncertain about whether that person will show up, offer to pick up the person yourself at the hotel or residence. Tell the guest exactly when to be ready and then show up slightly early. Allow for a few minutes of flexibility in case of heavy traffic on the way to the station and the possibility that the guest will not be ready on time.

Meeting the guest

For many, being on-camera is a strange and unsettling experience. This may be the first time the guest has ever heard her voice and looked at herself other than in a mirror. The guest will see an "image," and much of the time the image will be a disappointment unless the camera operators and director have carefully designed the video and audio to emphasize the attractiveness of the guest. The guest is often nervous, and the interviewer must put the person at ease and shift attention away from the interviewer.

To do this, the interviewer should greet the guest, at the door of the station if possible, and make him comfortable. The interviewer should then brief the guest on the layout of the station, noting where the restrooms are located and introducing key production personnel. It is helpful to advise the guest not to worry, to be natural, and to pay no attention to camera movements or crew. Explain the time cues and other signals. This conversation can take place in the greenroom. Some guests may relax with coffee and food, although such items may not be welcome in the studio. If guests bring family members or friends, see to it that they are properly taken care of and separated from the guest so that the business of the program can continue. On local programs makeup is frequently not applied to guests, even though they would look better if they were made up. Larger stations usually have a common makeup supply for guests. Some guests are unfamiliar with makeup, so a performer or a production assistant should apply it for the guest. Generally, if an interviewer wears makeup, the guest should, too. Familiarization with the studio, staff, and the program procedure will put guests at ease, or at least as much at ease as possible. Remember, guests want to look good.

Preparing the guest to go on

At an advance meeting, in the car on the way to the studio, or upon arrival of the guest at the studio, the main points of the interview may be covered, in decreasing order of importance. Some guests will not want to answer what you must ask, and so you will hold off asking those questions until you are on the air, or you can discreetly probe to find ways to the answers. Be assured that people who are in public attention expect you to ask the most important questions and know that if you do, you are doing your job. They have answers already prepared. Whether they will give your audience more specific information depends upon your skill and the confidence the guests have in you. In general, people will tell "everything" on-camera, or they will appear to do so. This may especially happen to folks who are new to the spotlight, either by choice or by fate, and are more innocent in regard to media. They may tell more than is good for them. Your program may benefit from this candor initially, but your acquaintances in the community may soon become wary of you if you have been too crafty. There is a delicate balance you will want to maintain. People want to look good in media, but at the same time you must seek the truth of a situation, the resolution of an issue, or the inner drives of a personality.

Some caution should be observed so that the subject and/or the guest is not exhausted prior to the broadcast. This is a real danger. Inexperienced performers tend to say the same things on the air that they said in the snack bar moments earlier. If they do, they may lead with, "As I was saying earlier," which is a dull opening at best. So, when on-camera an interviewer should tweak the guests' responses by asking questions phrased differently. When possible, an interviewer should not provide a verbatim list of questions or the order in which they will be asked, because a newly phrased question is likely to get a fresh response and generate a livelier discussion. Do not give a copy of your script in advance to the guest.

Visuals in the Studio

erformers often prepare visuals for informational television programs that are aired and/or recorded and distributed on DVD or online. If the visuals already exist, it is a matter of identifying, locating, and obtaining permission to use them. In the case of a performance that includes a guest, the guest usually provides these items, but the performer must be able to decide whether they are appropriate for media. Visuals, such as those in Figure 7.8, fall essentially into three categories: recorded materials, graphics, and three-dimensional objects. Visuals do a great deal to make a presentation stimulating; therefore, they should be purposefully built into a program. The principal guidelines for all visuals are included in Figure 7.9.

7.8 *Visual aids.*

Line graphs

Bar graphs

Pie graphs

Charts

Photographs

Slide shows

Videos

From microscopic . . .

. . . to large three-dimensional objects

Demonstrations in steps of process and examples of results

FIGURE

7.9 *How to use visuals effectively.*

1. Keep them simple.
2. Have the action and/or words in the center of the screen.
3. Have clearly defined images.
4. Be sure visuals are relevant to the topic.
5. Have enough visuals for good pacing.
6. Emphasize one point for each visual.
7. Use the aspect radio of 16 units horizontally by 9 units vertically for high definition.
8. Generally, use color, but remember that black and white can be effective.
9. Be consistent in the design and style of the materials.
10. Present complex information in a series of simple steps by means of visuals.
11. Use illustrations and/or words with data.
12. Be accurate.

RECORDED MATERIALS

Recorded visuals include moving pictures, slides, and photographs. Some stations or production companies have transferred entire series to new technology (VHS tape to DVD, often with retrieval devices). If they are not already in digital format, slides and still photographs are scanned and stored.

Film and videos

Entire motion picture segments, called "film clips," are available from guests, local libraries, public records, television stations, and many websites. They may be available in the original reel form or may have been transferred to DVD. These materials are especially useful in information features. Effective media presentations on travel, animal life, underwater photography, historical excavations, and medicine are only a few examples. Today digital cameras are recording events that you may want to capture yourself. As a performer, you never know when a newsworthy event might be an opportunity for you to appear on-camera, so have your camera ready. If you shoot the video, you will own it and may find a marketable use for it. No one can predict how valuable a video will become in later years.

Photographs

Photographs are commonly used as visual aids, and often they are pictures people cherish. For example, a war veteran has personal photographs that he is willing to share as he tells of the battle of Iwo Jima. If these items are not already in digital format, they may need to be mounted, scanned, or still stored before-hand so that they can be dropped into the program. If actual photographs are to be used live in the studio, they should have a matte or dull finish rather than a glossy one that may reflect overhead lights. The host or guest should hold them long enough for comment to establish relevance to the subject.

GRAPHICS

Graphics may include drawings, charts, and graphs, created either by hand or on a computer. Remember the value of graphics is to clarify what other-wise might be difficult to understand or confusing. Charts and graphs may be visually more instructive than tables of data. Charts and graphs are used largely for comparisons. Producing electronic graphics has become an im-portant aspect of news and information. Most schools have areas of study for electronic graphic development. Watching the computer-generated path of a hurricane is very impressive, especially if the hurricane is heading the viewers' way. Perhaps six paths are shown on the screen entering the coast at different locations. This is a valuable tool for weather forecasters and the public. Similarly, electronic charts can show the rise and fall of the stock market. The fluctuations of individual stocks become clearer through such charts as shown on cable networks FBNC, CNBC, and Bloomberg. For chil-dren's programs and some instructional programs, drawings can be very helpful. A host explaining what she is doing with crayons, brush, markers, or an electronic drawing program tends to fix the experience in one's mind. The basic sketch pad on an easel can still be quite effective if it is in the hands of a skillful performer.

OBJECTS

Statues, paintings, automobiles, boats, sports equipment, camping gear, cooking utensils, antiques, plants, and rockets are a few of the items that have inspired entire television series hosted by knowledgeable performers in the fields. Often these objects must be taken to the studio and returned safely. Such objects are excellent for demonstrations because performers are able to interact with them, picking them up, opening them, or even getting in and out of them. Examples include the three-dimensional treasures fre-quently seen on *Antiques Roadshow* (PBS) and numerous noonday features on commercial stations that are devoted to finding homes for animals. Re-member that in media everything is recycled at some point in time. Do not throw anything away; it may become the centerpiece for a new series that you will host or may prove useful to display in demonstrations.

Studio Rehearsals

Rehearsals are practice sessions for the performers and members of the crew. The more complicated the program, the more rehearsals a performer can expect; indeed, rehearsals may be regarded as stepping stones to perfection. The amount of time spent in rehearsals varies with the station or production company. Rehearsal at a local station is minimal, whereas large production companies and network studios may have many rehearsals. Busy newscasters at small stations may only have time to get wire service information or newspapers to assemble some continuity before the broadcast. As a beginning performer, you are likely to start at this level, because a small operation may be your best opportunity if you have little or no experience. Use these opportunities to hone your work, using feedback from station management, the public, and even friends and associates.

When rehearsals begin, certain guidelines, responsibilities, and privileges pertain to mass media that are based on a combination of precedent, practice, and common sense. As a performer, you are entitled to

1. an advance schedule of rehearsals and performance dates, including time, place, and a general idea of what is expected on each occasion.

2. concise and courteous direction from the director.

3. freedom to develop your role to the best of your ability, as long as you work within the concept of the director or producer.

4. consultation with the director if you do not understand your role.

5. cooperative assistance from the cast, production manager, and crew.

6. a reasonably quiet and orderly atmosphere during rehearsals and performance. It is difficult for a performer to work when there are noise and commotion in the studio, although practically speaking this is often the case.

7. a discussion of the director or producer's notes of the rehearsal that are relevant to you.

8. a share of whatever praise or criticism the production receives, regardless of your contribution.

In return your responsibilities are

1. to be present and prompt for every rehearsal. If an unforeseen event prevents this, you should inform the floor director and work out satisfactory arrangements for a replacement. An unforeseen event does not include a social engagement that arises unexpectedly.

2. to give your director complete and continuous attention and the rehearsal complete attention. When you are not on-camera or on-mike, you should attend to your needs for the show and not involve crew or others who are still rehearsing.

3. to advise the floor director of your whereabouts during the rehearsal, not going far, and never leaving until you are officially dismissed by the director or floor director.

4. to maintain a cooperative and positive attitude toward the whole company.

5. to remember a director in final rehearsal is probably concerned with (a) getting the program done on time, (b) meeting union requirements, (c) making broader artistic decisions, (d) maintaining client relationships, and (e) settling unanticipated problems. The performer should pay attention, perform as required, and remain silent.

NO REHEARSALS

As a performer, you will need to be ready if the director says there is no time for rehearsal; the expression is, "We'll have to **wing it.**" Under such stringencies, try to get program openings, closings, and transitions rehearsed, because these areas cause the most problems. If that fails, study the program format, the requirements of the guests(s), the phrases to be used, and the movements that will be necessary to show graphics. Much of this preparation can be done before you arrive at the studio. A wise performer anticipates extenuating circumstances and prepares in advance for them.

ABBREVIATED REHEARSALS

A form of abbreviated rehearsal is one that rehearses the opening of the program; all important transitions, such as movement from one set to another; and the closing of the program. A strong, well-rehearsed, well-delivered opening and closing, together with a confident, winning smile from the performer, can overcome public concerns about whatever technical errors occur, such as a microphone going dead temporarily or a breakup of the video on the air. Technology is hardly perfect. Partial blanking in scanning can become total picture loss. The human element may also contribute such things as airing the parts of a prerecorded program in the wrong order. Careful rehearsal of these elements can save a program from disaster. A performer must know exactly how the program begins, how it ends, and what the physical transitions are, so an abbreviated rehearsal is the answer.

COMPLETE REHEARSALS

The complete rehearsal is a series of stop-and-start rehearsals, frequently done in marked empty space, that result in a preliminary or dress rehearsal followed by recording the program or performing live. The complete set of rehearsals usually associated with new programs or dramas consists of the following:

1. A **first read-through.** This is a reading of the entire script aloud by the participants. The first read-through is essential for comedies and dramas but not news. Experienced professionals in a news organization work together almost every day and usually do not require a practice run. Occasionally a new reporter or anchor joins the group but immediately finds his or her place and rises to what is expected.

2. A **walk-through.** This allows the principals to physically walk from location to location. This is necessary so that the performers will be sure where they are to stand. For example, this can lead to smooth transitions during complex one-hour newscasts that move newscasters from the anchor desk to one or two other in-studio locations, commonly a weather board or an interview set. This is a "blocking" rehearsal. It may be very helpful if guests are to join this rehearsal.

3. A **dry run.** This is a live rehearsal that is not recorded or filmed. It omits the cameras so that the director is able to give more attention to the performers. Later, when everyone is in the studio, the director becomes preoccupied with the crew and numerous technical decisions, resulting is less time devoted to the performers.

The dominant impression of the organization, the warmth of the working environment, the confidence in decisions, and the nurturing of subtle, latent expressions—all are developed during these vital rehearsals. The director is the biggest guide, but the executive producer and program producer may also take notes for the performer and the total program.

Communication in the Studio

 hen a performer arrives at a studio, preparation should be complete. The script has been memorized or is on prompters, and the blocking has been rehearsed or is at least generally understood. Therefore, the performer focuses on getting acquainted with the performing area, and when appropriate, with special attire or makeup. If no technical problems arise, a rehearsal and airing or recording follow as soon as the director can possibly do them. To meet this schedule, the performer receives a series of checkpoints or cues, orally before the airing or recording and visually during the performance.

BASIC CUES

Oral and visual **cues** are given by the director or floor manager. Cuing is precise but informal unless the circumstances are complex. It is important to know who is giving the cues, where that person will be, and how visible the cues will be. Once cued, the performer must react instantly and do what is expected by the director. The audience is none the wiser, however. When the performer and director are in the same room, cuing is simple; but in television and film you will work through an intermediary, usually the floor director/manager, to talk to the director. You are in the studio; the director is in the control room. Consequently, cuing can be misunderstood or late. In such cases, if the instructions to the performer are simple, the director may use the studio intercom or loudspeaker. However, if they are complex, the director will come onto the studio floor to converse directly with you. Do not expect much direction. The amount you receive will depend on the individual director.

Typical oral cuing prior to the telecast is announced by the floor director: "One minute to air (or recording) . . . thirty seconds. Quiet in the studio . . . ten seconds. **Stand by.**" A countdown may then begin, but it is given silently. At the 10-second stand-by, the floor director raises a hand with the flat of the palm toward the talent or points an index finger toward the on-air lens. On a cue from the director received on the floor director's headset, the floor director points directly at the performer to begin speaking. The word or motion for **"action"** means the performers should begin the performance instantly.

Most visual cues concern timing, such as remaining minutes/seconds and the wrap-up, stretch, or speed-up before the program or segment is over. Some hand signals deal with movement. The floor director waves the performer from one camera to the on-air lens of another, especially if the talent cannot tell from the tally light which camera is on the air. Or the performer, by means of a prearranged signal, such as placing the palms of the hands on a desk, may indicate the intention to stand. Some signals have to do with content. If a floor director taps her palm with the index finger of the other hand, this signals the talent to go to a spot announcement. If the floor director points to an item on the set, you begin to discuss that item. For the most part, as long as you remain on your marks, stick to the script or program outline, and perform as the program was rehearsed, cuing is minimal. Basic cues are universal in performance, but a few may vary from studio to studio. Figure 7.10 shows some common **hand signals** that your director may use.

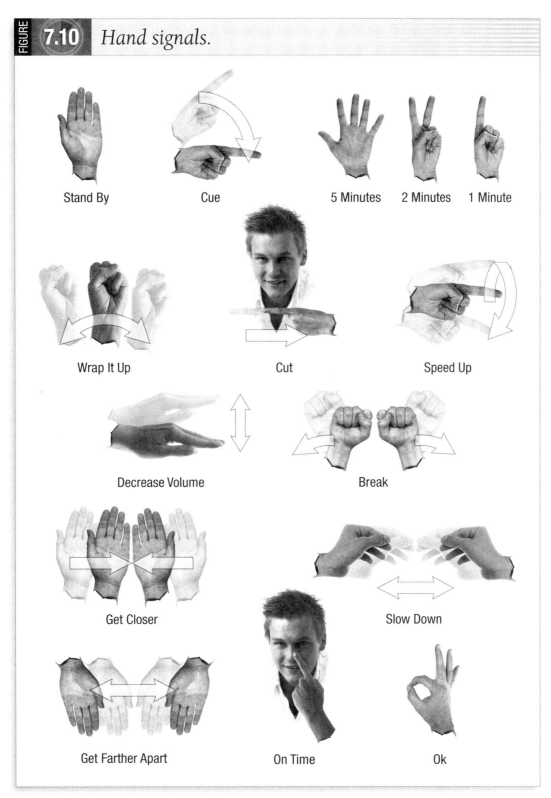

FIGURE 7.10 *Hand signals.*

Stand By   Cue   5 Minutes   2 Minutes   1 Minute

Wrap It Up   Cut   Speed Up

Decrease Volume   Break

Get Closer   Slow Down

Get Farther Apart   On Time   Ok

At the program's conclusion, you should not move until the floor director announces that the show is over: "That's a **wrap.** Thanks." Don't move until the cameras have obviously broken to another set. A common error for a novice is to move, especially to move the eyes from the on-air camera lens or to grimace prematurely. Such action might ruin the final shot.

At the very end, it's a nice courtesy to thank the crew for its work, both in the control room and in the studio.

HEADSETS

A performer, especially a newscaster, is connected to other members of the television production team through the floor manager and through a headset. The headset (IFB), which is a tiny button worn in the ear, enables the performer to listen directly to instructions, or **feed,** from the control room. Many news people feel more secure wearing a headset that is connected to a small, body-mounted transmitter. Headsets are not noticeable to viewers. Most intercommunication systems are controlled by the director, who receives messages from the studio floor, projection, engineers, remote locations, and elsewhere. The performer may hear some or all of this conversation.

PERSONNEL RELATIONSHIPS

If a performer becomes a celebrity, it is because of the talent, ambition, contacts, expertise, and cooperation of other performers, as well as countless people on the production staff. A performer is well advised to be reciprocally cooperative and generous. A staff member who likes a performer often gives an extra measure of attention to make that performer look good; but if a crew dislikes a performer, the reverse may result. For instance, as a performer you may not need a rehearsal, but keep in mind that your crew may need it. Do not be impatient with those who are trying to make you look and sound better.

Directors

In television, the public is hardly aware of the director's importance. In film, you may work with an outstanding director. This experience may be the highlight of your career or perhaps a turning point. Great directors and great performers need each other. The director or editor makes the audiovisual choices for the program. Usually the director is in charge, but the producer may also have influence. Once a performance is recorded, even if you could improve something, the producer will tell you that changes are prohibitively expensive. From time to time you may question a director's competence. If so, do it discreetly, usually through your agent, your news director, or your producer. Avoid trying to settle differences in front of the crew. Remember, the director calls the shots while you are on the air.

Floor crews

Remember, everyone on the floor crew counts. If someone fouls up an assignment by being noisy during the take or by making visible mistakes, the program is diminished, and you may be blamed by the viewers for the inadequacies of the production. This is especially true for remote segments where you have more control and responsibility. You cannot have thousands of viewers associate you with poor work. Ineptness in the crew may imply that you are inept as an anchor, reporter, executive, teacher, or talk show host. Be nice to the crew and be cooperative.

Many studio crews are being minimized—replaced by robotic cameras and automatic graphics equipment. In part, nearly every position in the studio may be replaced by systems that build the program instead of having people do it.

Summary

Even when you are the sole performer, it takes a team to televise your image. It can be daunting to enter the studio and control room for the first time, seeing all the equipment and wondering what each crew person does. However, the more you know about the equipment and how the crew interacts with it, the better your end product will become. The key components of a studio are described in this chapter, including the equipment, the crew, the scripts, and the guests. Each of these components has the ability to enhance or detract from your individual performance. The playback machine may lock up on a segment, a floor director may miss a cue, the script may not be written in a style you are comfortable reading, or a guest may freeze on the set and become uncommunicative. All of these issues present challenges to overcome, and you will learn how to respond to each as you gain experience. When all the aspects work well together, though, you likely will experience exhilaration.

CHAPTER 7   *exercises*

1. Chances are you live near a television station. Make a phone call to the news director or the assignments editor, asking if you can observe a newscast. Ideally, you would spend part of the newscast in the studio, quietly observing, and part of it in the control room. Afterward, send a handwritten thank-you note to the station personnel who were your hosts for the visit.

2. Check with your local community college or university to see what courses are offered. Ask whether the college airs its programs using

the college's own facilities or those of a commercial station. Visit those facilities and watch the programs.

3. Go to your local commercial station and ask if you can volunteer. Some stations have in-house internships, others are only through schools.

Other Sources

Benedetti, Robert, and Michael Brown, Bernie Laramie, and Patrick Williams. *Creative Production: Editing Sound Visual Effects and Music for Film and Video.* Boston: Pearson Education, 2004.

Foust, James. *Online Journalism,* 2e. Scottsdale, AZ: Holcomb Hathaway, 2008.

Gross, Lynn S., and James Foust. *Video Production,* 10e. Scottsdale, AZ: Holcomb Hathaway, 2008.

Spencer, Mark, and Jem Schofield. *Motion Graphics and Effects in Final Cut Studio 2.* Berkeley, CA: Peachpit Press, 2007.

Torelli, Joe. *Final Cut Pro 6 for News and Sports Quick Reference Guide.* Apple Training Series. Berkeley, CA: Peachpit Press, 2007.

Weynand, Diana. *Final Cut Pro 6.* Berkeley, CA: Peachpit Press, 2007.

Wohl, Michael. *The Craft of Editing with Final Cut Pro.* Berkeley, CA: Peachpit Press, 2008.

Zettl, Herbert L. *Television Production Handbook.* Belmont, CA: Wadsworth, 1997.

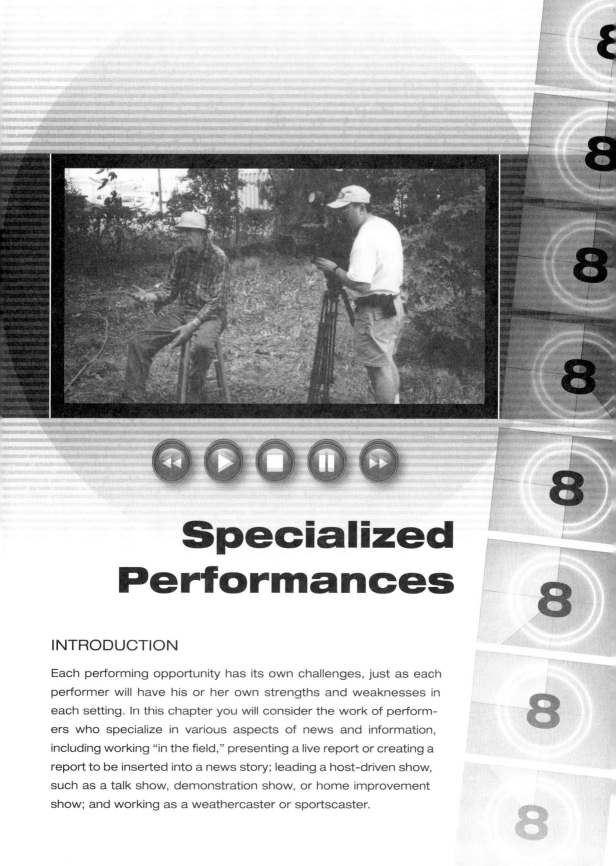

Specialized Performances

INTRODUCTION

Each performing opportunity has its own challenges, just as each performer will have his or her own strengths and weaknesses in each setting. In this chapter you will consider the work of performers who specialize in various aspects of news and information, including working "in the field," presenting a live report or creating a report to be inserted into a news story; leading a host-driven show, such as a talk show, demonstration show, or home improvement show; and working as a weathercaster or sportscaster.

Outside the Studio:
Electronic Field Production

he process of preparing a recorded performance in various locations outside the studio is referred to as **electronic field production** (EFP). This process grew out of television news departments' instant electronic news gathering, which was an effort to compete with the immediacy of radio. EFP is especially common for newscasts, for which it is common to travel outside of the studio to cover stories. Unscheduled events such as accidents and fires are covered by a reporter and videographer (or sometimes a reporter will do both jobs) at the scene. These individuals get the story and return to the station to edit it, or they may edit it right there on location.

MATERIAL

Gathering material begins when performers leave their desks and pursue news outside the building. These stories may be assigned by the assignment editor or a producer, or performers may be expected to generate newsworthy stories on their own, called **enterprise.** In such a role, you will be given a deadline for providing a complete story to be aired, likely in that evening's newscast. You must finish your fact gathering, your interviews, your B-roll (additional shots that supplement the story), and your pre-taped stand-up in the field in order to allow time for editing and assembling the pieces you have gathered into a story. This typically requires some degree of urgency while you complete your work.

Stories may also be generated by external events, such as a fire, a tornado, or a six-car pileup on the freeway. These events are called "spot news" or "breaking news." Such events require the performer to be at the scene, collecting information from emergency response personnel, the people involved, and eyewitnesses. Timeliness is a factor here, as breaking news becomes old very quickly. Plus, your competitors will be eager to report the story, perhaps before you do. These circumstances can create a tension-filled environment in which to work.

LOOKING POLISHED IN THE FIELD

Working in the field presents a challenge in keeping a professional and appealing appearance. You are now working outdoors in the elements, where temperatures may be extreme, or in buildings where it still may be too hot or too cold. At the same time, you are working hard to put together the necessary pieces to your story.

Hairstyles and makeup must look good despite the elements. If your hairstyle is too long or loose, hair may continuously blow across your face during a stand-up. Plan to use strong hair products (hair spray or gel) in heavier amounts than you do in your off hours. Makeup, even your portable makeup, can melt on your face or in your makeup kit, rendering it useless. Waterproof makeup may be your best choice, along with the use of loose or pressed powder and oil-blotting sheets. Your cheeks may be wind burned and chapped from spending hours in the wind, or sunburned from hours under the sun, so moisturizers and sunscreens are essential.

Being outdoors may mean your videographer will ask you to stand in bright sunshine where the light will be the most flattering to you. In addition, if you stand with the sun in your eyes, it's unlikely that shadows will appear on your face. Granted, it's difficult to keep from squinting in this situation. And nearly all performers, except for those at the pinnacle of their professions, are forbidden from wearing sunglasses on-camera. Keep your eyes closed whenever possible when standing in direct sunlight. When you are ready for your stand-up or live shot, open your eyes; it will then be easier to refrain from squinting for the duration of your on-camera appearance.

Clothes serve two functions—to create a professional image and to be practical and comfortable for the surroundings. Depending on the station's policy, you may be able to wear less-formal clothing to match the environment in which you are working. For example, you wouldn't interview people who unload fishing boats while wearing a suit and tie, nor would you report on a hurricane wearing a dress. Stations may embellish rain gear and umbrellas with their call letters and provide those items to reporters. If not, keeping a weatherproof coat and boots in your car will prepare you for reporting in adverse weather conditions.

When you report in the field, as a last-minute check ask your videographer or crew to visually inspect your hair and clothes. Is an unruly section of hair sticking out at an angle? Is your collar straight? After all, it's their job to make you look good, too, and a second set of eyes is helpful, particularly if you don't have ready access to a mirror. In the end, you are likely one of the best judges, once you review your recorded performances, of what looks the best on you—what works and what doesn't.

VOICE AND MICROPHONES

The voice you carefully craft for in-studio work is the same one you use in the field. Here, though, the environment can wreak havoc with your level of tension. As a result, you may not be breathing properly, or you may speak too rapidly, causing you to sound harried, ill-prepared, or inexperienced. Though these same sounds may add to the excitement of the event to an extent, your ability to keep the tension out of your voice will make you appear much more professional.

Figure 8.1 shows the basic arrangement of camera, microphone, and performer on an EFP shoot. A lavaliere mike or a handheld mike will be provided for you to use. If a handheld microphone is provided, hold it in your hand in front of your body. This microphone may have a cable attaching it

FIGURE **8.1** *Basic electronic field production setup.*

1. Camera on brace mount.
2A–C. Possible mike placements.
3. Transmitter behind the performer.
4. Receiver behind the camera.

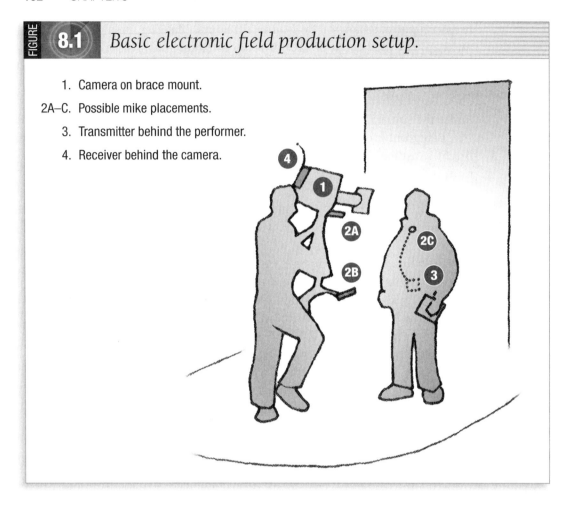

to the camera, enabling sound to be recorded, or it may be wireless. Place the microphone directly in front of you, bending your elbow at a right angle and locking your elbow into place. This prevents you from floating the mike up and down between your mouth and your sternum. If you place it too near your mouth you will block part of your face, and you may pronounce certain explosive sounds like p's with a popping sound in your delivery.

Your mike may have a wind screen—a foam cover that decreases the sound of wind. And at times you may be encumbered with a large headset.

Whichever type of microphone you use, avoid this common error: inexperienced performers will sometimes raise the level of their voice so that they are almost yelling at the camera located about 10 feet from them. They are mistakenly projecting their voice toward the camera. Though cameras do have a built-in microphone (called an **on-board mike**), the mike that is recording you is about six inches from your mouth, eliminating the need to overly amplify and distort your voice.

Above all, your ability to keep the tension from being revealed in your voice is key, because often that skill separates competent reporters from beginners.

STAND-UPS

Newscasters in the field will reserve a part of the story to tell themselves, called a **stand-up.** The reporter is visible in the scene where the story takes place, and in its simplest form, a reporter will stand stationary and deliver lines directly into the camera. Stand-ups serve many functions:

- They provide video when no other appropriate video is available.
- They can be written as a bridge in your story, creating a connection between two relatively disparate parts.
- They may allow you to demonstrate what the story is about, for example, breaking a car window with a tire iron to show how a car was burglarized.
- They may be a conclusion, where you wrap up the story and perhaps provide the expected next development as the story continues to unfold.
- In addition, they demonstrate reporter involvement—you were really there, conducting the interviews.

Stand-ups are an opportunity to showcase yourself, but be careful not to make the story about you. Because of that concern, reporters typically use just one stand-up per story. And stories rarely begin with a stand-up—the beginning of a story is reserved for your most compelling visual material, which isn't a talking head (you).

Stand-ups are brief to fit the format of broadcast news, where video shots are seldom used for longer than 10 seconds. You will need to memorize the lines you have written, or at least a general outline of what you want to say, so your material will typically be two to three sentences long, at the most. There are no prompters in the field. Crafting your words using broadcast style—keep one to two ideas per sentence; keep sentences short; don't use introductory phrases—will also help.

Although some reporters make stand-ups appear to be easy, almost to the point of being ad-libbed, they are not. It's best to practice before taping. As with most skills, practice helps you develop your ability more quickly. With less practice you are more likely to stumble, forget what you are going to say, and mispronounce words and names. Your missteps, because they are recorded, may even end up on YouTube or in a blooper reel.

Movement in stand-ups

Movement is broader and less contained when you are in the field collecting information than on a news set. In the field you are freer to move, and often you are expected to do so since movement on the screen attracts the eye and will make your reports more interesting. But as discussed in Chapter 5, these motions should be well thought out, planned, and without idiosyncratic movements that distract. You should review the recordings of yourself reporting in stand-ups. That way extraneous movement, such as swaying from side to side, swinging your arms, twitching your shoulders, and shifting your eyes are magnified so that you are able to work to overcome them.

Props can be incorporated into your stand-ups as a type of "show and tell." For example, a reporter may hold an electric bill for a story about mis-read electric meters or a can of spray paint during a story on graffiti artists. However, it can be overdone or strained. Use care in selecting meaningful props to contribute to telling the story. There's a fine line between a prop being a useful storytelling device and an inappropriate distraction. Handling props during your stand-up can be tricky, so make sure you are comfortable doing so. In the opening photo of Chapter 7, reporter Amy Davis is looking through a bag of mulch at the camera. Davis says this perspective introduces an element of surprise for the viewer. In the stand-up, Davis was recommending that viewers check bags of mulch they may have purchased recently since there were reports of a termite infestation in mulch shipped from Louisiana to Texas. She incorporated checking the bag herself into the story.

Reporters may move during their stand-up, perhaps by walking along a chain-link fence, replacing a gas pump nozzle when they finish filling up a car with gas, or pointing to the location of a crime. Again, this sounds simple and easy, but it needs to be planned. Preselect a spot to stop walking. Begin and end your stand-up stationary, which means begin walking after you begin talking, pick a spot to stop, and stop to finish your sentence and complete your stand-up there. As one reporter advises, don't walk just for the sake of walking—show the viewer something along the way. For example, if the grass is tall, don't just say it; walk through it to demonstrate its height.

Beginning and ending a stand-up

Remember to begin and end your stand-up with your mouth closed and your lips together. This makes it easier to edit your stand-up or insert it into your story. If your mouth is open when you first appear on the tape, you will appear to be caught off guard in midphrase. Closing your mouth at the end signals a conclusion. It alerts the viewer that you are finished and produces a cleaner edit or toss back to the live studio anchors.

CUTAWAYS

While you are working on an assignment in the field, you will need to provide some video shots to be used in editing—called **cutaways.** Your editor will want to have a few shots available to use to "cover" video edits. For example, you may want to put two different interviewee sound bites together (perhaps to edit out an "ahh" or "um" or to join two related sentences). A separate piece of video must be used to cover that edit, so the interviewee's head doesn't jump—this jarring effect is called a "jump cut."

These video shots are staged variations of your original interview setup, usually done without the interviewee present. You may be shot so it looks like the camera is filming over the interviewee's shoulder. You should appear to be interested in the comments the interviewee is making, but avoid nodding your head and writing in your reporter's notebook. Instead, you should be engaging in conversation so that the interviewee is talking and you are listening. This technique is so commonly used it is often mocked; therefore, it's important to appear and act as natural as possible.

FEATURES

Reporting a feature story provides some unique and more flexible ways to show your involvement with the story. Barbara Walters is well known for her celebrity interviews, and she interacts with her interviewees in several ways, often in their homes. For example, Walters and her interviewees are seen walking together on their property, touring their homes, cooking a specialty dish in their kitchen, or perhaps demonstrating a skill for which they are famous—throwing a football or swinging a golf club. These interactions can often yield private moments that give the audience an intimate glimpse of the celebrity. The feeling of fun and relaxation in that type of story is a hallmark of a feature story. As a result, these stories may actually be harder to master than the formulaic spot news or hard news stories. The emotion you are trying to convey with your subject and words needs to carry over into your voice and stand-up. Pay attention to the words you are saying; the emotion you project should follow easily. If you are reading robotically and simply letting words come out of your mouth, you are not in the moment and have lost your connection. If the story is about a bus accident where children were killed, be in touch with how you feel about it. You can search YouTube and find clips of anchors and reporters laughing during a somber story. On-air people have been fired for laughing at inappropriate times. One reporter with a few years of experience in several markets recommends varying your on-air demeanor to match the subject matter, with a note of caution not to overdo it. If you display your emotions too broadly—either smiling or talking gleefully, or speaking so somberly that it appears affected—it will be awkward, similar to bad acting.

TELEVISION REMOTE UNITS

Bigger electronic field production events, many of which are scheduled, may require a small truck with portable cameras and relay equipment, called a live truck, that may allow the newscaster to report from the scene before the event is over and often while the newscast is on the air, called a live shot. Recapping a story that took place earlier in the day, combined with questions asked by anchors in the studio, gives the story a sense of immediacy, even though it sacrifices the subtleties of controlled studio conditions. Occasionally transmission is uneven, and you find you must do an unexpected amount of ad-libbing.

Scheduled events of magnitude, such as entertainment from theaters, concert halls, and fairgrounds; sports; and some public affairs programs, are broadcast live or recorded by means of mobile television vans, sometimes called microwave trucks. Leased for special events, these trucks contain every piece of equipment required for putting on a complex telecast. The trailer area of a modest-size rig contains a small control room. In the rear is the engineering gear, and on the roof a microwave or satellite link is set up to transmit the signal back to the station.

If the director is in the truck, the only action the director sees is on monitors. Directors must rely on expert camera operators to pick up the action. The larger vans are accompanied by a utility support van. These units may have scores of cameras for national events, such as political conventions, parades, and sports coverage. Beyond those, some of the most spectacular field work is done from helicopters. A reporter, a videographer, and a pilot may have the only panoramic or close-up view of major traffic problems and disasters.

In the Studio: Hosting a Public Affairs Program

any television programs need a host—public affairs, entertainment news, home improvement/do-it-yourself, cooking, reality—and, as usual, proficient hosts make it look easy. (*Public affairs* refers to programming that focuses on matters of politics and public policy. In the early days of television, the FCC called on broadcasters to take a leadership role reaching beyond entertainment, sports, and sponsored news programming by airing programs in the public interest. Such programs are often produced primarily to satisfy regulatory expectations, and often are scheduled at times when few listeners or viewers are tuned in.)

MATERIAL

The basics of interviews and demonstration programs were covered in Chapter 2, but it takes more than knowing the format to host a program. You may have producers who provide content for you. They may select topics, schedule the guests, provide props, and provide questions for you to ask based on research they have done. Or, you may have to find your own topics and complete those tasks yourself.

Finding the best topics

As a beginning host, you may not have the experience to generate workable topics on your own. That skill will come with practice, but there is one thing you can do right now that may lead to ideas that make it on the air: Pay attention and listen to people as you go through your daily routine. One host of a public affairs program overheard people at the next table at the coffee shop talking about how the neighborhood used to be full of drug dealers and how new businesses had cleaned up the area, resulting in homes tripling in value. That one conversation gave her three topics: how the neighborhood responded to reduce crime, what prompted new businesses to locate there, and the growth in the housing market.

Gathering background information

The host must be prepared for the guest, preferably by having a biography on the guest and an outline of the subject matter. Printed or online biographies on guests may be available if they are well known. More likely the information will have to be obtained from the guests themselves, perhaps by e-mail, over the phone, by fax, or in a preliminary visit prior to the broadcast. Minimum information needed includes the following:

- the guest's name
- occupation
- title or relationship with the topic (Why is the guest worth listening to on this topic?)

Further information is anything that may relate to and enhance the discussion of the topic. Here are a few examples:

- educational background
- pertinent places the guest has worked
- honors and awards the interviewee may have received
- personal data that is relevant to the topic
- travel (to countries related to project developments or relevant to the topic)

The host picks out what is most valuable for the public. Although some do not care whether they know much about the guest in advance of the program, others like to know as much as possible. Occasionally friends, relatives, and business acquaintances can provide this information, but usually the guest offers it. A host or the studio may also maintain a personal biographical reference file on people who are well known in the field. Of course, a newspaper's back files and archives—often called a **morgue**—a library, or the Internet may be a rich source.

As to information about the topic itself, the host depends on things he or she has learned from other sources, and builds on that with research done at libraries, government offices, on-the-scene interviews, and personal observation. Naturally, another rich source is the Internet, but it must be accessed and used prudently because the information is sometimes inaccurate. Current publications, special news services, profiles, and attendance at events aid the interviewer in discussing a broad range of topics with guests. Fortunately, topics of great public interest get media attention, and this exposure will supplement a host's knowledge. The material can then be gathered into a quick reference, called a **fact sheet.** It will outline a list of titles or topics to be discussed on a program, and may provide the background or biography of a guest.

Asking the right questions

Program hosts typically have to engage a guest in conversation, and in order to ask good questions, paradoxically, you have to listen. It also helps if you learn to structure your questions using "how" or "why," as in, "Why did you decide to chase the robbery suspect?" This makes it harder for the guest to answer with a short "yes" or "no." Preparing the first question is perhaps the hardest task, because it can make or break the program. A host may try to begin with something fun that the guest doesn't expect to be asked. For example, KUHT-TV interview host Ernie Manouse asked writer/director/actor Kevin Smith if all films should have a message—to which Smith replied with an emphatic "no!" Smith explained that one of the reasons he wrote the film *Clerks* was he then had a girlfriend who insisted all films had meaning. He wrote it to prove her wrong but admits the film did, indeed, end up having meaning. Such openings set the tone for a more spontaneous conversation as opposed to seeking answers to questions guests may have heard hundreds of times. If you ask the same questions everyone else uses or if you begin by asking the guest something controversial, you run the risk of the guest shutting down or responding with the same tired answers. You want the guest to be open to the conversation as the interview progresses.

By the same token, how do you approach difficult topics with a guest? Perhaps the person's publicist has provided a pre-interview list of topics to avoid. An experienced host recommends taking the "back road" approach to asking people about their children, for example, when you know they do not want to talk about their family. Instead ask, "You know, a lot of people have written about how you don't like to talk about your children. Why?" Another common technique is to say, "You know I would be remiss to not ask you about (sensitive subject), but people want to know."

Next, listen to the answers and ask follow-up questions. Listening means really concentrating on what the guest is saying and not just waiting for your turn to speak. One experienced host attributes his ability to concentrate fully on a guest to his early habit of listening to books on tape while riding public transportation. He learned to block out distractions and focus on each sentence. This means you're not concerned about chaos occurring behind the scenes, how much time you have before the next break, or if your collar is still straight.

You may want to write questions out in advance and bring them to the interview, but it is recommended that you resist that urge. Though this may make you feel more confident, in reality during the interview you will be seen often looking down at your note cards or fumbling through them, looking for the next question. This does not inspire confidence from the guest or from the audience regarding your abilities. It also prevents you from really listening to the guest's responses. The most natural interviews flow from each response to the next related question, and so forth. Of course, you should thoroughly research your topic and guests so that you are prepared to converse with the guest in a relaxed way. You will be able to anticipate where the interview topics might lead you.

Preparing excess material

Collecting more than enough background material is rarely a problem. The more you know, the better you will be at interviewing. You will be able to guide the conversation along more constructive channels and add depth and new insight, and guests will be impressed that you have taken the time to become familiar with their work. Even big stars will be genuinely flattered.

A rule of thumb is to prepare 10 questions for every minute you are on the air. You may not need them. Yet, on the air, a host often finds that some of the questions unexpectedly merge into one, some answers that were supposed to be long are short, and vice versa. On the other hand, celebrities acquainted with media talk endlessly. Once, during the student-produced *College News Conference* at the University of Houston, students were in a discussion with architect R. Buckminster Fuller. Fuller spent the entire program answering a single question—the students were afraid to interrupt him. Celebrities are not going to permit dead air while they are being interviewed. Listen carefully and enter the conversation as often as possible. Remember, it is *your* program.

Nonprofessional interviewees do not always respond with consistency, and so the interviewer may end up delivering a monologue on the topic, the guest falling to near silence or an occasional "yes" or "no." At times like these it is good to be over prepared. Some news and sports situations place performers in periods when long ad-libs are necessary to provide continuity while nothing else is going on. Baseball games and golf tournaments may require a lot of fill material. An interviewer also hopes to avoid a situation in which the guest references some subject the host does not know and then asks whether the host knows about it. The host may hedge, saying something such as, "Why don't you brief our viewers?" The better response is, "No, tell us about it." Although this is usually a good chance to enlighten both the host and the audience, it may be embarrassing if the references are current common knowledge, which a sophisticated person in media is expected to know.

APPEARANCE

As a host, you are invited into someone's home via the television set. As such, it is important to look your best. It is respectful to dress conservatively: a suit and tie for men and a skirt or dress pants with an attractive blouse for women. If the program you are hosting is less structured and less serious than a hard news magazine program, reflect that in your clothing choices. Match your clothes to your content. If the topic is somber, wear darker-colored clothing. If the topic is playful or light, your clothing may reflect the same mood. Be certain that you select something to wear that is comfortable and looks good when you are seated.

MOVEMENT

The standard set for a public affairs program features two people, seated in chairs placed at approximately 45-degree angles to each other and to the camera. It may include some accessories, such as a table or a plant. Basically, it is you and the guest, seated. As such, movement is more about how you conduct yourself seated in the chair and less about bigger movements, such as walking. Sit so that you are comfortable, and fight the temptation to swivel in your chair (though stationary chairs are preferable for both you and your guest) or to cross and uncross your legs. Take a look at the monitor. Are your legs positioned or crossed in a flattering way? Observe the way interviewers you admire are seated on their programs and then try to mimic their style.

If you are nervous and fidgeting, your guest will reciprocate the tone you have set for the interview. The guest is only able to relax if you display a calm and collected demeanor. The preparation and research that you have done prior to the interview will also put the guest at ease. If you display that you know what you are talking about and that you have done your research, interviewees will have fewer things to worry about during the interview and will trust that they are in capable hands. In return, they may relax, open up, and provide responses that are easy and natural. Uneasiness is also transmitted to your audience. Your performance may make them so uncomfortable that they become uncomfortable, too, and they will likely stop watching you. Try taking several deep breaths, when you are able; this technique may help you to relax.

It is your responsibility to ensure you are able to see your floor manager, the person who provides time cues for the segments and may provide a cue that you are back on-camera after a break. If the floor manager is not positioned in your line of sight, ask him to move where you can see him. The ideal spot may be just behind the guest, out of camera range of course, so that you may maintain eye contact with the guest during the interview.

VOICE

Review the vocal techniques provided in Chapter 4. It is important for both your audience and your guest that your voice is clear and understandable.

A common belief is that hosts are able to talk less formally during their programs than a news anchor. This is thought for two reasons. The first is that the format dictates a more conversational tone than the tone used while reading news at a news desk. If, as the host, you speak in a more authoritative news anchor role and tone, sometimes referred to as gravitas, the guest may be put off or may try to match you in tone.

This approach is not conducive to the second reason for informality—the purpose. The reason for the interview, really, is to allow this guest to communicate to the audience. As one program host puts it, the host represents "the voice of the people." As such, hosts need to know they are not the focus of the program and instead showcase the guest. It is an opportunity for guests who are non-career performers outside the television industry to convey information about their areas of expertise and their opinions. The host may be on television every day, but this is the guest's moment in the spotlight. And, unlike other television performance opportunities, the host is required to step out of the way and let the guest shine.

Despite an informal tone, some common speech conventions that we use in normal interpersonal conversation may not be appropriate for televised interviews. Verbal responses, such as "uh-uh," other affirmations of agreement, and laughter may make it harder for the audience to hear everything the guest is saying. It's important, though, not to eliminate feedback entirely from the interaction. Instead, occasionally nod your head or smile, where appropriate, so the guest is put at ease, just as you would do in a conversation with a friend off-camera.

In the Studio: Demonstration Program

emonstration programs have different requirements than interview programs. As host, you are facilitating an informational presentation to the audience, be it a home improvement show, a cooking show, or a craft show.

APPEARANCE

It is difficult to watch someone participating with a guest in an activity, such as kneading bread dough, in a formal suit coat and tie. Clothing should allow the host to become as involved in the demonstration as needed. For example, an apron might be appropriate for a cooking segment, and jeans might work for a home repair segment. Of course, it is possible that clothing may become stained during a segment. If that happens, it is best to keep quiet about it if the audience is not likely to notice it. Acknowledge it quickly if it is an obvious mishap and move rapidly to the next step in the demonstration process.

MOVEMENT

Remember, there is an audience at home, so make sure that the product is shown adequately on-camera during each step in the step-by-step process. The demonstration process should be well planned and calculated: begin at this table, mix these ingredients, then move to the stove, sauté this meat, place in a baking dish, and move to the oven to place it inside. Next, display a finished dish, prepared prior to taping or broadcasting the segment. The ingredient list is likely provided to the audience in a graphic. Allow the guest to be the main demonstrator, helping as instructed. During the segment, be aware of where the camera is. Move the product if needed for a better close-up camera shot. Make sure the finished product is featured at the conclusion of the segment.

VOICE

Be loose and ad-lib. But be careful not to dominate the guest's words in doing so, and avoid making comments or jokes that undermine the demonstration or disrupt your guest's process. Guard against becoming lax with your diction or overly comfortable using slang. Slang words common in your geographical region or with your friends may not translate to a larger audience. The audience needs to understand what you are saying.

Strive to speak naturally, just as you do with your friends and family. If you do not use a natural inflection when you speak with people on the air, your voice will sound mechanical and emotionless. Remind yourself that you are simply having a conversation with someone. Listen to hosts you admire and begin to notice the natural pauses they use—between words and between sentences. Try to mimic their rhythm of speaking.

BECOMING A DEMONSTRATION SHOW HOST

How does a person prepare or train for this type of host position? Often, people match an interest, hobby, or career with photogenic qualities and abilities. Cable channels are awash with specialty topics—history, cooking, decorating, home improvement, golf, travel. You can likely find a channel that features an interest or skill you possess. As with topics, there is a wide variation in what you may be required to do for the program.

You will likely work for a separate production company that sells the program series to networks and cable system operators. You may tape the program in front of a studio audience, or you may tape all aspects of program content in the field, or on-location. You may be responsible for writing each script, scouting field locations, and scheduling guests, as well as hosting. Or you may just need to show up and record an introductory and concluding segment, as well as some transitional material used between segments. You may be "hands-on" and participating in the activities, such as cooking or constructing a house. You may be a contestant on a reality show, competing for a slot week to week, in order to earn a reward at the conclusion of the series.

The paths to these careers may be as varied as the topics: some people work as reporters in television news; others may secure a small role in a weekly segment on a local television station's news programming. Others may practice a sport or work in a particular industry, such as touring as a semi-pro golfer or working in a gourmet foods grocery store. These people then take the expertise they have learned, perhaps drawing on photogenic qualities, creativity, and public speaking abilities, and attempt to secure hosting work.

Ernie Manouse, talk show host with the PBS affiliate KUHT-TV in Houston, Texas, stresses that you have to be friends with people on the other side of the lens. "The audience will forgive you anything as long as you are honest and sincere. Faking it doesn't work. If you care about people, information, and television, a naturalism will come out." And that may be the most important skill of all.

Special Performers: Weathercasters

uring the mid-twentieth century the development of radar and television changed the public perception of the value of weather information. Previously, the public accepted the wonder of four seasons in the northern half of the United States; the warm, wet climate in the Southeast; and the hot, dry climate in the West. With the development of radar and television, people slowly began to recognize the importance of weathercasting in planning their daily activities. Color television, weather satellites, and cable distribution that appeared during the last quarter of the twentieth century yielded rapid distribution of information gathered throughout the nation by the National Weather Service. As such data and predictions are constantly improving and becoming more precise, weather reports can be found everywhere, from an entire channel dedicated to them (The Weather Channel) to various weather services on the Internet.

The weather map shows typical elements, like those in Figure 8.2, including (1) a radar scan that is color coded from blue to dark red violet showing light rain to severe storm cells, (2) the jet stream, and (3) the path of a Pacific Ocean hurricane. In large metropolitan areas a traffic report frequently accompanies the weather, especially during drive times. This is another transfer from radio. The traffic report offers street maps and measures the speed of cars on principal highways, with helicopter reports on even gloomy days. With TVs and GPS in automobiles such maps have become more popular. Traffic reporting may be presented by a television traffic specialist, an in-station staff announcer, or a radio reporter speaking over a still graphic.

KEYS TO BEING A SUCCESSFUL WEATHERCASTER

Weathercasters themselves have been indispensable over the decades. The principal differences in weathercasting from one local station to another are the way the information is organized and the personalities of the weathercasters. These personalities can range from someone who gives a factual report to one who prefers humorous presentation. To this day the personality of the weathercaster, who is often a meteorologist, is the lik-

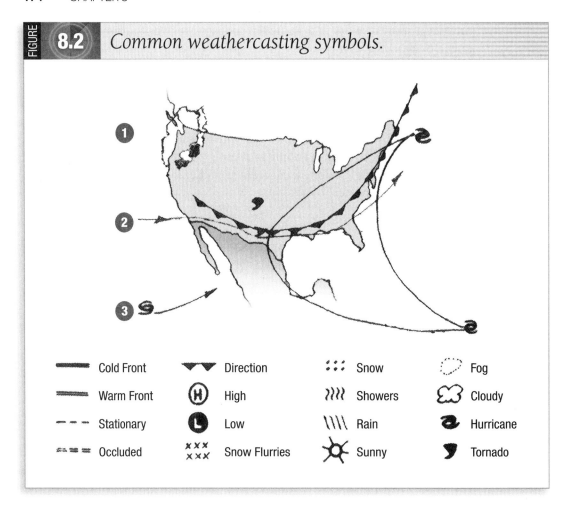

FIGURE 8.2   *Common weathercasting symbols.*

▬▬▬	Cold Front	▼▼▼	Direction	⋮⋮⋮	Snow	◌	Fog
▬▬▬	Warm Front	Ⓗ	High	⁾⁾⁾⁾	Showers	☁	Cloudy
- - -	Stationary	Ⓛ	Low	\\\\\	Rain	🌀	Hurricane
▬▬▬	Occluded	xxx xxx	Snow Flurries	☀	Sunny	✎	Tornado

able asset that viewers watch. Key traits are a pleasant appearance, a good voice, and experience.

Like sports, the weather is presented mainly in about three minutes, consisting of current conditions, the previous 24 hours, projection for the day, and projection for the week. At the national level the weathercast is mainly useful for travelers flying or driving from state to state, and is a minor supplement to daily homestyle talk shows. Nevertheless, the national weathercaster may have or build significant recognition and a reputation that enables him to become a national celebrity, such as Al Roker.

WEATHERCASTING AND THE COMMUNITY

Regions that are subjected to intense storms, hurricanes, and floods have encouraged weathercasters to use the latest technology, such as high definition Doppler radar, moving icons, large display maps, and inserts of destruction. When the same scene of a category 5 tornado moving over a community is shown repeatedly, it is being shown not only for its informational value but for the station's promotional benefit. Therein lies the danger of weathercasting. Fear spread by the weathercaster, even if it is unintended, can instill panic in the public. As a public servant the weathercaster does not want to create panic by alleging the potential severity of a storm that never materializes, yet she must be honest and accurate. Weather forecasting has become a big business that affects regional emergency evacuation plans, as well as decisions such as whether the roof of the baseball stadium should be open or closed for the game. Thus, today's weathercaster must be a delightful personality and someone the public trusts. The public cannot give enough praise to those weathercasters and reporters who risk their lives covering a severe storm for many hours or days, and a local station for devoting its resources to warnings and updates.

Weathercasters must be good performers because the day-to-day weather has an element of entertainment in it. When the weather is not so nice, experience and credentials—such as a degree in meteorology—become more important. Meteorologists who are weathercasters look at raw weather data and weather models from the government and create their own forecasts. They put the forecast on paper, build the graphic elements and maps to be used in the program, and determine what to say during the weather segment. Often they must condense information into a three- or four-minute weather segment, without relying on meteorology jargon. The weathercast is entirely ad-libbed or delivered by memory—there are no scripts on prompters for this segment. Even talking about weather for the local region may be challenging because viewers judge newly hired weathercasters harshly if they mispronounce names of areas in the community. If in doubt about a pronunciation, ask someone.

Weathercasters rely on the public's trust in their credibility, as indicated above. One way to convey credibility is through the use of formal conservative attire, typically a light-color shirt and dark suit for men and perhaps even a tie. Female weathercasters have a bit more freedom in selecting their clothing; however, it is better to be too formal than too casual. Light makeup, such as pressed powder, is recommended for men to reduce the shine skin naturally creates. Selecting a shade one step darker than your natural complexion will prevent you from appearing "washed out" or too pale under the bright lights in the studio.

A weathercaster in one of the top markets in the United States says the way he sounds on the air is the way he talks in person. (In fact, he says he wants viewers to think he's sitting in the room with them while they watch television.) This underscores the importance of cultivating a natural conversational tone for your on-camera appearances.

The weathercaster is likely the most active member of the news team on set. She may begin her weathercast at the news desk and then walk to the "weather wall," the chroma key screen that she controls with a remote unit in her hand to insert maps and other graphic representations. She stands in front of the chroma key screen watching images on a monitor just out of the camera's view. Weather people typically use their arm and an open hand to point out items on the map that help illustrate the forecast. As the weathercaster wraps up the forecast, she likely is walking back to the anchor desk to talk with the news anchors as the segment finishes.

It may take you six months to become comfortable during your weather segment. Delivering a weathercast daily, though, is the only way to learn. It's the rare person who is able to master the job during an internship where you might sporadically tape a weathercast when the studio is not being used.

Weathercasters embody a somewhat strange mix, especially meteorologists, because they are scientists on television who walk a fine line between entertainment and information.

Special Performers: Sportscasters

Sportscasting is another specialized form of reporting. A sports summary on a local station usually consists of news items, scores, interviews, and commentary. Local sports appears mostly on evening news programs. Historically, women have tried to compete for sports announcing jobs and success came slowly. Decades ago Anita Martini pioneered an effort in Houston to enter the men's locker room after the game so that she could get the same information the players shared with male sportscasters; but progress was slow and challenging. At the network level the sportscaster has become as much of a personality as the players, and in many cases as well known because his exposure is consistently greater. Some unique sportscasters—past and present—are visually attractive (Bob Costas), vocally distinctive (John Madden), and/or critically perceptive (Dick Button).

Scripts for local sports are printed out on paper and sportscasters read from them if they are unable to depend on prompters or data are too complicated to remember. Typically, the sportscast that is included in the local evening news is about three minutes long and may have its own sponsor. Some stations have only one sportscaster, others may have three or four including a sports director, who is both on-air and the manager of the group. To avoid broadcasting more than a blur of statistics, the teams and players are personalized as much as possible. To do this, extra programs are allotted during the season. Half-hour feature programs introduce the players and outline the season. A **color** commentator, the second person on a two-person sports announcing team, contributes facts and statistics about the players and teams and may play off the other sportscaster's comments.

These programs are supplemented by weekly summaries of the game of the week, and discussions by former coaches and players abound. The teams depend on sportscasters to showcase them, thereby promoting the sale of tickets and merchandise.

SPORTSCASTERS AS SPECIALISTS

Because sports entities are so large and complex, sportscasters tend to specialize in one or two sports. Many sportscasters were high school or college athletes who did not have the qualifications to become professional players on major teams. Many of them are virtual encyclopedias of data about the games and the players. They have personalities that are gregarious and pleasing to the companies they work for, the leagues and players they write and talk about, and a cadre of avid viewers and supporters. Nevertheless, the relatively few top sports announcing positions are as difficult to get as the positions obtained by the players.

Seasonal sports are central to the program, with baseball, football, and basketball providing most of the annual calendar. The main reports largely concern the local teams, led by the most profitable businesses (professional and college teams) and ending with high school games. NASCAR racing has become a well-attended sport, and hockey and soccer are making steady progress in capturing public attention, although this trend has been slow. So, sportscasters who are especially knowledgeable in these sports are gaining prominence. Some individual sports such as tennis, golf, and horse racing do well locally. Some personal sports (such as roller skating) have youth appeal, but are not regularly reported or sponsored. Numerous water sports (sailing, surfing) and winter sports (skiing) are more popular where climate and facilities permit them. Hunting and fishing are seldom covered, although they have a big following. Contact sports (boxing, wrestling, and martial arts) have held their special fan base since television's earliest days, but only at the national level. The prospects for performers who are producers suggest that much more could be done in local sports.

KEYS TO BEING A SUCCESSFUL SPORTSCASTER

The material conveyed during a typical sports broadcast is different from other news content only because it is focused on a game or event; its primary purpose is similar—to tell a story. These stories are often about overcoming adversity or some obstacle. For local affiliates the focus is on coverage of area teams.

The sportscaster is faced with the challenge of distilling the pertinent sports information of the day into perhaps a two-minute segment during each newscast. Unlike news anchors and reporters, sportscasters are encouraged to include more of their opinions in their reports. A sports segment is supposed to be fun. Try to connect with your viewers by giving them a humorous bit of information or making a comment to someone else on the set.

Professional dress is expected. That means a suit (and a tie if you are a male). One sportscaster approaches his segment as if he is giving a business presentation every day, and so he dresses the part. Good grooming is a key component. Sportscasters need neat hair and pressed powder makeup to control shine while on the set, and eyebrows may need to be trimmed or shaped.

Your voice should convey energy and yet sound natural. Beginning performers sometimes think talking loudly conveys energy, but unnatural volume detracts from your words. If you are passionate about sports and the stories you are telling, the energy will be conveyed naturally.

Your movements during the sportscast can convey energy, too, but only if the movements are natural. Any forced arm gestures or facial expressions will make the viewer uncomfortable, and you will appear to be stiff, not relaxed. Strive to be yourself and make use of the same types of movements you might use when telling the story to a friend. Like a weathercaster, you may choose to move around the set. Perhaps you will stand in front of a monitor or next to the anchor desk. Choosing to stand rather than sit will inject your delivery with some added energy.

Being physically fit is a key aspect of feeling comfortable and at ease with your body as a sportscaster. But being fit serves another important purpose, too: it will convey credibility to the players you interview and to the viewer at home. If you are in good physical condition, players will be more likely to respect you and recognize the commonality you share. As one sportscaster noted, how can viewers take you seriously when you talk about athleticism when you don't look the part? Of course, not everyone is able to be as fit as a professional sports figure, but if you exercise regularly, you will better understand the challenges, injuries, recovery time, and rewards that are an integral part of athletes' lives.

Discipline is required when working behind the scenes. Attend practices; be visible so players know you are serious about your job. Build relationships with the coaching staff and the players. Some sportscasters have that encyclopedic knowledge of game and player statistics, but it is not a requirement because any information you might need is easily found with a quick Internet search.

A sportscaster is a storyteller. As a sportscaster, strive to be the person everyone wants to sit down with to talk about the game. (See the box below.)

Sportscasting on the World Stage

Obviously people like competitive sports, whether live or as virtual games. An array of sportscasters, therefore, narrate, report, comment, investigate, promote, and speculate on them. Nowhere is this spectrum of sportscasters more evident than at the Olympic games. Although sports in the United States is huge, for the two weeks or so the Olympics are held, the world stage is much larger. The Olympic games are held in various on-location venues and so it can be said they are mainly a series of electronic field productions (EFPs) held together with sportscaster continuity.

Continued

The 2008 presentation of the Olympic games was an example of the enormous enjoyment they bring to people throughout the world. Chinese earthquake victims watched China play the USA in basketball on television receivers in the rubble.

For the 2008 Olympic games, NBC, which obtained the games through network rotation and millions of dollars, had to cover the events, the city, and the general area. For 17 days NBC Sports, headed by Dick Ebersol, chairman of NBC Universal Sports and Olympics, and David Neal organized 3,000 announcers and technicians, with about 2,400 in Beijing and 600 in New York, to bring the Olympics to the world by way of NBC's seven English-language broadcast and cable channels, the Spanish-language Telemundo, and the Internet. This immense undertaking in high definition (HD) television was financially supported by a billion dollars in advertising revenue. The opening ceremony, featuring about 15,000 performers, averaged 31.2 million viewers, compared with 25.4 million for the Athens games and 27.3 in Sydney in 2000.[1]

The Olympic events were seen in a series of programs. The time difference between New York and Beijing is 12 hours, so many daytime programs, hosted by Jim Lampley, were recorded and played the next day. The opening ceremony was a delayed broadcast aired and anchored by Bob Costas in primetime viewing from the Beijing National Stadium, referred to as the Bird's Nest. Afterward, Costas anchored from behind a table to list the evening's live and recorded events, usually in an exclusive NBC set and using his dominating voice and lightly humorous, no-nonsense style. Lampley anchored from behind a table, also. Both men depended on scripts and prompters. To provide continuity and to focus on the games, Costas and Lampley announced the sports experts, usually two or three, who would moderate and comment on each of the events. Costas included some news references to controversies and the murder of an American that occurred in the city. In addition, Costas held some interviews from comfortable sofas and led into feature material about Chinese tourist attractions, food, and sites that was prepared in advance to fill time for transitions from one event to another. He was often seen at these venues.

The feature or color commentators ad-libbed an abundance of comparative data and prepared background comments about participants from 25 venues: the Bird's Nest, the Water Cube, the Olympic Green, marathon locations, and 350 miles away at the sailing venue at Qingdao. The sharp critiques of those commenting on gymnastics and diving proved they were especially adept at calling and explaining the points the athletes would or would not accrue and why. The action was shown in actual and slow motion time to reference the accuracy of their judgments.

All of this illustrates how extremely well prepared a sportscaster must be in advance in order to be a competitive announcer. Volumes of instructions are gathered and digested in order to present such an impressive extravaganza that in the end filters down from the glamor of the world stage to the familiar on-campus EFP.

Summary

Television performances can take a variety of forms; each, as you might realize, requires something different from the performer. As a news reporter, you may be responsible for creating news stories in the field, culminating with a live shot during the evening newscast. Here, you often have no producer to guide you; you may be part of a crew, or you may have the sole responsibility of shooting your own footage. A reporter may travel to spend the day with a hometown girl who has achieved fame in Los Angeles, creating a feature story about how the celebrity's life has changed. You may be a host of a public affairs program, moderating a political debate in the studio between mayoral candidates in your city, or you may have the task of demonstrating how to make a casserole on the cooking set. Weathercasters and sportscasters share a role where knowledge about their subjects adds to their credibility. They are specialists whose on-air persona is critical to their success.

CHAPTER 8 *exercises*

1. Practice reading out loud. Read newspaper stories from the sports section or stories about the weather. Newspaper stories are written in a specific print style, which includes longer sentences and phrases than you would find in a broadcast story. As you read, try to adapt the style as written to a style that is more conversational in tone and phrasing.

2. Experiment with adding inflection or excitement to your voice. This activity will help you when you do read material written in broadcast style.

Note

1. Data is summarized from NBC Olympics broadcast and promotional information.

Other Sources

Compesi, Ronald J., and Ronald E. Sheriffs. *Video Field Production and Editing.* 4th edition. Boston: Allyn & Bacon, 1997.

Medoff, Norman J., and Tom Tanguary. *Portable Video ENG and EFP.* 5th edition. Stoneham, MA: Focal Press, 2007.

Nisbett, Alec. *The Use of Microphones.* 2nd edition. Mountain View, CA: Mayfield Publishing Company, 1996.

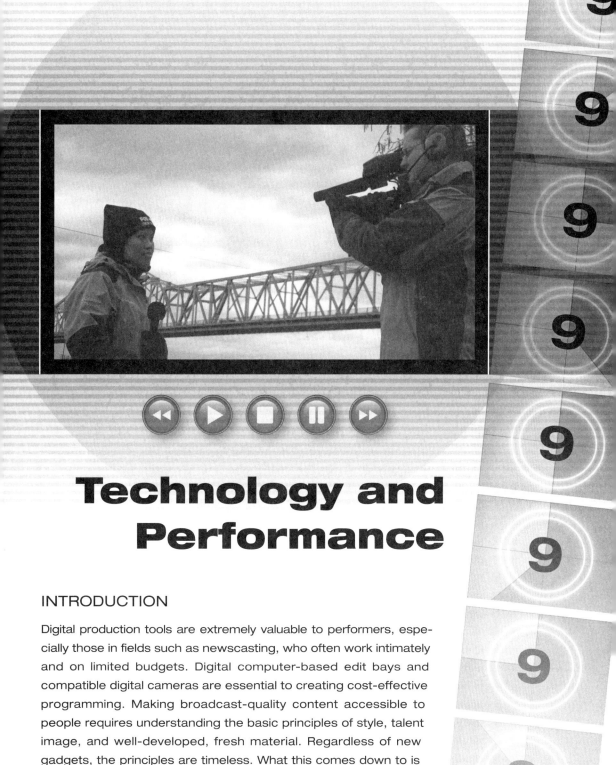

Technology and Performance

INTRODUCTION

Digital production tools are extremely valuable to performers, especially those in fields such as newscasting, who often work intimately and on limited budgets. Digital computer-based edit bays and compatible digital cameras are essential to creating cost-effective programming. Making broadcast-quality content accessible to people requires understanding the basic principles of style, talent image, and well-developed, fresh material. Regardless of new gadgets, the principles are timeless. What this comes down to is more opportunity and competition for the performer. You need to have a large, cohesive set of skills and know how to use the new technology to work out imperfections so that you can develop your image into a marketable performer.

This chapter discusses the essentials of technology and suggests various performance possibilities.

Technology and Television

Production is not content. It is not what is in the copy, or what is said on the soundtrack, or what is in the pictures. Production maximizes this content by showing it at its best so that the picture resolution is optimum, the sound is clear and understandable, and the material is presented to viewers in an attractive way. With the introduction of computers and digital technology into the production arena, huge advances have been made in every area of the process, from content acquisition and management, to camera and sound equipment, to editing and graphic solutions, and now to the distribution of content.

DIGITAL VERSUS ANALOG EQUIPMENT

Digital foundationally refers to the form in which information is recorded and transmitted, namely, through the use of "0" and "1." An infinite combination of zero-and-one sequences can accurately communicate vast amounts of information. Millions of 0's and 1's in unique combinations represent any image, audio, or sound that is captured.

Predating digital recording, the **analog** method creates an electronic signal that physically describes the image, and another magnetic head involves a recording head that reads the information. The best quality comes from the first analog tape, the one from the camera. Then it may be dubbed to a second tape, creating a second generation that provides a signal of lesser quality. Over time these signals deteriorate further, to the point where the signals create color and image problems. For this reason, wide videotape strips were used, to get as much electronic information as possible on the tape. Early broadcast videotapes were two inches wide, then one inch. Three-quarter- and one-half-inch videotapes, such as VHS, were commonly found in homes.

Similarly, digital equipment captures the image and creates an electronic signal, but unlike analog, the electronic signal is sampled and compressed using a standardized algorithmic formula. This binary digital information is then recorded onto the digital tape or other media. The media can be inserted into a compatible device that inputs the content into a computer for editing or sends it to a monitor for viewing. As opposed to creating an inferior second-generation dub from the original source as analog does, the digital information is simply copied as a computer file. The result is an acquisition and editing system that essentially maintains the original quality of the source material. For performers, it is important to remember that higher resolution digital images can be more detailed, harsher, and more revealing than analog video.

CAMERA TECHNOLOGY

Many cameras today can claim "broadcast quality" because of digital and image compression technology. Of the numerous products and manufacturers, Sony's BetaCam and DigiBeta cameras were long recognized as the preferred digital broadcast standard. Recently accepted standards for digital video (DV) have brought about new professional formats such as Sony DVCAM, Panasonic DVCPRO, and variations that provide this broadcast quality and are rivals in the world market. Cameras once used tubes that absorbed light and color and created an electronic signal from the image information. Today, cameras are solid state and use CCD (charge-coupled device) chips, or more recently, CMOS (complementary metal-oxide semiconductor) sensors, which promise to merge still photography and videography by allowing users to capture a high-resolution still image while shooting at high speeds. Previously, capturing a single frame from a video recording resulted in a low-resolution, blurry image. The size and quantity of the imaging chips or sensors in the camera determine the image quality. These electronic chips have a photosensitive surface that reads the image and creates an electronic signal. Most broadcast-quality cameras use three CCD chips that specifically target the color or chroma components of an image. They also read luminance or light.

RECORDING MEDIA

Videotape is a Mylar plastic strip with a magnetic coating. As the tape passes across the magnetic recording heads inside a camera, electronic information is recorded on the tape by rearranging the magnetic particles. The heads create multiple, separate **tracks** or channels for video and audio. Other tracks are generated for special uses, such as captions for the hearing impaired. Professional cameras break down the video signals into component video. Most consumer cameras do not break down video as completely. They create a video signal that is a composite of all colors and light.

Digital cameras have also used "tape" to record digital information, but today most use alternative media for source materials such as recordable DVDs, hard drives, and flash memory sticks. Some use wireless camera systems that send content to a remote truck, base station, or server, which eliminates the traditional cabling, reduces production costs, and expedites delivery to the audience.

EDITING AND DISTRIBUTION

With the digital transformation completed, television stations have replaced their analog tape-based linear edit bays with computer-based nonlinear editing systems. **Nonlinear editing** refers to the ability to edit out of sequence, something that is possible only because of digital technology. News stations now use nonlinear editing because news records directly to a hard drive, which is fast and inexpensive.

Computers within a station are networked so that they can call up digitized video content stored on the station's server. A **server** is a computer with large hard drives interconnected for the sole purpose of storing and serving digital content to local workstations. A server removes the hassle of having to cue up commercials, feature stories, and other brief items; instead, this material is logged, stored, and retrieved across the network, and can be displayed whenever editing sessions or broadcasts require it.

Journalists no longer have to rush a tape to the station or even to a remote (live) truck to get the story on the air. They may report a story from a faraway place and upload the edited content directly to the server at the station. For instance, reporters in a foreign country may shoot with small, compact digital broadcast cameras. They shoot the footage and then use a laptop computer or portable editing device to assemble the finished story. They can then upload that content to the news server at the station, network, or news wire service so that it can be called up and shown on demand. It is typically uploaded across high-speed, broadband Internet connections or microwave systems.

GRAPHICS

A major leap forward in television production has resulted from the new flexibility and ease of graphic production. Technology offers almost endless options to create complex images and to display them in numerous ways. Keys or mattes used in connection with special computers can eliminate unwanted details and add shadows and depth to an image, such as for a weatherperson in front of a forecast map. Computers can create convincing illusions such as placing a reporter who is actually on a small set with no background in front of an elaborate image of a virtual set that looks like a huge studio. Digital technology is completely revolutionizing the way news content is captured, edited, and distributed.

STATION PROMOTION

News stations, shows, and performers may benefit from technology in another way—promotion and interactive communication, especially across the Internet. Most news stations have a website for **promotion**, which is any planned activity that furthers the growth and development of a network, station, or programming, such as showing their brands frequently and having sophisticated communication with the audience. ABC and KTRK-TV, Houston, provide a sophisticated website, with real-time program streaming and instantly updated news bites that complement each story. By contrast, the KTLA, Los Angeles, website is slower, and so is

CNN's. How well a network or station shows its video online reveals its level of sophistication.

Websites may provide services to the audience with written stories, transcripts, links to other resources, and video clips. Some stations stream their broadcasts live and in real time across the network or to cell phones and similar wireless devices. They use this technique both to promote their content and to extend their reach to their audience. They may create online surveys for use as part of their broadcasts or use other audience feedback methods via e-mail or instant "chat." Weather updates, program notes, traffic alerts, or other news can be sent automatically to an e-mail or cell phone. Stations can track what online content viewers watch, the frequency and length of time they look at it, and where the viewers are located on the planet. This information helps them direct their content. They also use this information to attract advertisers wanting to target certain segments of an audience.

One-Man Bands or Videojournalists

hile the heart of the news program is the story, journalists should be familiar with the use of technology, both for maximizing their image and for displaying the performance skills they need to compete. At some smaller companies, reporters are hired with the expectation that they will report, shoot, star in, and edit their own stories, and this is becoming common at larger studios as well. This trend toward cost-effective **one-man band** (also called videojournalists or "multiplatform" or "backpack" journalists) news gathering is why journalists take production courses in addition to performance work in building their repertoire of professional assets. Performing is still the heart of any news report. But just as a second language is a welcome asset, the abilities to skillfully use a digital camera and edit in the field with a laptop and editing software can boost the performer's career.

DTV: The New Era of Broadcasting

ederal law required that in June 2009 all full-power television broadcast stations stop broadcasting in analog format and broadcast only in digital format. Congress mandated the conversion to all-digital television broadcasting, also known as the digital television (DTV) transition, because all-digital broadcasting frees up analog frequencies for public safety communications (such as police, fire, and emergency rescue).

DTV enables stations to provide dramatically sharper pictures and better sound quality. By transmitting the information used to make pictures and sound as data bits, like a computer, television stations can also carry more information using digital broadcasting than was possible with analog broadcast technology.

MULTICASTING

Compared with analog TV, local broadcasters can now send pictures, sound, and other information over the public airwaves in smaller packages. The result is that local digital TV stations can broadcast not just the traditional single channel, but many more channels of content at the same time on the same digital frequency. This is known as "multicasting" and has been one of the prime incentives driving the conversion to digital television. Televisions equipped with a digital tuner may receive channel 2 from a local station as well as separate, additional programming on channels 2.1, 2.2, and 2.3 on the digital band. For example, a local station may provide its regular broadcast in digital format on channel 2.1, provide a continuous weather channel with an emphasis on local forecasts on channel 2.2, and provide programming centered on regional cooking and craft shows on channel 2.3. Multicasting capabilities increase your opportunities as a performer, because the stations need to fill channels with viable content that attracts their target audience and thus advertisers.

DTV IMAGE FORMATS

Digital television can include broadcasts in different formats, depending on the source material from which it was created and the capability or choice of the broadcaster. Essentially these are defined as standard definition or SDTV and high-definition or HDTV formats. The picture resolution of these images is described in pixels. A pixel or picture element is the smallest piece of information in an image arranged in a two-dimensional grid using dots, squares, or rectangles. The resolution of an image is described by the width and height in number of pixels.

SDTV offers an aspect ratio of 4:3 and a resolution of 720 pixels by 480 pixels and is comparable to the former analog TV broadcasts. The picture and sound quality, however, are noticeably better because digital transmissions are free of snow, ghosts, and static noises—though the downside is that, in some areas where television reception has been difficult, this may result in no signal at all where a lesser image was acceptable previously to the consumer.

HDTV offers significantly improved images at a higher resolution of 1,280 pixels by 720 pixels and an aspect ratio of 16:9. This image is comparable to the viewing experience on a computer screen or at a movie theater and is commonly called widescreen. The actual resolution varies based on American (NTSC) or European (PAL) standards as well as the capability of the viewing device. Higher resolution images will no doubt follow as capacity expands.

Though full-powered TV stations have converted to digital broadcasts, they are not required to offer high definition broadcasts. But, because most digital TVs sold in the United States are high definition to meet consumer desires, many stations deliver some type of HD programming and are adding more.

VIDEO ON DEMAND

A recent area of interest is developing in the use of video on demand technology, or VOD. VOD has actually been around for decades. One early, familiar application of VOD was in the hotel industry. When a guest ordered a movie, the request was sent to the hotel's VCR player bank and the movie would be sent to the television set in the room. To manage system load, starting times would be staggered. Today, digital technology allows vendors to feed movies via satellite to the establishments and then directly to televisions in guest rooms.

Cable companies have also used video on demand for some time to offer movies to subscribers first through pay-per-view and now through provider-specific channels. The Internet now allows users to watch TV on their own time, whether through network sites like NBC.com or through sites such as www.hulu.com that provide shows from multiple networks.

The question has been how stations and providers can derive ad revenue from VOD. Dynamic digital ad insertion in VOD content enables a more effective and relevant form of advertising and the promise of an additional revenue stream. Targeted ad insertion is a very attractive proposition for advertisers because the commercials are more pertinent to the subscriber and, therefore, are more likely to generate product sales. The deployment of targeted VOD ads is predicted to dramatically increase revenue for cable operators as it can target audience segments for advertisers by cities, neighborhoods, and even specific demographics in each area.

INTERACTIVE TV

DTV allows a station to broadcast more than video channels. By transmitting computer data across part of its data stream a station can not only offer new services to new people but also tap new sources of income.

For example, the Texas Public Broadcasting Educational Network uses part of the DTV broadcast capability on the state's 14 public TV stations to send large amounts of digitized educational content to personal computers equipped with low-cost DTV tuner cards. The new network is comparable to a university's LAN or intranet, connecting stations across the state and capable of serving rural area consumers with high-speed Internet access where it has previously been too expensive. The network downloads material over the air into computers with hard drives, providing vast amounts of video and data that can be stored for users to tap on demand.

This technology also provides for the transformation of television from a singular experience, where programming is broadcast to the consumer, to an interactive service where customers see what they want, when they want to see it.

IPTV

IPTV, or Internet protocol television, uses the same World Wide Web standards as the public Internet. Usually associated with DSL or digital subscriber loop delivery, it is equally applicable to cable and to combination delivery systems that use IPTV over a data network with broadcast delivery on cable, satellite, or land-based broadcast systems. IPTV allows viewers to choose what they watch and whether to watch it live or on-demand, and to control content by skipping ahead, going back, and so on. The possibilities of this technology extend far beyond traditional broadcasting of content.

Most IPTV systems offer movies, special interest channels, and compelling interactive services ranging from gambling and Karaoke on demand to simple gaming for children. Recently Disney signed a deal with Italian-based Fastweb to provide American programming to that country across an IPTV system, meaning more exposure for performers involved in this programming. This technology will allow content producers to deliver programming anywhere high-speed internet is accessed. (See the box on the facing page.)

Performing on the Internet

From the most experienced performers to the least experienced performers, the Internet provides a delivery system, audience, and archive for their work. And whether one person or millions see you, it's possible to appear professional and have some fun with it.

USING THE INTERNET TO YOUR ADVANTAGE

Ideally, you are performing on the Internet because you know something or do something unusually well. The public is interested in learning something new or watching a person who has perfected a talent. Focus your remarks on your knowledge or skill so the public has a clear understanding of who you are and what you do. Discuss what you know, avoid what you're not sure of, and do not speculate. If you are a demonstrator, keep your performance brief and crystal clear. The length of a typical appearance is from 20 seconds to three minutes. Exceptions may be found, of course, but many Internet stories total five to six minutes long. Five minutes is considered a long time, even for a professional performer. For the most part, the content should be the essence of what you do, and generally you will be expected to provide the content.

IPTV in Education: Early Training for Future Performers

PTV technology is already being used extensively for corporate communications, for distance learning services for universities, and for on-campus broadcasts and programming created by students in K–12 schools. Houston Independent School District's J. Will Jones Elementary, working with media literacy/technology consultant the Production Company in Austin, Texas, has pioneered the use of an IPTV broadcast system in elementary school education to teach media literacy to disadvantaged students and broadcast live student-produced educational programming.

The campus has created a turnkey television station and media lab that models similar technology used in professional settings, working with a mix of consumer and professional camera and editing equipment. Station KJWJ-TV has a multicamera setup with a switcher that sends the program to an encoder to compress the signal and broadcast it through the existing high-speed Ethernet and wireless campus local area network. Classrooms tune in on any computer in the building and can see programming in real time. Students are also able to produce stand-alone reporter packages on science, history, social studies, or current events that are inserted into the morning show with the aid of specialized software. Such sophisticated software provides a user-friendly environment while producing a high-quality product on a single computer equipped with a camera. Students write the copy, rehearse, and shoot with the aid of an integrated prompter. They also edit and add titles, graphics, and music. Students can even use a chroma key feature to create the illusion of placing themselves on various sets.

Students who participate in the program gain technical expertise, but moreover they learn discipline and timeless principles of performance, appearance, and content. These students graduate from elementary school and progress through media programs available within the district's Central Regional feeder pattern at Lanier Middle and Lamar High School, where a professional-grade digital production studio is available. Graduating with a skill set that used to be associated only with college students seeking production or communication degrees, these students know how to produce and distribute their content out to the market using services such as Facebook, MySpace, and YouTube to immediately broadcast and promote themselves as performers and content producers.

Organize the material

One of the unique aspects of the Internet, compared to broadcast or cable outlets, is that time is infinite. In theory, you have as much time as you want to present as much as you want, limited only by bandwidth and download time. However, it is just as easy for your viewers to move on to something else they find more interesting. Think through what you intend to say and how to say it in the fewest possible words. Your comments should be concise, preferably in short, easy-to-understand sentences. If you take time to think on-camera, the presentation or conversation will seem slow and dull. Don't expect to ramble or fill time. Interviewers who want to know more should ask additional questions, one at a time. Anticipate the questions, rehearse your phrasing, and plan tentative answers based on what you think the public must know or wants to know. Do not sound mechanical, of course, but do sound precise, knowledgeable, and articulate.

Have visuals ready

Besides verbal preparation, performers should have visuals fully prepared. Be sure these items are properly mounted for presentation or electronic storage, are easy for viewers to recognize, and are arranged in the order of use on the program. If you are to show these items, hold them steadily in one place and in view of the proper camera lens for about five seconds. Frequently, visuals are shown in "detachment" or "limbo," that is, in a separate area, and then edited into the program.

Retain control

Performers who appear sporadically, especially on the Internet, usually look satisfactory, are well thought of for a moment or two, and are quickly forgotten. This is the place of the amateur in media. As a professional performer in media, on the other hand, you will want to make a positive appearance in a vehicle that is remembered and recycled for a long time, such as in an Internet clip, which may reach viral status. When you become a successful celebrity, and own the show, you will have great control over the product or program series, and you will reap the financial benefits. Top performers who reach a certain level must decide what is best for their future, win or lose. From humble beginnings a profitable program may grow.

Even as a beginning performer you can retain control through being sufficiently prepared to do a good job in the first place. The key to doing a good job is having a script outline. Very little in television is ad-libbed, even though it may seem that way. By preparing in advance you may produce something really fresh for viewers to experience.

Boost your performance image

The Internet can be a valuable tool for the individual performer. Having a website, especially one that is well designed, is an asset to those who want to be in front of an audience.

One way you can use the Web is by creating your own information or news service, so to speak. This is a great way to develop your image, talents, and skills. For instance, you might create a simple page to post videos you have created and reporting you have done. You may be lucky enough to break an important news story that is picked up by a wire service. This break could lead to sufficient recognition for employment on the air or on cable. Remember content is king. The content has to be good if you are going to get viewers, and frequently that means it has to be a specialized feature.

If you are already employed as a performer, perhaps a career journalist who works for a television station, the Internet represents an opportunity to further market yourself and your work. You have an audience that is potentially unlimited and that includes people who are in a position to provide more prestigious opportunities for you. Consider placing your résumé and other material on social networking sites, YouTube, or your own personal website. If you lack the skills to post your material, ask a friend with those skills to do it, or pay someone to do it for you.

On your website, you can create an interactive résumé with photographs and video clips that furnish a comprehensive presentation of you and your talents. Whether your target is a general audience or a potential employer, the Internet can provide access to your information and image on the screen for everyone to view and assess—so make sure that you look and sound good. Knowing what opportunities are available and having the skills to do this type of work can be very valuable to a performer.

ONLINE NEWSCASTS

Internet newscasts are evolving; most networks either stream their newscasts live or provide them online after the newscast airs on traditional television broadcasts. Others may scrap the standard newscast format almost entirely and create a newscast designed in format, content, and style to appeal to people who prefer to get their news from the Internet. For example, *ABC World News* experimented with a newscast that was just half the length of the regular nightly news broadcast. The program was recorded with "shaky cam" approach, a video style best described as a loose or freestyle approach, where the camera is not mounted on a tripod. The resulting video is not steady, and conveying an informality that can be fitting to the setting and topic. The news anchors' performance style was less constrained as well. One of the substitute anchors, Dan Harris, says it was his favorite newscast to anchor because, he said, "I feel less pressure to wear a tie, sit up straight, and make sure everything I say is perfectly enunciated. I have an opportunity to be much closer to who I actually am, instead of a TV version of myself."[1]

BLOGS AND VLOGS

Career journalists at broadcast networks and stations probably will spend part of their working day preparing a **blog** or a **vlog** (video blog). Typically a blog consists of a story synopsis, background information that would exceed allotted airtime or space in newspapers, and ways for viewers to interact with the journalist personally. Such interaction has become very popular with increased use of the Internet.

Technorati, a blog-tracking company, reported that 65,000 blog posts are made hourly; and it counts more than 100 million blogs globally.[2] Their CEO estimated in 2007 that there were 120,000 new blogs created every day.[3] The content of blogs ranges from the serious to the playful. So, you must be aware of how your work appears and who might see it. One reporter noted that as a working professional performer, you must strive to be objective in any work you create because your reputation and your employer's reputation depend on it. However, by definition a blog is usually maintained by an individual and includes his or her opinion. A journalist who also writes a blog must walk a fine line with the content. An opinion expressed in a blog, if publicized, can damage your credibility as a reporter or anchor.

Journalists such as Bill Moyers are able to enjoy the sophistication of a larger organization, such as PBS, to disseminate their work in a variety of applications. His series *Bill Moyers Journal* focuses on political issues, and visitors to his blog, www.pbs.org/moyers/journal, can choose to listen to a **podcast** (a "broadcast" downloadable from the Internet in mp3 format), watch video clips or sound bites, watch a vodcast (a video broadcast), read transcripts of the program, and leave comments on the blog, all in addition to watching the hourlong program on television.

Some bloggers are individuals from various professions who want to promote their businesses and themselves or offer public service information. The largest group consists of ordinary citizens who want to express their personalities and opinions to those who will view their site. The information these groups offer is usually designed for readers who are in a hurry and prefer short notes and sound bites. This may result in less well-documented information that skews toward impromptu responses. The pleasure from immediate feedback from around the world is a primary reason for blogging. The performers are casual in dress, the language may be colloquial, and the blog may be loaded with commentary and playful remarks.

Bloggers may appear as performers by making brief appearances in a larger video story or by narrating. Sometimes these appearances lack the polish that we traditionally see in visual storytelling, but that is not necessarily a sign of amateur work. Picture this: There is no elaborate background or backdrop. Instead the performer appears to be simply standing in the center of the frame, directly facing the camera, and is wearing a plaid shirt with a collar but no tie. He is indoors. The background is a gray wall; a large plant is positioned over his right shoulder and a water carafe on his left. In another story, the blogger appears outside a convention hall. His identification badge is blowing in the wind and is partially concealed by his sports jacket. He is not wearing a tie, and he's wearing sunglasses. He appears from the midwaist up or in a medium shot. His appearance is recorded with the shaky cam approach mentioned earlier. You might guess that these two performers run their own blogs with few visitors; but these bloggers actually work

FIGURE **9.1** *News blogs.*

http://onthescene.blogs.foxnews.com/author/adamhousley/

http://onlinejournalismblog.com/

www.cjr.org/

http://video.on.nytimes.com/

http://abcnews.go.com/Technology/blogs

for the venerable *New York Times*. These two examples illustrate how the Internet is continually changing the traditional aspects of performance. You can compare these with the news blogs in Figure 9.1.

Creating a blog, podcast, or vlog is a way to expose your work to people who otherwise might not see it. You can create your own blog with website publishing tools such as Wordpress or Blogger or seek work with a blogging organization solely set up to feature such work, or perhaps you will be asked to write a blog for a news or information organization.

CITIZEN JOURNALISTS

According to the organization Educause (www.educause.edu) the term **citizen journalist** applies to ordinary, everyday people contributing news or commentary about news events. Citizen journalism content may be divided into two categories: the first includes what's called nonprofessional reporting, such as YouTube's *Citizen News,* www.youtube.com/citizennews, or Yahoo!'s *You Witness News,* http://news.yahoo.com/you-witness-news, both places where viewers may access news and information content generated by nonprofessionals. The second encompasses citizen journalist submissions featured on traditional media websites, such as CNN's I-reporter, where a small percentage of the content submitted is used on-air.

In general, the definition of the term does not automatically conjure up visual images of packaged performances. However, citizen journalists' content comes in many forms. The majority of citizen journalism content may be found posted online as either text or photos. Video images that document news events may also be found; this is commonly weather video, such as images of a tornado, or some type of news event that occurs when television news crews are not present. Some citizen journalists do package their material using standardized television news templates. The story that is created may be similar in length, camera angles, editing techniques, and production values to a television news story, resulting in a formal effect.

At the other end of the spectrum are stories that are informal, recorded with a small handheld video camera with a corresponding drop in the production quality. The shots are not framed, the audio may sound fuzzy, and often the reporter is also the camera person. Subjects in the stories are interviewed by a disembodied voice (the camera person/journalist). Or the story may resemble a television live shot where the reporter is first featured in an opening stand-up and then takes the viewer for a behind-the-scenes look at, for example, delegates attending a political convention. A series of on-the-street interviews may appear, where each person tells, in a brief sound bite, why he or she is voting for the candidate. It is raw video in its most basic form.

In another story, the reporter takes the viewer into a recording booth at the convention, where individuals are recording their own sound bites explaining why they belong to the party. The reporter is never seen in the story; only his voice is heard as he holds the camera to record these pieces of news. The video is likely pieced together on a laptop computer without any digital effects. The tradeoff for quality is the ability to capture news as it happens, perhaps highlighting an event that bigger news and information outlets would not have the time to explore. As such, stories produced and placed on the Internet by individuals will continue to evolve into their own style or format.

Content may be distributed by utilizing any of the avenues available, cheaply and easily, such as blogs, vlogs, or podcasts. Using one of these methods to post your work could certainly be a reflection of personal initiative. Plus, you do not have to purchase a television station to transmit your work! You have the same tools at your fingertips as professional journalists.

On a related note, you have likely heard of potential employers checking on applicants by conducting an Internet search. Applicants may see their employment opportunities disappear when decision makers observe them, perhaps on social networking sites, engaged in embarrassing social situations that cannot be erased. Posting photographs or video of you and your friends at parties does not generally inspire confidence in news directors or others who may wish to hire you.

Summary

The technology required to transmit or communicate your performance to an audience is always changing. That said, certain basic features and techniques remain the same. In the field, the process begins with acquisition of images and sound and ends with postproduction (assembling the images and sounds, or editing). In the studio, digital conversion has replaced the standard definition (SDTV) format used for analog broadcasting. High definition (HDTV) is a digital format with a higher resolution image and an aspect ratio of 16:9—similar to the screen on a computer or at a movie theater.

In the broader sense, the conversion to digital broadcasting has created a myriad of platforms for performers: television station websites, station multicasting, IPTV, personal websites, online newscasts, blogs, vlogs, and citizen journalism websites. All of these have the potential to provide many more venues for a performer. Additionally, a performer looking for employment in a smaller media organization may need to work as a one-man band, requiring the acquisition of certain skills. Citizen journalists, of course, use these tools, too.

Production is not content, but it is one of the tools, along with your material, appearance, voice, and movement, that will help you tell your story.

CHAPTER 9 *exercises*

1. Arrange several opportunities to "shadow" media professionals who work at television stations. Ask to spend the day with a director, editor, videographer, and Web producer to see firsthand and compare the duties they perform daily.

2. Cover an event in your area and post the story to a citizen journalism website. Use photographs, audio, or video to help tell the story.

3. Use consumer-grade electronic equipment, such as a video camera and computer software, to shoot and edit a story yourself. Post to a suitable website.

Notes

1. ABC Reshapes the Evening News for the Web (October 12, 2007). Retrieved August 25, 2008, from www.nytimes.com/2007/10/12/business/media/12abc.html

2. P. Hirshberg. Discovery, News, and Blogs on the New technorati.com. Retrieved April 13, 2008, from http://technorati.com/weblog/2007/120405.html

3. Seven Things You Should Know About . . . Citizen Journalism. Retrieved October 5, 2008, from Educause Learning Initiative website: www.educause.edu/eli

Other Sources

CBS Interactive. www.cbs.com/sales

Federal Communications Commission (FCC). www.fcc.gov

Local News (Television Series). New York: Lumiere & WNET, 2001. A five-part series of work-behind-the-scenes at a television news organization.

Newslab. www.newslab.org. An online resource center for television newsrooms.

Radio-Television News Directors Association. www.rtnda.org.

Sony Electronics. www.sony.com.

The Business

INTRODUCTION

This chapter shows that in order to advance your career as a performer, you must have the tools to market yourself. Course work, internships, letters of introduction, résumé recordings, job interviews—all should be approached with one goal in mind: to gain the tools, skills, and contacts you will need to succeed.

Some of these considerations may not seem to relate to you at this point. As time goes by, however, you will begin to realize how very versatile you are and success may bring additional needs. This is largely because of unexpected demands for your image and voice once you are considered popular talent. Then, you will find more applications for your abilities in multimedia, and greater distribution of your work worldwide.

A Performer's Career Cycle

For those who want to make a living from performing, some knowledge of the business aspects is essential. This begins with understanding the typical life cycle of a television performer.

Here's an ideal scenario for you as a performer: Appropriate schooling comes to an end with a bachelor's degree that includes an internship at a prominent television company. Through contacts and job applications, you eventually land a full-time position on the air. After six months to two years on the first job, you are already looking for something better. You have some experience and move to a larger market. Your abilities and ratings begin to give you recognition. Network scouts and talent agents may be looking to negotiate your future contracts. Success and recognition follow.

Unfortunately, relatively few professional performers are so fortunate. Instead, they apply their on-air experience in behind-the-scenes roles or related work. Some aspiring performers have gained recognition by forming their own company and packaging their own series. For example, a stockbroker created her own television series on investing and a house repair expert on radio expanded his audience through audio recordings and endorsing various building products on television. Frequently, your recognition in news and information will enable you to expand your career fields into public relations for industry, government, and education.

Very few people, including performers, know what they want to do at an early age. Opportunity has a great deal to do with this decision. Sometimes performers are not ready to take advantage of the opportunities they get. Each professional career in journalism or entertainment requires a different type of preparation. Late anchorwoman Jessica Savitch once said that a performer must "get in the right line." If you want to be in news, enter it with a desire to report and present the news and realize that a news director wants a qualified journalist with an attractive appearance who may increase ratings. If you want to be an on-air presenter, develop confidence in your writing skills and present yourself with style so you will be noticed. Do not be dissuaded from becoming a performer because someone else says, "There are no jobs." There still may be a job for you. No one can make your decision for you, because no one else can say how much time, energy, imagination, and work you are willing to devote to your career, or what opportunities will come along. If you know what you want, opportunity will come along. Be ready to take advantage of it when it does.

Getting a Job

"In order to get a job, I've got to have experience. To get experience, I've got to have a job!" This frustrating dilemma is partly true and partly nonsense. With rare exceptions, you must have experience to get a paying job. Getting a job, any job, consists of finding an opening and being qualified to fill it. Talent agents, some schools, and a few placement offices know where the jobs are, and they match their clients or students with them. The task of matching performers with the right job is so varied that station personnel departments are constantly looking for new talent and replacements. They cannot depend solely on talent agents and schools to furnish the right human resources when they need them. A performer, therefore, should provide résumés and photos to talent agents, schools, placement offices, and media personnel. Figure 10.1 contains a list of typical entry-level jobs, though starting positions can vary and may even be surprising.

LETTERS OF INQUIRY

About the time of graduation many performers blanket the top markets with letters of application. Some performers send out as many as 200 letters. This is often a waste of time because you may receive only one or two responses per hundred letters. More helpful is a letter addressed to a department head at a station in a city that you intend to visit. The letter should be neatly typed and grammatically correct. It should indicate that you would appreciate touring the station and the department you are interested in, and that you are seeking the advice of the department head, whose name you mention, concerning a career in media.

If a response is not forthcoming, send follow-up inquiries and try to make an appointment when you are in town. Basic information on stations, networks, agencies, and production companies is found online, in libraries,

FIGURE 10.1 *Entry-level jobs.*

Typical entry points for television performers include the following:

- part-time, weekend, and odd-hour reporters for television or radio news departments
- community or public affairs directors with their own programs
- local station sportscasters, weathercasters, and farm reporters who may also cover general news
- presenters on closed-circuit television who are instructors, announcers, or narrators for education, business, and medicine
- actors in commercials
- representatives of trade or community organizations, philanthropic groups, churches, and legal and medical societies
- fund-raising advocates in public service series
- press or public relations spokespersons for business and industry

Cable television, especially public access channels, and schools probably offer inexperienced talent the greatest variety of on-air opportunities, including everything from announcing to presenting gymnastics programs.

and in some bookstores. The book *Broadcasting & Cable Yearbook* identifies markets, companies, and associations. Job openings are listed in the weekly *Broadcasting & Cable* trade publication and online at www.broadcastingcable.com. The Radio-Television News Directors Association (RTNDA), www.rtnda.org, has a job information service, and broader placement listings are provided by state organizations of the National Association of Broadcasters (NAB), at www.nab.org. Educational journals and newsletters may list openings in public broadcasting.

INFORMATIONAL INTERVIEWS AND STATION VISITS

News directors may get scores of applications each month; however, they see few applicants. To an extent, employment depends on making a strong impression by letter or in person. Try to see the potential employer, either the personnel head or the news director, so that you can sell yourself in person. This may be difficult, but do not become discouraged. *Networking* is important—ask relatives, friends, teachers, and mutual acquaintances involved in the industry to help you get an appointment. Ask for an informational interview, which allows you to talk to a director in order to gain knowledge and information. Most department heads are very pleasant, will probably be flattered that you have studied their operation, and are very interested in promising, fresh talent. However, in an informational interview, avoid asking directly for a job. Chances are the department head will not have one at the time, and the visit could end abruptly without your having time to leave a favorable impression. Instead, ask for whatever help the department can provide, such as suggestions, contacts, job leads, or anticipated opportunities. Rarely does an opening materialize at the moment of the interview, but sometimes one does later, and the department head, if favorably impressed, will contact you, assuming you have the necessary qualifications.

A distant station may or may not pay travel expenses. Be willing to go to the station at your own expense. Some network jobs have been obtained by aggressive people who were willing to invest in their own future. A department head is quick to notice an aggressive, yet attractive professional approach. Dress appropriately and conservatively. Some stations conduct internship programs, which give them an opportunity to observe talent before hiring. Eventually, you may be asked to fill out routine personnel application forms that are held for future reference. Update these forms every six months.

RÉSUMÉS

The basic résumé is a one-page list of your accomplishments. Your strongest credits should appear first (college degree, on-air employment). List facts without embellishment ("I'm an *excellent* writer"). High grades, awards, and scholarships speak for themselves. Study the suggestions in Figure 10.2. Online résumés may be useful as well.

10.2 *Résumé suggestions.*

Include:

- Your name, address, phone, fax, Internet contact
- Your professional objectives: short-term and long-term
- Your strongest asset: professional credits or education
- Education: degree, name of school, location, date granted. (Include most recent degree first, grade point if distinguished, perhaps high school if it is in career track.)
- Media employment: paid work. Identify position, company, dates
- Media experience: unpaid. Identify responsibility, organization, location, dates, and related activities
- Publications: titles, publishers, dates
- Honors: scholarships, prizes, academic/athletic/artistic recognitions
- Skills: Languages, computer, abilities, principal hobbies, significant travel
- Membership in professional organizations

Note that references are available upon request and that audio or video recordings are available.

Head shots

Nearly every employer appreciates an in-hand reminder of the talent. A **one sheet,** with a single photograph or **head shot** showing a close-up of the person and giving limited vita (name, contact numbers, e-mail, address, hair color, and one or two other details you want to provide) is a common way of doing this. The pose should be appropriate for the job you are seeking, and the photograph should be made by a professional photographer who is in the business of taking head shots. Glossies may be preferred to matte photographs. A small color photograph attached to a résumé is good for news (often it is scanned into the upper corner). Casting agencies for hosts, spokespersons, and entertainers often want 8-by-10-inch black-and-white or color pictures of different facial expressions and poses. If these poses are printed as a single photograph, it is called a **composite.** Modeling and theatrical work use composites. Assemble whatever credits you have in an attractive book that documents your achievements through pictures, reviews, and comments that assess your career. Some television directors may only read Internet submissions, but a personally written letter and photograph may distinguish you from the multitude of submissions.

Résumé tapes and recordings

A brief recording can be made at a professional recording studio. Some schools have such studios and can do a respectable job. The performer is shown close up most of the time. The recording begins with a simple identification followed by about 10 minutes of excerpts from on-air programs or other material you have. Video recordings can be expensive and should be sent in duplicate with return postage guaranteed. Needless to say, everything about the recording should be perfect. Remember, it is designed to showcase you and your abilities, not the cleverness of the director, although imagination in selecting flattering material and other help from the director should be encouraged. A brief digital recording or **air check** (an excerpt from one of your previous broadcasts that best shows how you look and sound on the air) might include your identification and on-air samples of your work in news and interviewing.

Credits

Employers always ask applicants, "What work have you done, and where have you done it?" You should have a list of previous employment, especially on-air work. These are your **credits.** You should strive to be associated with top stations, film companies, networks, recording studios, and well-known people in the business through connections, internships, and jobs. This association helps you to establish your reputation. As your work experience increases, your record should show that you have progressed to better stations, bigger markets, and more responsibility, more money, and more benefits. Some beginners, listing their credits on their employment forms, are surprised to learn that experience is more important to an employer than education. You should expect this. Paid experience indicates that you are a professional performer progressing in a highly competitive business, that you are aggressive enough to get a job, and that some employer was willing to pay for your services. As a novice, be sure to list and make the most of each credit you are entitled to, since you may not have many at this point. As years go by, only principal recent credits should be listed—until you become so well known that the networks, stations, and film companies feel fortunate to get a contract with you.

AUDITIONS

If there is an opening at present or in the near future, you will be asked to **audition.** An audition usually shows whether a person's appearance, movement, and voice have sufficient impact to impress the station management. It provides the management with something concrete to look at and listen to and pass around to others for an opinion—few hiring decisions are made by one person. Despite being nervous, you need to read in a confident style as fluently as you can. Don't fret about mistakes. Turn on the charm by radiating your personal warmth and unique personality; that is, present yourself as someone marketable. You may be asked to read copy without preparation. Some news directors want to test whether a person is fluent at sight reading. This tells a lot about how the performer would sound in an ad-lib situation, where potential errors may show up in manners or judgment, and whether the performer has skill in word recognition. Generally, professional employers do not want to train nonprofessionals, for stations are not in the business of training people. They will acquaint you with the specific way they handle content and operate their equipment, but they do not have time to train a novice. So the audition is to show what you can do as a professional employee. An audition can be nerve-wracking, but you should keep in mind that you probably would not get one if there was not already interest in your ability. Even a short audition takes staff time and equipment.

Performers may also be hired through a casting department retained by a local advertising agency or through an independent casting firm. Some photographers serve as casting directors. Acquaint yourself with local casting agencies.

If you get a call back after an initial audition, try to perform the same way the second time, for your work was apparently acceptable. Numerous auditions are often held to cast one role. Regardless, preserve an air of confidence.

Professional Assistance

If you become successful, you may gather quite a collection of other professionals to assist you. The first is likely to be one or more instructors to develop your talent; the next, an agent to get more work; the third, a business manager to invest your money; the fourth, a lawyer to draw up contracts; the fifth, a personal assistant to handle correspondence, personal maintenance, and in some cases, security. In addition to your own assistants, a major program may require more than a hundred people who directly or indirectly assist you: producers, writers, directors, editors, production assistants, secretaries, camera operators, and business and legal assistants. Fortunately, they are not on your payroll. While many performers find the best assistance comes from experience and practice, there are other places and people who can help you along the way.

COLLEGE AND PROFESSIONAL SCHOOLS

Although some professional schools may be able to train commercial announcers and others in specific vocational fields, most performers need a much broader education to succeed. Colleges and universities help develop talent within the context of a liberal arts education. Concentrated studies in communication—radio, television, film, and journalism—are supplemented by traditional disciplines such as languages, history, political science, the arts, natural and physical sciences, and mathematics. Decades ago, on-the-job training at wire services and newspapers was adequate; nowadays professional performers and subject experts really need a college degree.

Even after you attain some success in your chosen career you may want to improve your skills through further education. There are schools designed to keep performers mentally and physically fit through discipline. The benefits of these professional schools are listed in Figure 10.3.

FIGURE **10.3** *Why attend a professional performing school?*

- A performer keeps in practice, which is very useful when the performer is not working constantly.

- A performer gets a chance to perfect skills, including voice, appearance, and movement, and to bring these skills to the same degree of accomplishment as the competition provided by other performers.

- A performer becomes acquainted with other performers so that he or she can draw upon them for ideas, inspiration, and comparison. This is *networking.*

- A performer often finds work through professional schools, especially entry-level jobs, before he or she is experienced enough to attract an agent.

Schools can be very expensive and time consuming; therefore, you want to be certain the time and money spent will promote your career objectives. Make a list of your preferred schools and look them up on the Internet. If a school looks promising, try to visit it. None of the schools considered here should be confused with those that claim shortcuts to success. There are no shortcuts at any price. You should examine the reputation of a school before enrolling in it. Ask for a list of graduates, and get the opinion of professional performers, if possible. A school depends on its faculty and its graduates for reputation, so you should also get biographies of the faculty and see the facilities to which the program has access. A school contributes much to a performer's career. Therefore the proper choice is extremely important in the long run.

INSTRUCTORS AND PERSONAL COACHES

An instructor or coach is not necessarily a performer, but must be someone who knows what it takes to be a performer. These instructors or coaches may not have the appearance, voice, or other characteristics of a performer; instead, they may have patience, concern, understanding, knowledge, and an intuitive sense for developing talent. Sometimes they search for talent. A good instructor is very important to a performer. Besides discovering those with the greatest potential, instructors encourage performers with the care of a gardener nurturing tender plants, giving discipline, encouragement, and attention when they need it, and finding opportunities for them. Your instructor may be the only source of hope and inspiration you have through the early stages of your career. Regardless of your successes or failures, the teacher will be the one understanding person who knows the struggle you are going through. Many fine instructors are found in high schools, colleges, universities, and professional schools. Personal coaches may be hired, or you may be put under their direction during professional employment. You may even be fortunate enough to continue your education under the supervision of a highly respected news director, television or film director, talent agent, producer, or other mentor.

TALENT AGENTS

After you are sufficiently well trained to be placed for continuous work, you are ready for a talent agent. Sometimes talent agencies take performers who show promise at an early stage; however, agents essentially want people with abilities and a track record they can sell. A talent agent is a salesperson whose chief function is getting the performer jobs at the highest salary possible. For this service the talent agent gets a percentage of the payment negotiated for the talent, at least 10 percent of the gross. Thus, the more money the talent makes, the more the agent gets. Some of the benefits of a talent agent are listed in Figure 10.4.

Local talent agencies provide performers with job leads in the immediate vicinity. Agents in New York and Los Angeles provide talent for major markets and often for programs distributed nationally. Many celebrities, whether in journalism, the talk show circuit, or sports, have agents. Generally, per-

FIGURE 10.4 *Should you work through an agent?*

An agent is beneficial because this person can provide

- an intimate knowledge of what is happening in the industry.
- an optimum presentation of the performer's assets to buyers.
- ongoing contacts with talent buyers.
- a detailed negotiation of the contract.
- the knowledge to give advice about career development.
- in some cases, the ability to provide the security of a friendly counselor.

The principal drawbacks are that

- the agent may have to divide his or her attention among many clients.
- the agent may be entitled to receive a commission from work the performer obtained alone.
- an agent may tend to favor the position of major buyers in negotiations.
- the agent's advice may be bad, and the agent may benefit more from the association than the performer, in which case the performer should get a different agent. Always be sure you are able to get out of a contract.

formers at this level do not talk to anyone seeking their services; instead, they refer potential employers to their agents. The agent determines whether the performer should do the work and whether there is enough money, prestige, or both in the job. The performer receives a secondary benefit in this arrangement: any blame for being unwilling to meet a request is placed on the agent and not on the performer. An agent schedules the performer's commitments, making certain that amenities such as accommodations, receptions, and billing are met in accordance with the contract. A large talent agency is active in every type of media performance for national networks and film companies. These agencies represent performers, or they may package entire programs.

There are four ways that you as a performer may come to the attention of a major agent:

1. If you are referred by a mutual acquaintance
2. If you are performing where an agent can see your work, such as on the air or at charity benefits
3. If you become an established performer
4. If you are aggressive enough to take your résumé and photographs directly to the agency and are able to get an appointment with an agent.

From time to time agents set up appointments with performers who look promising. Meanwhile, working with a smaller agency may meet your needs as well as or better than a large agency. Some talent agents want three-year, **exclusive contracts,** which bind the performer to the agent, but performers may negotiate for shorter periods and with more than one agent, because many agents specialize in different media. Be sure to read your contract very carefully before you sign it.

MANAGERS

A performer may need a personal manager, business manager, or lawyer. A personal manager performs tasks similar to those of an agent, but having few clients, he or she gives the performer custom service. The combination of an agent and personal manager may amount to one-quarter of the performer's salary; this expense should be able to be more than offset by the performer's revenues.

Business managers and lawyers (they may be the same person) specialize in handling a performer's money. If you earn a lot of money, invest it wisely. There may come a time when you are out of work, with nothing to live on for months or even years except money from investments that were made when you were working steadily. Many performers are wealthy because of the money they invested, with the help of managers, in real estate, stocks, and other businesses. Money management involves a risk, of course, and you should choose a completely reliable manager who will make certain your money is accounted for and your investments are sound. Though performers appear to make vast sums of money, frequently they spend equal amounts. For contracts involving considerable money or complex commitments over a long period of time, a performer may need the advice and services of a lawyer who specializes in talent contracts.

PERSONAL STAFF

Performing can be a lonely life, especially for speakers who are on the road and also appear in media. Many performers take along a personal assistant. This employee may handle appointments, take phone calls, and assist with the performer's personal upkeep; but the assistant is usually much more than a secretary, giving friendly advice and encouragement when needed. Occasionally even a local performer—for instance, an investigative reporter who is threatened or a reporter at the scene of a riot where someone has been stabbed or killed—may need protection through a bodyguard or security service.

PRODUCTION COMPANIES

A media celebrity often forms a small production company for the express purpose of producing the programs in a series. This unit, an independent business, employs experts who collectively produce the vehicle in which the performer regularly appears. In fact, the resulting series may then be owned not by the network but by the performer's company, which syndicates the series for years to come with a profit continually flowing to the performer and financial backers. Once the prerogative of the rich and famous, many others now package an entire series for broadcasting, DVD, or CD markets that the performer's company may own, at least in part, and lease. Personal advice (on physical fitness, investing, food) information is often sold to viewers through such production companies.

CONSULTANTS TO THE STATION

Companies that provide advice to station management on how to improve their programs, specifically newscasts, are called consultants. Their advice may range from story content to stand-up techniques (such as including movement or props), image, and voice. It's important to keep in mind that if consultants have no suggestions for you, there is no reason for them to be in business and be paid. Expect a **critique,** which is some feedback from them, but take their advice only if you can use it. If the research conducted for a station's newscast indicates people think it has a staid or too conservative image, the consultants may advise the on-air personnel to loosen their ties and use more conversational phrases, such as "check this out" or "here's what's we found." Ultimately, station executives and on-air personnel will only change what improves the operation and is cost effective.

Legal Affairs

L
egal and ethical considerations are a fact of life for performers, and aspects of the legal field may take many forms throughout their careers. Content for on-air delivery may occasionally create a situation for a performer where legal action may be threatened by a guest or by someone included in the program. Nearly all television and Internet outlets have legal counsel that they may consult—primarily because often the legal and ethical issues are not sufficiently clear-cut for lay people to understand or make decisions. However, several journalistic organizations have prepared legal and ethics information catering to on-air personnel. Some of those resources are included in Figure 10.5 and at the end of this chapter. On a more personal level, you will need to educate yourself about legal matters specific to your career—namely contracts and relationships with agents.

CONTRACTS

Performers should be aware of the common provisions in contracts, so that they can balance the desirability of these provisions with the chances of getting a job. They must be aware of certain laws pertaining to the limitations of program content, and the conduct of a performer on the air.

A performer may become involved in several kinds of contracts. The main one is for continuous employment with benefits. Other contracts may be written for scripts, musical compositions, performer endorsements for advertising or promotion, and for the development of audio and video recordings, films, DVDs, or other media entities that may be distributed for profit. If the performer has an agent, the agent usually handles the contract, because it is in the agent's best interest for talent to be well cared for. A performer who does not have an agent may want a lawyer to go over an individual contract with a television station. Figure 10.6 lists the basic components of a contract.

FIGURE **10.5** *Legal and ethical resources.*

- **Ethics advice for journalists:** Free service provided by the Chicago chapter of the Society of Professional Journalists and Chicago's Loyola University. 866-DILEMMA (866-345-3662)
- **Online training for ethical decision making in journalism:** www.newsu.org
- **Poynter Institute for Media Studies:** www.poynter.org
- **Radio-Television News Directors Association Code of Ethics:** www.rtnda.org/pages/media_items/code-of-ethics-and-professional-conduct48.php
- **Read ethical cases online:** http://journalism.indiana.edu/resources/ethics

FIGURE

10.6 *Common contract provisions.*

1. Basic salary and increments

2. Amount of work to be done on and off the air

3. Compensation for personal appearances

4. Time off for vacations and holidays

5. Fringe benefits such as insurance, retirement, vehicle expense, and office accommodations

6. Release time to do other projects

7. Billing and credits on the program

8. Use of the performer's image or voice for endorsements or promotions

9. Residuals, if any

10. Expense account

11. Staff assistance

12. The period of the contract, with provisions for early termination or renewal

SALARIES

Your salary is based on the demand for your services. As a novice, your compensation may range from unpaid exposure to a few dollars above minimum wage an hour. Ten to 50 dollars for a single appearance is not uncommon. A beginner prizes opportunity even more than money. A great deal depends upon how much money is available for the job and how highly the employer rates your work. One novice sportscaster paid his own expenses to travel with and learn from a network crew on location. Often a second job pays the bills. If possible, get a related second job, but remember you are taking it mainly for the money. It is a means to an end. A college graduate who enters the information business should be able to subsist on the company's salary. You are usually so busy that you do not have time for a second job. Because of the hazards of starting out in a large market, you are far better off if you can go to that city with some money in the bank or financial support from your family.

Estimates of salaries for radio and television performers are difficult to make due to variations in station profits, market size, and requirements of the job. Visibility in the community and on the air pays the most. Of course, station management will attempt to get talent for the lowest possible figure, while the talent or his or her agent will try to get as much as the market will endure. Typically, the annual entry salary in news is in the midteens. Once a performer is established, about two years later, it jumps to the midtwenties and thirties. Anchors get more money than rank-and-file reporters: $25,000 to more than $100,000 per year in small to medium markets. Company benefits may add another 10 to 20 percent. Although a comfortable living can be made in news and information programming, the much publicized multimillion-dollar contracts are rare.

RESIDUALS

Sometimes a performer is very successful in a single role, and may or may not be successful in anything else. This role may be in a media series or a commercial. The initial payment to the performer is followed by smaller amounts paid every time the television series, spot, or film is shown. These are known as **residual** payments. You may receive payment for a number of years from a television program or series that ran only briefly.

UNIONS

Network operations and major film companies—those businesses that make a great deal of money and whose programming has wide distribution—are usually unionized. Some exceptions may be found in states like Texas that have right-to-work laws, where broadcast stations are nonunion. Non-union performers get whatever compensation the market will bear; union performers get whatever the union contract agrees to or more. Generally, to enter a union, a performer has to be employed in a job covered by a union contract. Some performers belong to more than one union. The **American Federation of Television and Radio Artists** (AFTRA) and the **Screen Actors Guild** (SAG) represent media performers. Contracts include all work whether live, film, tape, television, or radio. Actor's Equity Association (AEA) represents those who appear live on the legitimate stage, in stock companies, and in industrial shows; and the American Guild of Variety Artists (AGVA) covers nightclub performers. The American Federation of Musicians (AFM) represents musicians, and the Writers Guild of America (WGA) has jurisdiction over writer contracts in its independent chapters, WGA-East and WGA-West.

AFTRA includes newscasters, such as news presenters, reporters, and sportscasters; entertainers, such as singers, dancers, and animal acts; and commercial announcers. SAG, which is a theatrical motion picture performers' union, represents performers in all television shows and commercials made on film. AFTRA and SAG have established minimum wages, called **scale**, as well as minimum rehearsal days and hours for a day and for a week. Wages are tied to the length of the show and the use, whether local, regional, or national. There are various scales depending upon the number of lines the performer has.

AFTRA and SAG contracts are complicated and long, in part because they address various categories of performers, such as those in news, commercials, or drama. Essentially, contracts concern payment to and working conditions for performers. A **player** (performer) is paid specified fees for each session. SAG has per-day fees, but AFTRA works on a per-program basis. Player compensation is determined by whether

- the player is on- or off-camera.
- the player is appearing in a large or small market.
- the duration of service requires overtime, overnight, weekend, or holiday work.
- the program is distributed nationally or internationally, in which case residuals are paid.

A player may also be compensated for use of his or her own makeup, hairdressing, street or evening clothes, and travel time.

There are certain working conditions that a player may expect, such as adequate dressing rooms, travel accommodations, rest periods, and protection from pay loss due to injury on the job. The contract may provide protection clauses concerning dangerous or hazardous circumstances, foreign duty, and conditions for living overseas. Union contracts include nondiscrimination clauses that encourage the employment of women and minorities. Contracts define penalties to producers and players if the conditions are not met.

RESTRICTIONS AND ETHICS

Although your contract may be your initial concern, once you gain a measure of prominence, you will sense the care with which you must conduct your public and often your private life. Performers and the companies they work for may, justifiably or not, become the targets of litigation. Whether in news or entertainment, the basis of the litigation is usually fairness, or the perception of fairness when bringing to public attention the actions of individuals and companies. Because of the enormous power of television, a performer may inadvertently harm someone else, damage a company, or destroy a cause.

Anchors, contributing reporters, commentators, moderators, panelists, analysts, and talk show hosts must aspire to the highest levels of presenting material fairly. In recounting the day's events, in assigning meaning to them, in allowing an exchange of views and criticism, the performer must check the accuracy of data, attribute statements, divide fact from allegation, and allow reasonable presentation of all points of view, even those he or she may not share. Without such efforts, performers expose themselves to possible litigation, severe criticism, and public disfavor.

You will find it worthwhile to consult federal and state laws concerning fraud, obscene language, libel and slander, and the assurance of fairness in contests and in the treatment of political candidates and public figures. Most companies retain attorneys to guide you in these matters, but the majority of problems will never occur if you retain high ethical standards in your judgment of individuals and situations.

Your First Job in the Real World

bout a year before you plan to work, begin to make your contacts. Review opportunities on the Internet and talk to your friends. Use all of your contacts, even old ones. Use your parents' contacts in media, too. Remember that the best approach is to visit the stations where you really want to work. Meet the news director and other station executives who will decide whether to hire you. The best way to sell yourself is in person.

Your first job is temporary. Here, you will get acquainted with the daily routine of working for a company. Two years later you will be experienced in ways you cannot know before you are actually working. Stations and the areas they serve are all different. You must get along with those in your working environment and with the public. Be flexible and optimistic.

If you pursue it, the journey will be more exciting and worthwhile than you ever imagined.

Have a good time with the performing experience. Most subjects and acts, even if briefly sad, are light and pleasurable. Keep them that way. The public should enjoy them to the utmost. You must enjoy telling about the subject or presenting your work. Energy, a smile, and appropriate laughter are enormous aids in presenting the material favorably. Even though you are nervous, and most performers are, concentrate on the value of your information or the ability demonstrated in your work. Have fun interacting with the people you meet along the way.

Now go out and do your best with high hopes for success. Luck plays a part. Whatever happens, do not be hasty in making judgments or drawing conclusions. Give yourself a chance to gain experience and to mature. Do not expect instant feedback and recognition, but if it comes, enjoy it.

Summary

our first job in the real world may likely be an entry-level position that you obtain using a combination of sound strategies. Strategies that help you reach this stage include completing an internship (at least one), seeking feedback on your résumé and résumé recording, networking through professional organizations (here you may find people willing to critique your résumé and recording) and through your letters of inquiry, informational interviews, and station visits. You may exhibit promising skills during your internship, and the internship host may offer you a position. Or you may demonstrate capability and promise during an audition. Your instructors and personal coaches will likely help you to sharpen your performance skills, too.

Once you gain experience and obtain more prominent positions, you may work with image consultants under contract to your station. You will become acquainted with the world of contracts and contract provisions, residuals, and unions. And you may enlist the services of talent agents, managers, personal staff, and production companies as your career grows.

CHAPTER 10 *exercises*

1. Read the codes of ethics and various ethical scenarios from the organizations listed in Figure 10.5. Consider the following questions for discussion:

   ▪ Would you accept a gift from a news source?

   ▪ Why have reporters been fired for dating a source?

   ▪ What are the ramifications of participating in a political campaign?

   ▪ Are there guidelines to consider before you air a 911 call?

2. Contact on-air personalities (local or national) and request informational interviews. Ask them about ethical situations they have encountered in their work and how the situations were resolved. Write a story to present to the class.

Other Sources

Cooper, Anderson. *Dispatches from the Edge: A Memoir of War, Disasters, and Survival.* New York: HarperCollins, 2006.

Engel, Richard. *War Journal. My Five Years in Iraq.* New York: Simon & Schuster, 2008.

Ethics Advice for Journalists. Free service provided by the Chicago chapter of the Society of Professional Journalists and Chicago's Loyola University. Call 866-DILEMMA (866-345-3662).

Nantz, Jim, with Eli Spielman. *Always By My Side. A Father's Grace and a Sports Journey Unlike Any Other.* New York: Gotham Books/Penguin, 2008.

News University. www.newsu.org. Online journalism training on ethical decision making (free to sign up).

Poynter Institute for Media Studies. www.poynter.org.

Radio-Television News Directors Association Code of Ethics. www.rtnda.org.

Russert, Tim. *Big Russ and Me: Father and Son: Lessons of Life.* New York: Hyperion, 2004.

School of Journalism, Indiana University. Read ethical cases online. http://journalism.indiana.edu/resources/ethics.

Society of Professional Journalists. www.spj.org.

Glossary

Act: A performance. A display of a performer's ability.

Action: A verbal or physical cue from the director to begin performing.

Actor/Actress: Performer who appears in dramatic roles usually portraying someone other than him- or herself.

Actuality: The voices or sounds of an event as they are happening at the scene, the presentation of a story as it occurred.

Ad-lib: Spoken remarks not written in the script.

Air check: An excerpt from a broadcast illustrating how a performer sounds and looks on the air.

American Federation of Television and Radio Artists (AFTRA): A talent union, commonly pronounced "Aff-truh."

Amplification: Magnification of the voice so that the audience can hear it better.

Analog: An electronic signal that physically transcribes images and sounds onto magnetic tape. A second magnetic head reads the information.

Anchor: Performer who provides continuity for news and information programs; likely to work as part of an anchor team.

Announcers: Various performers who present information, news, commercials, sports, and weather. Narrowly defined, an announcer reads commercials, promotional spots, and station continuity.

Arc: A camera movement command that means to move the camera mount in a curve to the right or the left of the performer.

Articulation: Any sound made in forming words clearly and precisely so they are understood instantly and easily.

Attack: Forceful tone or energy with which to begin your performance.

Audiovisual(s): Any presentation using sound and sight, especially materials designed for that purpose.

Audition: A selection and testing process whereby producers and casting directors determine which performers to hire.

B-roll: Secondary video that is used to amplify a story, typically with voice-over narration.

Back timing: Predetermining in a script where a performer or program should be (near the end of a segment or show) so with careful judgment the program will end on time.

Background (B.G.): Maintaining music or sounds or both at a low enough volume so that the performer can be clearly heard.

Bidirectional: A microphone pickup pattern resembling a figure eight that allows two or more performers to speak opposite each other while using the same microphone.

Blackout: Deletion of audio or video during a live performance.

Bleep: An electronic interruption in verbal continuity, usually deleting a word or phrase considered in bad taste or legally injurious.

Blocking: The plotting of action by the director during rehearsals.

Blog: A combination of the two words "web" and "log." Online written commentary, regularly updated, that may include photos and video.

Book: A multipurpose term referring to contracting a performer, the periodic listing of program ratings, a performer's collection of credits and photographs, or a script for a musical show.

Break: To stop action, that is, to take a break. Also to move talent and cameras to another location.

Breakaway: Scenery, properties, or clothing designed to break or come off easily.

Breaking news: Hard news that interrupts regular programming because of a current live event.

Breathy: Vocal characteristic caused by allowing an abnormal amount of breath to escape the mouth with each utterance.

Build: The gradual development of interest or tension in a narrative story.

CCD/Charge-Coupled Device or CMOS/Complementary Metal-Oxide Semiconductor: A light sensor used in digital cameras to convert light into an electronic signal.

Call: A warning to performers, who are usually in the greenroom, that a rehearsal or on-air session is about to begin. Also, a posted notice seeking talent; that is, a casting call. A call for many performers is referred to as a "cattle call."

Canned: A completed filmed performance that is in the (film) can. Hence, any recorded performance.

Cardioid: A heart-shaped microphone pickup pattern.

Career performers: People whose income primarily comes from performing and whose occupation primarily revolves around performing, whether on television, on the stage, or in the movies.

Character: A performer portraying an individual he or she may not resemble in age or personality.

Character generator (CG): An electronic device that creates words and designs.

Charisma: The ability of a performer to consciously or unconsciously exude a compelling aura that allows that person to captivate an audience.

Cheating: An effort by a performer to create the illusion of speaking to someone directly as in an interview, while positioning the body for a maximum open relationship with the camera.

Chroma key: A production technique that electronically inserts a performer into a television picture.

Circular response: The delivery of a message from a performer to the audience and the return of the audience's response to the performer.

Citizen journalist: Someone not employed by a news organization who produces content for it.

Climax: The highest point of tension or interest in a program or performance. The moment of resolution.

Close: The conclusion of a program.

Closed position: A body position relative to the camera that allows the least expression by the performer and tends to close out the camera operator from getting a full range of shots.

Close-up (CU): A close-up shot, usually the face.

Clothing: Ordinary street clothes worn on camera, as opposed to costumes.

Cold: The reading of material without prior knowledge or rehearsal of it.

Color: The second person on a two-person sports announcing team, who contributes related facts and statistics about the players and teams.

Communication: The ability of one person to evoke a response from and/or create an impression on another person.

Composite: A collection of photographs printed on a single sheet illustrating the versatility of a performer.

Concentration: Undivided attention.

Condenser: A high-fidelity microphone.

Conflict: Dramatic opposition of the protagonist with one's self, another human being, society, or fate. The most compelling news stories have conflict.

Continuity: A continuous flow of a segment or program.

Control room: A room often adjacent to a studio or in a vehicle. It contains audio and video consoles that are utilized by producers, directors, and engineers to control and record program content.

Crane up/down: Camera movement command that elevates or lowers a camera filming overhead.

Credits: A list of work experiences including live and media performances. Also, a list of names and titles at the beginning and/or end of a program.

Critique: Feedback from consultants.

Cross: A movement from one place to another by a performer on stage or on camera.

Cue: A hand signal for a performer to begin the action. The first words spoken may be referred to as the incue or intro.

Cue cards: Large cards that have dialogue written on them for prompting performers. Sometimes called "idiot" cards.

Cut: A signal to stop action or a break between scenes created during editing.

Cutaway: An editing technique where a related piece of video is used to cover an electronic edit, add complexity to a scene, or provide flexibility when using just one camera.

Cyclorama: A huge drape or plaster wall (hard cyc) providing the backdrop for a setting in a studio.

Denasality: Loss of airflow through the nose, such as when you have a cold.

Diaphragm: A large muscle located between the lungs and the abdomen. It serves as a bellows in the breathing process. Also, a flexible element in a microphone producing electronic impulses.

Digital: Information transmitted as an infinite combination of zero-and-one sequences that can communicate vast amounts of information accurately.

Direct contact: Eye-to-eye contact with a live audience and/or by means of looking into the on-air camera lens.

Directional: The dominant pickup pattern of a microphone; that is, uni-, bi-, omnidirectional, or cardioid.

Director: The principal person responsible for the artistic development of a production and its presentation on-air.

Dissolve: A transition that overlays the previous shot with the new one.

Dissonant: Unpleasant, unharmonious sound.

Dolly: A camera movement command that means to move the camera toward or away from the performer.

Dry run: A live rehearsal that is not recorded or filmed.

Dynamic: A common type of rugged microphone that picks up sound from all directions.

Editing: Assembling video shots and sound bites to tell a story.

Electronic field production (EFP): Segments shot live or recorded at the scene of any event.

Electronic news gathering (ENG): The process of recording and presenting news events live from the scene.

Enterprise: A story that is generated by a reporter as opposed to one assigned by an editor or boss.

Entertainer: A performer who makes a career out of providing fun or enjoyment for others and is usually the reason for an event or performance.

Entrance: A performer's movement into view or recognition on microphone.

Exclusive contract: A legal agreement that binds the performer to one company or agent.

Exit: A performer's movement out of view or microphone pickup.

Extra: A performer without lines who contributes to the background or atmosphere in crowd scenes, most commonly seen in documentaries and dramas.

Fact sheet: An outline and/or list of titles or topics to be discussed on a program, sometimes called a rundown. A background sheet or biography of a guest.

Fade: A transition between shots that takes a longer amount of time to move from one shot to the other, or to black on-screen.

Falsetto: An artificial range of high pitch in a person's voice.

Featured player: A performer requiring special identification, although not a star.

Feed: Messages sent from the director to a performer, usually over a headset. Also, a wire news summary known as an electronic feed.

Feedback: A response from the public, critics, and those associated with the production.

First read-through: A reading of an entire script aloud by the participants.

Format: The overall structure of a program or series. Also, a type of script listing major steps in carrying out the segment, such as opening, interview topics, and closing.

Freeze: To maintain an exact position. A pose held until the segment is complete.

Fricative: Sound produced by consonants when air is forced through a narrow opening, such as pressing the lower lip against the front teeth in pronouncing the letter "f" or curling the tongue to pronounce an "s" sound.

From the top: An expression meaning to start at the beginning.

Grayscale: Colors converted to a scale from black to white.

Greenroom: Area where performers wait before going on air.

HDTV: Digital television broadcasting system called high definition television. A system of scanning more lines per second that produces a sharper picture. (Standard or analog television has a 4:3 aspect ratio versus the 16:9 ratio for HDTV letterbox format.)

Hand props: Personal properties carried by a performer.

Hand signals: A silent method of sending instructions to performers while they are on the air.

Hard news: A news story about an event having significant current impact, usually on many people. Hard news often deals with disasters, economics, and political events.

Head shot: A close-up picture of the face.

Hoarse: Describes a voice with a "frog in the throat" quality.

Hot: On the air.

Hot set: A set where a program is live or being taped.

Image control: Presenting the public carefully selected and supervised elements of one's personality and appearance; showing what you want and nothing more.

Interpretation: An intellectual effort to present the depth of text in order to display its further meaning in a performance.

Key light: The brightest major light source for a performer.

Kicker: A brief humorous story at the end of the newscast.

Kill: To cut, remove, or get rid of action, lines, stories, or production elements.

Lavaliere: A tiny microphone attached to a performer by a clip or lanyard.

Lead in/lead out: The opening or closing sentences of a story or other program information.

Leading man/woman: A performer who has the major responsibility or role in a program, such as documentary or drama.

Level: The volume of a voice or sound as registered on a volume units (VU) meter on an audio console.

Level check: Listening to an audio signal to make an adjustment if it is too loud or too soft, or to determine if a mike is working. "Give me a level" is an engineer's request for the performer to keep talking until audio equipment is adjusted properly.

Lines: The spoken words or dialogue a performer must deliver.

Live: A performance in which the talent is working in the presence of an audience. Also, the direct transmission of a performance at its time of origin.

Long shot (LS): A full-length view of the performer.

Look: A performer's distinctive appearance, the direction in which the performer is asked to face in order to match a previous shot, or a facial expression that prepares an audience for action, or indicates the location of a person or object in the shot.

Looping: The addition or substitution of voice(s) in post synchronization after a program is mainly complete. Also called dubbing.

Makeup: Cosmetics applied to improve a performer's appearance.

Marks: Designations usually taped or painted on a studio floor indicating positions for the performers.

Master: The original recording of a program, disk, or film.

Material: The content or the substance of what you say during a broadcast. Scripts for print, film, and electronic systems that convey messages.

Medium shot: A view of the performer from the waist up.

Mixer: An electronic board, usually an audio console, used to combine sounds.

Monitor: A television receiver without sound placed on a studio floor or news desk, or in the control room. Also, any of several audio receivers found in television, radio, or recording studios.

Morgue: A reference file of stories, photographs, films, and tapes.

Nasality: Quality of a voice when it resonates in the nasal cavity; air is expelled though the mouth and the nose when speaking.

Newscaster: A performer who reports stories about other people and events throughout the world using multimedia.

Non-career performer: An individual who has another occupation but uses the media to communicate with the public.

Nonlinear editing: Electronic cut and paste technique of piecing together a video story. Source content may be accessed in any order. Also, a non-chronological sequence of events.

Off-camera: Out of view although possibly participating in the scene.

Omnidirectional: A microphone that picks up sounds from everywhere.

On the air: To be on the air, camera, or microphone.

On-board mike: A mike built into the camera for recording ambient sound.

On-camera: Actively in scene and usually in camera view.

One-man band: A person who acts as videographer and reporter.

One sheet: A photograph with minimum vita, used for résumés.

Open position: The relationship of the body of a performer to a camera that allows fullest expression. To open up means to have freer movement and interpretation.

Outcue: Those words constituting the final seconds of a segment, such as the final seconds of a sound bite. An outcue is critically timed to match the upcoming segment. Sometimes called an outro.

Pace: The overall rate or flow of continuity in a production.

Package: A complete report, usually from a nonstudio location. Also, a group of marketable items such as a group of films, or a collection of advertisements cut to various lengths (e.g., 60, 30, 20, or 10 seconds).

Pad: A period of flexibility in the continuity that can be expanded or cut near the end of a segment or program so that it comes out on time. Extra material a performer can go to if he or she runs short.

Pan: To move a camera horizontally right or left.

Pancake: A water-soluble makeup foundation.

Pantomime: The silent expression of an idea or emotion through body movement.

Pedestal up/down: A camera movement command that is used to raise or lower hydraulically operated cameras.

Performer: Anyone who appears on-camera and/or on-microphone, especially those who are paid to do so (career performers) and community experts who do so because of their knowledge in areas outside media (non-career performers).

Personality: The innate charm or essence of an individual. Also, a performer whose personal characteristics dominate whatever role he or she portrays.

Phonation: The formation of a sound by means of the vocal mechanism, dominantly the lips, tongue, teeth, and surrounding areas.

Pickup: The range within which a microphone can get a sound signal. A pickup pattern refers to the shape of the sensitive area surrounding a microphone. Also, to accelerate the pace of a program largely by means of responding more quickly to cues, or to begin where the action last stopped.

Pitch: The range of vocal sounds a performer can produce, from deep tones with relaxed vocal cords through falsetto.

Playback: The replay of a performance on magnetic tape or disk.

Player: A performer; a common term used in union contracts.

Plosive: Sound made while speaking when air is expelled quickly, such as saying the letter "p."

Podcast: Audio or video files that may be downloaded via the Internet.

Post-synchronization: A process in production in which the sound is added after the picture has been recorded. The performer re-records the words while trying to match the movement of the lips.

Prepared statement: A speech that is completely written out in advance of delivery.

Prerecorded: Edited events that are prepared and recorded in advance of an airing date.

Presence: The optimum clarity of sounds. Also, the psychological status of being in the same room or present.

Producer: The executive who arranges the business aspects of a production, including the contracting of a director and major performers.

Production staff: The behind-the-scenes crew who take care of most technical and artistic aspects of the production, from lighting and sound to sets and makeup.

Promotion: An announcement that arouses favorable attention for a show or a person; abbreviated as "promo."

Prompter: An electronic system of cuing a performer.

Pronunciation: An accepted way of saying syllables or words, using emphasis and intonation.

Props/properties: All objects necessary for the completion of a setting and for use by performers. This includes furniture and smaller personal items (hand props).

Public image: The relatively few characteristics that a performer and associates wish to convey about the performer.

Publicity: Attention that media, especially news, gives to a performer or show without charge.

Quick study: A performer who can remember lines easily.

Radio Television News Directors Association (RTNDA): A group devoted to improving standards for news.

Range: The extent to which a performer can produce high to low pitch levels. Also, the extent of one's ability to perform in various capacities.

Rate: The pace at which words are spoken.

Ratings: An index of the relative number of persons tuned into a radio or television program during a given time period.

Rear screen projection (RSP): An older method of projecting images behind a performer, using an optical device that displays a photo or image on a screen.

Relaxation: A state of physical and mental rest.

Residual: Small payments to a performer made every time a series, spot, or film is shown.

Resonance: The reinforcement of a vocally produced sound by means of physical structure, acoustics, and electronic devices.

Résumé: A brief summary of a performer's background and abilities.

Ribbon: A type of microphone that selectively picks up sound in a long, thin, bidirectional pattern.

Rip 'n' read: A hasty presentation of news by means of tearing copy directly from a wire machine and reading it on the air. May be referred to as reading copy cold.

Roll cue: A transitional line that enables a performer to yield his or her presentation to another person or segment.

Rundown: An outline for a segment or program that usually lists the order of events. Sometimes referred to as a fact sheet.

Scale: Minimum union wages.

Scene: A portion of a drama or documentary, typically from the entrance to the exit of a performer from a camera's field of view or microphone pickup.

Screen Actors Guild (SAG): A union representing actors.

Script: A printout of what is read on the air.

SDTV: Standard television, a digital transmission format that has an aspect ratio of 4:3 and a resolution of 720 pixels by 480 pixels and is comparable to analog television broadcasts.

Server: A computer set aside to perform specific functions, such as storing graphics, DVD, or video for playback during a newscast.

Set/setting: The scenery (walls, landscape, panoramas) for a production.

Share: A give-and-take relationship between performers, as in an interview or a documentary. Also, a part of a viewing audience or market used for rating systems research.

Shot: The basic visual unit of a program or film, during which action may or may not occur without interrupting physical continuity by cutting or editing.

Soft news: A feature story having high human interest value, such as humor, novelty, gossip, and so forth.

Sound bite: A brief audio-video insert or segment in a news report; often about 10 seconds, used for attribution.

Source: An original event; a person providing information for a story; equipment picking up audio-visual information.

Spokesperson: A representative of a person or a group, such as an agent, publicist, or press officer.

Spot: A commercial or public service announcement. Also, a brilliant white light emphasizing the main performer. A place in the organization of a program is referred to as a spot.

Stand-by: A verbal or visual cue given just prior to a rehearsal or on-air program, usually indicating 30 seconds to air.

Stand-in: A substitute for the actual performer, used to check lights and final preparations.

Stand-up: A taped or live segment of an on-scene report, typically featuring a reporter in a medium shot.

Still store: Photographs electronically scanned and kept in a computer for later use.

Story angle: The way a story is told, the facts on which it is based, or the person highlighted in telling the story. A reporter's perspective on a person or event.

Straight: A role similar to a performer's natural characteristics and age.

Strident: Describes a voice produced by strain and tension.

Studio: A specially equipped room in which a performer rehearses or presents his or her material or act.

Style: The unique way a performer presents material.

Summary: A prepared statement with which a moderator closes a program.

Switcher: An electronic control panel that executes changes from shot to shot.

Tag line: A performer's final line of a speech, or the final line of a story, segment, or program.

Talent: A collective term for all performers. Talent implies that a performer has exceptional ability and/or knowledge.

Talking head: A camera shot of a person talking, typically in a medium shot. Considered a derogatory term if a story doesn't capitalize on television's ability to display interesting or compelling visuals.

Tally light: A tiny light atop a television camera that indicates the camera is on the air.

Tease: A short enticement at the beginning of a program; a preview. In news, it consists of headlines; in documentaries it may be a dramatic highlight presented in or out of story sequence.

Texting: A means of sending word messages via small electronic wireless devices and systems.

Thin: Vocal characteristic of lacking resonance.

Throw away: To underplay a line or scene.

Tilt: To move a camera vertically up or down.

Timbre: Tone and quality of sound; what makes voices unique.

Time: A term that means the segment is over. Running time is the duration of any program or segment, often measured in seconds.

Timing: A term that refers to a performer's judgment in the delivery of material to cause maximum impact on an audience.

Trachea: Commonly referred to as the windpipe, it is a tube that extends from the larynx to the bronchial tubes carrying air to the lungs.

Track: The portion of a film strip or tape that carries the sound impulse. Sophisticated sound uses multitracks.

Truck: A camera movement command that means to move the camera right or left on its mount in relation to the performer.

Unidirectional: A narrow microphone pickup pattern projecting in a single direction and designed for a single talent.

Variety: The use of the voice in an unexpected way.

Video prompter: Mechanical device attached adjacent to the on-air lens of a television camera that reveals the script line by line to the performer.

Videotape: Any of several strips of plastic cut in various gauges and coated with metallic oxide for different purposes such as recording sounds and pictures, filling blanks, mending, and providing leader.

Vlog: Video blog or a blog with visuals.

Vocal cords/vocal folds: A part of the throat that vibrates to produce sounds and speech.

Vocal quality: The audible characteristics of a voice, including all of its nuances. A voice with a broad range of clear tones is considered to have high quality. A voice having excessive or unpleasing nasal, breathy, harsh, or strident characteristics has poor quality.

Voice over (VO): A performer reading copy over silent tape or film.

Volume: The loudness of a person's voice or of audio.

Walk-through: A rehearsal in which the participants physically move from location to location as the script requires.

Wind screen: A porous covering over a microphone that eliminates extraneous noise, especially wind.

Wind-up: A signal to end a segment, commonly the final 30 seconds. Also called the wrap-up.

Wing it: To perform a program without rehearsal.

Wipe: An electronically created transition between shots that uses a variety of geometric configurations to change from one scene to the other.

Wrap/wrap-up: The conclusion of a news story or the end of a show or broadcast; a signal given by the director to indicate that the recording is over: "That's a wrap."

Index